EDWARD MCWHINNEY is Professor of Law at Simon Fraser University. His most recent books are *Quebec and the Constitution 1960-1978*, *Conflict and Compromise: International law and world order in a revolutionary age*, and *Constitution-making: Principles, process, practice*.

The debate over 'renewing' Canadian federalism in response to the 'Quiet Revolution' in Quebec and the more recent economic demands of English-speaking provinces forms part of a greater response to the challenging problem of rebuilding the federal system and the Canadian constitution in an attempt to meet new cultural, social, and economic demands.

This volume follows on Professor McWhinney's *Quebec and the Constitution 1960-1978* but is more than a mere sequel. McWhinney draws on wide knowledge and extensive personal contacts to portray the players and the events in this last, complex chapter in the patriation drama. He shows how Quebec's special claims have given way to a regional approach; how the prime minister sacrificed the possibility of a genuine Canadian-made constitution by trying the old 'made-in-Britain' amending route one last time; how the British government properly and firmly resisted the meddling in Canadian matters proposed by the Kershaw committee; how the Supreme Court has taken an increasingly activist role in interpreting constitutional law; and how the people of Canada may yet take a major role in the coming second phase of constitution-making now that the BNA Act has finally come home.

Extensive appendixes provide invaluable primary material: various versions of the constitutional resolution, including the complete final version approved by the Canadian and British parliaments; the Guy Fawkes Day accord between the prime minister and the nine premiers; and extracts from the Supreme Court's decision on Senate reform, from the decisions on patriation by the courts of appeal of Manitoba, Newfoundland, and Quebec, and from the Supreme Court's famous ruling on the 'legality' and 'conventionality' of unilateral patriation, which produced the final round of constitutional negotiations between Ottawa and the provinces.

EDWARD MCWHINNEY

Canada and the Constitution 1979-1982: Patriation and the Charter of Rights

UNIVERSITY OF TORONTO PRESS
Toronto Buffalo London

© University of Toronto Press 1982
Toronto Buffalo London
Printed in Canada

ISBN 0-8020-2478-5 cloth
    0-8020-6501-5 paper

Canadian Cataloguing in Publication Data

McWhinney, Edward, 1926-
Canada and the constitution 1979-1982

Includes index.
ISBN 0-8020-2478-5 (bound). – ISBN 0-8020-6501-5 (pbk.)

1. Canada – Constitutional law – Amendments – History.
2. Canada. British North America Act. 3. Canada –
Constitutional history. I. Title.

JL65 1982 M39   342.71'03   C82-094521-8

**The Canada Council
Conseil des Arts du Canada
1957-1982**

Publication of this book has been assisted by the block grant programs of the Canada
Council and the Ontario Arts Council.

Contents

Preface

Quebec and the Constitution 1960–1978 was published in May 1979 and reissued before the end of the year. Rather than attempt a new edition of that book, I have decided to write a new study – both a sequel to *Quebec and the Constitution* and a delineation of the new and larger constitutional events, which transcend immediate Quebec issues.

The several years of shocked reaction to the Parti québécois victory of November 1976 have passed, and the 'Quebec problem' has begun to resolve itself. The best and most lasting resolution of the Quebec problem will be one that maximizes Quebec's special interests within a more comprehensive and inclusive pluralism and the renewal and modernization of the Canadian constitution and federal system as a whole. Our founding fathers saw the federal government as an independent entity in its own right and not merely the sum of one or more of its particular ethnic-cultural or regional groupings and this view has now prevailed.

In preparing this book I have used evidence that I gave the Special Back-Benchers' Committee on the Canadian Constitution (the Aitken Committee) of the British Parliament, in London on 9 April 1981 and remarks I made to the British-Canadian Studies Association at its Annual Meeting held at Lincoln College, Oxford, on 10 April 1981. I have drawn also on public addresses I gave during 1981 and early 1982, to the Department of Political Science, Faculty of Law, and Faculty of Management Studies of the University of Calgary; the Institute of Intergovernmental Relations of Queen's University, Kingston, Ontario; the Annual Meeting of the Indian Association of Alberta (Treaty Nations 6, 7, and 8); the Canadian Institute of International Affairs in Victoria; the Municipal Affairs Workshop of the Board of Trade, Vancouver; the Annual Meeting of the Canadian Club of Vancouver; Judges

Day at the Annual Meeting of the Canadian Bar Association, held in Vancouver; and the Meeting of Canadian Lieutenant-Governors and Territorial Commissioners, under the Chairmanship of His Excellency the Governor-General, held in Victoria.

Douglas Verney recently reminded me of an analysis I made, more than a decade ago, concerning bicultural constitutionalism and the differing conceptions of the scope of constitutional law and government taught in Quebec universities and in those of the other provinces. (See *Ontario Advisory Committee on Confederation, Background Papers and Reports.* vol. 2 [1970], 50ff.) English-Canadian schools seemed preoccupied with two sections, 91 and 92, of the BNA Act; Quebec schools had a far broader and more eclectic range of concerns, 'designed to equip the lawyer, as citizen, to grapple with the as yet only partly discerned and partly answered political-constitutional problems of this revolutionary age ... to face the unknown with some modest confidence, by exposing [to students] some of the range of the constitutional options and alternatives in any remaking of our constitutional order' (ibid, 52). In *Quebec and the Constitution* I argued that the new constitutional ideas of the 1970s were all either Quebec-inspired (as part of the heritage of the Quiet Revolution) or else essentially reactive responses by English Canada to those ideas. The Quebec 'dualist' side of the debate has been largely documented in *Quebec and the Constitution*. The more recent 'regionalist' emphasis has come unaccompanied by any substantial new ideas from English Canada.

The basic raw materials of the recent and dialectical constitutional process are therefore the frequent armed encounters of the period 1979–82; the primary sources are the governmental memoranda, position papers, 'agreed negotiating texts,' *aides-mémoire*, and the like – very often confidential in character or restricted in circulation. The best evidence is often to be found in official 'leaks' (contrived or otherwise), journalists' reports, and personal correspondence or interviews, the latter still on an 'off-the-record' basis. Wherever possible I have made reference to published sources. When that has not been possible, the proposition put forward has been checked or verified in at least two, and usually more, places.

'Law,' as Jeremy Bentham noted, 'is not made by Judge alone, but by Judge and Company.' The constitutional patriation company includes federal and provincial ministers, parliamentarians, and senior civil servants; British ministers, parliamentarians, and senior civil servants; professors, publicists, and editorial writers (francophone and anglophone) specialist in the constitutional question. It is a relatively small company, linked by professional ties, and sometimes personal friendship, extending over the many years of constitutional debate. More complete citation, though perhaps desirable, would not have been possible, as much of this material is personal and/or confidential.

I shall argue that the opposition to the Charter of Rights and Freedoms was centred in an alliance of convenience that brought together rather disparate groups, including some obscurantist and regressive forces. Some quite respectable arguments can, of course, be made against any sudden reception in Canada of an American-style policy-making supreme court. Some of these arguments were cogently advanced by Donald Smiley, Peter Russell, and others.

One technical weakness in the federal government's approach was its failure to recognize or to admit publicly that the new charter would compel profound changes in the constitutional system and particularly in the Supreme Court. The project might sensibly have been accompanied by proposals for structural and procedural changes in the judicial arm of government and in the judicial appointment processes. Similar proposals were widely and enthusiastically canvassed by Quebec jurists in the 1960s. Such fundamental changes are going to come anyway, from the sheer weight and agony of the Court's transformed work-load; but they are likely, now, to come on an ad hoc basis.

Some colleagues have asked me to comment on the constitutional alternative that was *not* adopted by the federal government: going not to a foreign country (Britain), however well loved it may be, but directly to the Canadian people as the ultimate source of constitutional power and constitutional legitimacy in Canada. The federal government decided to use one last British statutory amendment to the BNA Act as the legal means of achieving constitutional patriation and thereby effectively foreclosed any direct participation by the Canadian public.

The Canadian people never became involved emotionally in the patriation project until the frantic bargaining and trading that produced the 'compromise' of 5 November 1981 between the nine English-Canadian premiers and the federal government. The nine premiers made the cardinal error of appearing to be trying to deny or take away women's rights and Indian and native rights in the proposed new charter. Angry public reaction occurred quickly and spontaneously and compelled an immediate and substantial retreat by the premiers. This public intervention produced the final collapse of lingering provincial opposition to patriation and the charter (apart, of course, from the Quebec government).

Why didn't the federal government try to enlist direct public support and co-operation right from the outset? The charter is the product of a committee of federal functionaries, a heavy, technical-legal draft and not a 'people's charter' like its great American and French predecessors, which have always engaged popular understanding and support. For reasons still not clear, the prime minister's closest advisers apparently dissuaded him from trying to play a Thomas Jefferson role and personally writing the charter. A clear, direct, and easily comprehended text could easily have been defended in any electoral campaign that might have to be fought upon it.

However, the prime minister's approach to law-making and legal change generally is somewhat traditional and conservative: in technical terms, 'positivistic.' As he said in an interview in Vancouver in the winter of 1981, when his constitutional fortunes seemed at their lowest ebb, it would have been a legally revolutionary step to bypass the pre-existing processes of constitutional change, however undignified, anachronistic, or irrelevant they might seem to Canadians today. So it would have been, of course, just as it was in Britain in 1688–9! But the events of 1688–9, which created the juridical foundation of the British constitution of today, are still hailed as the 'Glorious Revolution.'

Very few countries base their new constitutional systems on the forms and the formulae of the old, particularly where these seem anachronistic or just plain absurd in contemporary terms. The starting-point (or *Grundnorm*) of a new constitutional system is a *pre*-legal or *meta*-legal fact. Its political and constitutional legitimacy comes from the fact of its popular endorsement, the act of constituent power. The 'people's' route, via a referendum, to a new Canadian constitutional system must remain one of the great 'might-have-beens' of the patriation conflict. It would certainly have been far less irritating for the British government and prime minister than the route actually followed by the federal Government, which brought Mrs Thatcher a whole nest of internecine squabbles as a result of the activities of provincial lobbyists.

If Canada really did obtain its full juridical sovereignty and independence with the Imperial Conference of 1926 and the Statute of Westminster of 1931, it would have been possible to argue that it would be constitutionally anachronistic and 'unconventional' for the British Parliament still to legislate amendments to the BNA Act, even at the direct request of the Canadian government. Mrs Thatcher seems to have decided from the beginning to grit her teeth and press ahead with the only remaining 'conventional' course, of acting on the advice of the Canadian government. It was a legal position she maintained, politely and firmly, and with splendid detachment throughout, and she was amply vindicated by subsequent events. It was an object lesson in political realism and statecraft, the more so perhaps because her private sympathies may well have been with the predominantly Conservative provincial premiers.

Two other women may also be singled out for special mention. The Canadian high commissioner in London, Jean Wadds, a Conservative, presented, loyally and with quiet effectiveness, the federal government's case to parliamentary back-benchers who were being wined and dined, at very considerable expense, by the agents-general of the dissident provinces. And the Queen, from the moment the constitutional resolution arrived in London, let it be known that she would attend the ceremonies in Ottawa to celebrate final patriation of the constitution to Canada. Such an announcement was constitutionally premature and 'unconventional' (if not downright unconstitutional) for the head of state. But, as an apparently spontaneous gesture, it seemed to demonstrate practical wisdom and political common sense, in its generous recognition both that Canadians themselves must be the ultimate arbiters of their own constitutional future and that the issue had already been resolved with the final vote in the Canadian Parliament in December 1981.

I was honoured to have the opportunity to test some of the hypotheses in this book before a French audience in February and March 1982 when I lectured in Paris at the Faculté de droit, Université de Paris I (Panthéon-Sorbonne); the Centre Universitaire de Recherches (Centre de Droit Constitutionnel); and the École Nationale d'Administration.

This study represents the third volume in a 'constitutional trilogy' stimulated by the vast political, social, and economic changes in Canada in recent years and their impact upon existing institutions and processes. *Quebec and the Constitution* (1979) examined the main intellectual impulses of the Quiet Revolution in Quebec, and English Canada's responses to them. *Constitution-making* (1981) set out the general lessons or axioms from comparative constitutional legal science as to *when*, *why*, and *how* one should approach the elaboration and adoption of a new constitutional system, and the main errors or pitfalls to avoid. Now comes *Canada and the Constitution* (1982).

I am considering yet a further volume, in anticipation of the Supreme Court's expanded and radically different constitutional role under the new Charter of Rights and Freedoms. This book will again draw on comparative constitutional legal science. In it I shall attempt to establish some general principles as to judicial policy-making and judicial legislation and their prudent constitutional limits, much as my earlier book, *Judicial Review* (first edition, 1956; fourth edition, 1969), attempted to do in an earlier era of general societal and constitutional change.

I would like to acknowledge the generous co-operation and wise guidance extended to me in my work on the 'constitutional trilogy' by the University of Toronto Press 'team,' and especially Prudence Tracy and John Parry. I am indebted, as in the past, to the administration of Simon Fraser University, to Dean Robert Brown and his staff, and to Elsie Trott who typed the various drafts of the manuscript for publication.

E.McW.
English Bay, Vancouver
April 1982

CANADA AND THE CONSTITUTION 1979–1982

Introduction: from dualism to regionalism

In *Quebec and the Constitution 1960–1978*, I advanced the general thesis that the spate of constitutional activity in Canada throughout the 1960s and 1970s was a direct consequence of those vast intellectual, social, and economic upheavals within Quebec that we today characterize as the Quiet Revolution. Many of its early leaders were legally trained and tended to verbalize their desires for change in constitutional and legal terms. Some sought 'special' or 'particular' constitutional status for Quebec within the existing Canadian federal system.[1] Some wanted a more or less unique 'associate state' status for Quebec, involving a redefinition of the Canadian federation as a whole.[2] Others desired constitutional separation and the secession of Quebec from Canada. All the initiatives and all the original ideas on constitutional change were coming from Quebec. The positions taken by English-Canadian leaders tended to be reactive – delayed responses, too often belated solutions to problems of yesterday, or even the day before.

The Parti québécois victory in 1976 certainly accentuated English-Canadian concern over Quebec. The federal government sought new constitutional and legal formulae for accommodating Quebec's special demands within Canadian federalism. Prime Minister Trudeau put forward a draft Constitutional Amendment Bill in 1978[3]; yet another all-party, joint Senate-House committee on the constitution, the Lamontagne-MacGuigan committee,[4] and a further special Senate committee on the constitution were set up[5]; and a federal commission, the Task Force on National Unity (or Pépin-Robarts commission) was appointed.[6]

At the same time, however, Canada, along with all other post-industrial societies, had been experiencing economic difficulties since the OPEC cartel began to raise oil prices in 1973. A general industrial recession was accompanied by high inflation and high unemployment, and the 'Long Parliament,' from 1974 to 1979, had shown itself unable to resolve these problems. The issue came to a head with widespread political disaffection in those regions of the country that had particularly suffered. This and the vagaries of political representation and the electoral laws seemed to ensure that important areas of the country would not return government members to Ottawa and would therefore not participate in federal decision-making. As a result there emerged onslaughts on the federal system as a whole, and on the federal government as the prime symbol thereof, that quite transcended Quebec's special complaints and demands. Often, too often, these latter-day onslaughts came from provincial administrations that seemed to be looking for convenient political scapegoats for their own inability to comprehend or control their own intraprovincial economic problems.

Whatever the combination of reasons, however, the nature and character of the constitutional great debate changed from one in which Quebec had seemed pitted against Ottawa and English-speaking Canada as a whole, to a pan-Canadian confrontation in which all the provinces seemed to be joining together to make a common war against the federal government. Other participants in the debate seemed to pick up the cue at the same time and offered a new constitutional synthesis of Quebec's earlier claims and the assorted, essentially fiscal and economic, complaints of the English-speaking provinces. We can thus observe, from the end of 1978 onwards, a shift in direction and emphasis: a 'dualist' (*deux nations*) approach to Canadian federalism was replaced by a more broadly pluralist, 'regionalist' (*dix nations*, if you wish), conception. In a new constitution there would be a massive decentralization and devolution of decision-making powers from the federal government to the provinces.

Such a lateral shift in focus was not without its risks for Quebec and those of its leaders who chose to espouse it. It could dilute the strength of Quebec's historical and sociological particularity in the cause of a larger, but necessarily far more diffuse (and artificial) alliance of all the provinces. A compact theory of Confederation, resting on international law arrangements between two founding nations, French and English, and on their peaceful coexistence since 1759, comes closer to blending historical folklore with present-day sociological reality.

This claim, however, can hardly be advanced to explain relations between the federal government and the nine English-speaking provinces. Indeed, here the compact theory becomes contrived and factitious; the historian knows it to be untrue, and it clashes with all common law-based theory of federalism. The English-speaking provinces were only relatively recently wrested form their original, aboriginal inhabitants and settled by Europeans;

thereafter, they have been characterized by large-scale immigration and movement and transfers of population. Any notion of an original, English-speaking, founding nation with an original sovereign title surviving to this day (save possibly for Newfoundland) is nonsense.

That almost pre-Copernican vision of Confederation which we saw in the 1960s and most of the 1970s, when the whole constitutional universe seemed to rotate around Quebec, has disappeared. There has been a consequent decline in Quebec's importance in the federal system, noticeable even before the Quebec referendum.

The 'Long Parliament' of 1974–9 exhausted the range of constitutional options that included accommodation with the Parti québécois government. Till the defeat of Trudeau's government in May 1979, there had been an essentially consensual process of constitutional adjustment to Quebec's special claims – inter-governmental diplomacy and exchange and barter between the federal government and the ten provincial governments, including Quebec. The short-lived Conservative interregnum minority government collapsed in the December 1979 budget debate, as much through its own internal weaknesses and tactical mismanagement as through external political pressures; and it was defeated in the February 1980 election. Trudeau, who had momentarily contemplated, and certainly publicly announced, his retirement as Liberal party leader in the autumn of 1979, stayed on for the general election and was restored as prime minister.

Political events in Ottawa and Quebec City now waited on the Quebec referendum on separation. It had been promised by Premier Lévesque in the 1976 campaign, but had been delayed in the pursuit of the most favourable political timing. The normal, four-year governmental mandate was approaching its end, and the referendum was finally held on 20 May 1980, with a deliberately watered-down proposal of 'sovereignty-association' instead of outright separation of Quebec from Canada. The defeat of this rather modest proposition seemed to indicate a marked decline in the political fortunes of the Lévesque government and to presage its defeat in the next election.

In *Quebec and the Constitution 1960–1978*, published in May 1979, I identified several possible scenarios. When the provincial election was finally held, on 15 April 1981, scenario three – defeat of a separatist proposal in the Quebec referendum, followed by re-election of the Lévesque government – ensued. Some (especially English-language) observers had predicted defeat of the Lévesque government and election of a new Liberal government under Claude Ryan. The result was greeted almost with equanimity by

Prime Minister Trudeau. Analysts could see in the apparent turn-around yet another application of those checks and balances between federal and provincial politics noticeable in Quebec as elsewhere in Canada. Canadian voters tend to balance a strong mandate for one party at the federal level by an equally strong mandate for a rival party at the provincial level. Separation had been disposed of, and Lévesque had promised during the spring 1981 campaign *not* to hold another referendum during any new term of office. The overwhelming mandate given by Quebec to the Trudeau government in February 1980 could now be balanced by a renewed mandate for Lévesque.

In terms of the constitution, one of the key events for the present volume has been the release of the three-volume report of the Task Force on National Unity (Pépin-Robarts commission) in early 1979. It contained an impressively detailed analysis of the current constitutional malaise and offered prescriptions for constitutional changes of a more general, pan-Canadian character as a remedy for particular Quebec-based ills.

The Quebec Liberal party, with the installation of its new leader, Claude Ryan, moved immediately to establish its own constitutional commission. Its report – *Une Nouvelle Fédération canadienne*,[7] popularly known as the *Livre beige* – was released in January 1980 and seemed closely linked to the Pépin-Robarts report. It, too, appeared to opt for some more generalized, Canada-wide constitutional decentralization at the expense of the federal government, rather than to look to Quebec-oriented remedies for Quebec's problems. This seeming dilution of the particularity of Quebec's constitutional demands occurred just when English-speaking leaders seemed prepared to accept such particularity. This dilution may have contributed to a weakening of the Ryan forces' standing with the French-language voters of Quebec.

The Parti québécois government, in preparation for the referendum campaign, issued its own white paper, *La Nouvelle Entente Québec-Canada*, sub-titled *Proposition du gouvernement du Québec pour une entente d'égal a égal: la souveraineté-association*: This was released at the end of 1979 – too late to be commented on or directly responded to in the *Livre beige*.

Several other important works on the constitution appeared during this period. Léon Dion's constitutional essays appeared in *Le Devoir* of Montreal during the referendum campaign; they were collected in book form, in mid-1980, under the title *Le Québec et le Canada. Les voies de l'avenir*. This volume appeared soon after Chief Justice Jules Deschênes's *Les Plateaux de la balance* (1979) and Gérald Beaudoin's *Essais sur la constitution* (1979).

The Supreme Court of Canada, in December 1979, rendered its advisory opinion[8] on the Senate reform aspects of Trudeau's Constitutional Amendment Bill, 1978 (which had already lapsed with the defeat of Trudeau's government). The Senate, through its Standing Committee on Legal and Constitutional Affairs (the Goldenberg committee), published, in November 1980, the report of the special Lamontagne subcommittee, entitled *Report on Certain Aspects of the Canadian Constitution*, an analysis and synthesis, and at times a devastating critique, of the disparate proposals for changes in the upper house advanced by various English-speaking premiers as part of their own constitutional platforms.

The federal-provincial first ministers' round of conferences on constitutional change was summoned by Prime Minister Trudeau immediately after the Quebec referendum and ran from June to September 1980, before its total breakdown. The federal government subsequently launched a solo initiative for repatriation of the BNA Act, together with an entrenched constitutional bill of rights and a constitutional amendment formula. Intensive lobbying by the premiers in London followed, aimed at blocking unilateral repatriation. The premiers challenged unilateral repatriation before provincial courts of appeal, and later in the Supreme Court.

By this stage, the debate had transcended Quebec's demands for national self-determination. Regionally based political and economic special interests had begun to challenge the post-Keynesian conceptions that had dominated Canadian political thinking and political practice since the Great Depression of the 1930s and the Second World War – a strong federal government and strong federal direction and leadership to political, social, and economic planning throughout Canada.

1

Constitutional interlude 1979–80

At year's end 1978, Prime Minister Trudeau made two high-level appointments that seemed designed, in part, to counter critics of central Canadian
domination in Ottawa. He named as the new governor-general the former
New Democratic Party premier of Manitoba, Edward Schreyer. And he
named a member of the British Columbia Supreme Court, William McIntyre, to replace Mr Justice Spence on the Supreme Court of Canada. There
had been no Supreme Court justices from British Columbia since Chief Justice Sir Lyman Duff's retirement more than thirty years before. Usually
three of the nine justices come from the Ontario bar, to balance the statutory
requirement that three of the nine must come from the Quebec bar; Premier
Davis of Ontario is understood to have privately waived any insistence that
Spence, from the Ontario bar, be replaced by an Ontarian, as a gesture to
western feelings, in the interests of national unity. The new justice, however,
was reported to be close to the federalist thinking of Chief Justice Laskin and
therefore hardly likely to see himself as a regional or provincial 'representative' on the court, as some of the more strident western critics of the court
had been demanding. Legal education in Canada has always managed to
achieve a national, rather than a sectional or regional, dimension and the
geographical accident of birth or even residence is thus likely to be transcended, on the Supreme Court, by other, more truly pan-Canadian considerations.

The Pépin-Robarts commission was appointed in July 1977. Its report was
released in early 1979, in three volumes. The all-important prescriptive volume I, *A Future Together*, containing conclusions and detailed recommendations, appeared at the end of January 1979. The terms of reference of the
commission were somewhat vague and general – 'to enquire into questions

relating to Canadian unity'; and the commission was given authority to 'hold public hearings and sponsor public meetings,' to 'support and encourage ... the efforts of the general public,' and to 'assist in the development of processes for strengthening Canadian unity' (135–6). It was, however, during its brief life, most active and thorough in consulting public opinion, mounting an impressive series of public hearings in all major Canadian cities and producing the only really detailed study of what the general public wants in a new federal system, all this being published in a special, third volume, *A Time to Speak. The Views of the Public* (March 1979). A second volume, *Coming to Terms. The Words of the Debate* (February 1979), is an erudite attempt to cut through semantic confusion over terms such as community, culture, race, ethnicity, nation and national community, multiculturalism, duality, regionalism, federal government, devolution and decentralization, secession and separation.

The commission's report must, in the end, stand or fall on the authority of its first volume, *A Future Together*. The commission, in approaching the task of making recommendations for the renewal of Canadian federalism – a leap from its mandate to 'enquire into questions relating to Canadian unity' (I, 135) – had two main possibilities open to it. It could relate its proposals to what the general public and the various pressure and interest groups appearing before it had demanded by way of constitutional change; this would have given its report its greatest authority, granted the exhaustiveness and apparent representativeness of its hearings. Or it could start its own research program and seek to develop its own constitutional plan accordingly. However, the public hearings absorbed most of the energies of the commissioners until the end of the spring of 1978, and the research and interaction between the commission and research staff had to be confined to a few months. The commissioners had to rely on other people's and other organizations' research, without always being able to verify their empirical quality or their disinterestedness.

Much of the constitutional special pleading that had characterized English-Canadian reaction to the Parti québécois victory turned up before the commission. It was subject to the same flaws as the arguments advanced by various English-speaking premiers, professional groups, pressure groups, and special interest associations and foundations.

What is striking, however, is that the commission did so well, in such a short period. Its report is lucid and often sparkling in its literary style and presents an impressive analysis and synthesis of the main currents of Canadian federalism. In its most striking section, the report asks the rhetorical question 'Does Quebec possess the right of self-determination?' and concludes: 'If, in the course of the next few years, Quebecers decided, definitively and democratically, to secede,' then the answer should be 'an unequivocal yes,' as 'a virtual corollary of our acceptance of the democratic process, (I, 113). This was to dare to speak the politically unspeakable and to answer the hypothetical question before it should have arisen concretely. It was in keeping with the courage, intellectual honesty, and generosity of outlook with which the commission approached its task. The commission went on, in this same spirit, to recognize Quebec's 'unique position' based on its 'distinctive culture and heritage,' and though rejecting 'special constitutional status,' it seemed to embrace it nevertheless on an informal de facto basis when it recommended that all of the provinces should be alloted powers 'in the areas needed by Quebec ... but ... in a manner which would enable the other provinces, if they so wished, not to exercise these responsibilities and instead leave them to Ottawa' (I, 86–7).

The commission opted clearly for the principle of provincial protection and hence provincial determination of the scope of language rights within the province, and also had some not unfavourable words for the Lévesque government's Bill 101 making French the official language of Quebec.

This unofficial recognition of a species of 'particular,' if not indeed 'special,' status for Quebec had to be balanced against the more detailed recommendations for a substantial decentralization of the federal system in the name of a more generalized 'regionalism.' The commission's approach to a renewed Canadian federal system involved a three-part constitutional conception of federalism, dualism, and regionalism, with a continuing interaction between the three and with the appropriate accommodations – particularly between dualism and regionalism – to be made in particular contexts in regard to particular problems. This approach allows for, and indeed compels, the exercise of a large degree of constitutional pragmatism. But this part of the commission's work, in its very specificity, seemed more questionable and open to technical objections as well as the understandable political criticisms. The commission had no mandate to act as a constituent assembly; it was not an academy of jurists; and it had neither the time nor the staff to conduct research in order to venture upon generalizations about the lessons to be derived from foreign experience.

The commission succumbs too easily to the 'numbers' game: the Supreme Court was to jump from nine to eleven judges; a new federal upper house was to have sixty members; there were to be sixty new members elected at large for the federal lower house (I, 128–31). There was a rather quaint coexistence of a new federal upper house, composed, like the conclaves of the Holy Roman Empire, of princely 'delegations' named by the premiers (I,

128), and direct popular election, by proportional representation, of the sixty new members-at-large of the lower house (I, 131).

The commission members may have applied a lesson of Weimar Republic constitution-making: when differences cannot be reconciled in the drafting committee, put them all in together and leave it to history to resolve any contradictions. The commission's detailed recommendations did not always seem self-consistent or necessarily to flow from the earlier conceptualization of the problem and identification of its key antinomies. They could, however, be viewed as alternative models available for the give-and-take that should certainly follow in the next few years.

For reasons beyond its own control, the commission tended to be passed by historical events. The report had hardly been read or digested before the federal election campaign arrived. Succeeding political events eventually brought different federal constitutional initiatives that made the report seem dated or irrelevant before anyone had seriously tried to apply its detailed recommendations.

The first ministers' conference on the constitution in the fall of 1978 marked the end of the inter-governmental diplomacy inaugurated by Ottawa and the English-speaking provinces after the Parti québécois victory. By the close of 1978, the Trudeau government had already well exceeded the normal four-year parliamentary term and was approaching the limits of the five-year statutory term. Dissolution of Parliament could not be postponed beyond mid-1979. Knowledge of that reality, coupled with predictions of defeat for the government, persuaded the solid phalanx of premiers opposed to Trudeau – Lévesque and, the predominantly right-of-centre premiers in the other provinces – to withhold co-operation from Trudeau and to await the installation of his successor. Joe Clark was generally considered more sympathetic or adaptable and capable of accommodating the demands of provincial governments and the interest groups that supported them.

One last hurrah was the first ministers meeting of early February 1979. It opened amid predictions of a new federal bill, to be introduced before the end of the session, involving unilateral federal initiatives in areas within federal jurisdiction, such as changes to the Supreme Court and entrenchment of human rights and linguistic rights in the constitution.[1] The federal government argued that some degree of constitutional movement was required before the Quebec referendum, in order to persuade Quebec voters of the federal government's and English-speaking Canada's sincerity about change. While differences on most issues seemed as intractable as ever, some form of consensus did seem possible on issues such as increased provincial powers over marriage and divorce; curbing the federal 'spending power' in areas of otherwise clear provincial jurisdiction; enshrining in the constitution the principle of financial equalization, involving federal payments to economically disadvantaged provinces; modifying the federal declaratory power by requiring provincial concurrence or at least prior federal consultation with the provinces, in certain cases; and, finally, the retention of the monarchy.

The gloomy predictions about the conference were soon vindicated. Quebec was joined by British Columbia, Alberta, Manitoba, and Nova Scotia in rejecting a federal proposal that all children of the two official language groups, French and English, be guaranteed freedom of choice of language of education, throughout Canada, wherever numbers warranted this. Quebec indicated also that it would not consent to repatriation of the constitution and an amending formula until all contentious issues of division of legislative powers (sections 91 and 92 of the BNA Act) had been settled.[2] On these key questions the conference foundered, even though a substantial consensus was attained in a number of other areas – granting the provinces power to licence cable television; allowing them to impose indirect taxes on natural resources; giving them complete jurisdiction over family law; enshrining the equalization principle; and retaining the monarchy and entrenching constitutionally the existing status of the Supreme Court. With a federal election, the Quebec referendum, and a Quebec provincial election approaching, the bargaining process was adjourned *sine die*.

The federal election of May 1979 ended the long-reigning Liberal government by returning a minority, Progressive Conservative government. The new government seemed to start out under favourable constitutional auspices. The Tories, long out of power, had no backlog of past ideas to which they could be held prisoner in a rapidly evolving Canadian society. The slight and evidently rather hastily prepared party white paper of early 1978, *The Constitution and National Unity*,[3] could be fairly easily disposed of as earlier, partisan advocacy, in no way binding on the new government.

The patently non-charismatic personality of the new prime minister meant a more low-key approach to constitutional issues than that of his predecessor, and this seemed to promise fewer personal frictions and inter-governmental accommodation on a pragmatic basis. These expectations were hardly disappointed, but they did lead to the charge, in the next election, that the price of such federal harmony was an abandonment of strong and legitimate national interests.

Prime Minister Clark made no overt constitutional blunders in his nine-month term, from June 1979 to February 1980 – no sins of commission at least. But he seemed to lack a body of positive constitutional ideas of his own, other than the rather vague conception of Canada as 'a community of communities.' This seemed to point to a new constitutional pluralism, but in what form and through what institutional modalities? If the provinces were the relevant 'communities,' we would presumably have a generalized delegation or transfer of decision-making powers to the provinces. If, however, the 'communities' were the new ethnic and cultural groupings in a Canada that had increasingly become a multi-national society, then we would presumably be looking at some form of cultural and linguistic self-determination, going beyond cultural dualism and bilingualism in the federal government. Perhaps, again, Clark was using 'communities' in the sense of two founding nations and making a modest plea for some institutional recognition of that fact: in that case, he would be reverting to the politically courageous 'deux nations' position advanced by Conservative leader Robert Stanfield in the election campaign of 1968, with politically unfortunate consequences.

Lacking any blueprint for constitutional change, Clark announced the formation of a special constitutional research group within the federal Conservative party. It was to be headed by Arthur Tremblay, a retired Quebec civil servant who had held senior posts under the Lesage government and its successors but was not associated, in the public mind at least, with Quebec's 'new wave' constitutional thinking. Clark appointed Tremblay to the Senate, and the government's constitutional policy became one of waiting on Senator Tremblay to develop ideas to guide constitutional decision-making. Unfortunately, this work had not been completed – it had hardly, indeed, begun – by the time the government was defeated in the House in December 1979.[4]

The defeat in the House was on a relatively minor aspect of the budget. The Pearson government was defeated, in early 1968, in a snap vote when key government members were absent; Pearson chose *not* to treat the vote as one of no-confidence warranting his government's resignation. There are a number of similar British precedents since the First World War. Clark was under no constitutional obligation to resign, but could have carried on. There is evidence that Governor-General Edward Schreyer asked Clark to consider his alternative options (including carrying on the government), before granting dissolution, which was not granted immediately on Clark's visit to the governor-general but only after a delay of several hours and a telephone call from Schreyer to Clark. Whether through faulty staff work and constitutional advice to Clark, or simply through over-confidence (again the product of faulty advice), Clark chose the gambler's option of dissolving Parliament and calling an election.

During the succeeding campaign, Clark was tempted to offer concrete gestures of his willingness to abandon areas of federal law-making competence to the provinces. He indicated that he would yield federal jurisdiction to the provinces in regard to control of lotteries and, more controversially, offshore oil resources.[5] This latter promise, at the insistent demand of Premier Peckford of Newfoundland, was apparently without any awareness of the Supreme Court's advisory opinion on offshore oil, that had declared such jurisdiction to be wholly federal.[6] It simply could not be disposed of in a campaign promise and by simple executive decree, but would require a formal constitutional amendment before it could be acted upon.

A document released by the Clark government in early January 1980,[7] at the height of the campaign, purported to establish a frame of reference, for the Tremblay study group, on renewal of the federal system. It set out three premises: that there is a Canadian identity; that the Canadian reality is constituted by a series of diversities – of peoples, of governments, and of economic regions; and that the regional aspirations and dynamisms have evolved throughout the past two decades to produce regional and community consciences, variously expressed. Flowing from these premises were certain basic principles. The federal government had the prime responsibility for the development of the Canadian identity; for developing policies to ensure economic progress and to stimulate and harmonize exchanges between the different communities, regions, and provinces; and for maintaining national criteria and sharing financial resources. But the different communities, regions, and provinces were the first artisans of their development. There should be a system of delegation of responsibilities, to correct formal rigidities. Finally, constitutional revision must take account of the rôle of the state and its presence in the life of individuals and collectivities.

The paper invoked the Pépin-Robarts report as its model for the rebuilding of Confederation.[8] It promised a new spirit of openness and détente in the federal government's approach to federal-provincial relations. It envisaged a federal green paper for the fall of 1980, to be submitted to a Senate-House joint committee, accompanied by similar provincial government ventures. The whole was eventually to be submitted to a first ministers' conference which would try and reach consensus on substance, and then on the stages and modalities of constitutional change.

This skeleton outline was hailed by Michel Roy in *Le Devoir* (8 January 1980) for its embracing of the principle of regionalism – already signalled by Pépin-Robarts – as an escape from the notion of a 'special' or 'particular' status for any one province and thus of 'every form of discrimination in favour of one Province rather than another, all of them having access to a system of delegation of which only some would take advantage.' The project was 'philosophical ... a project for a list of matters,' it seemed also to approve the Conservative decision not to hurry with constitutional revision pending the referendum vote and the next Quebec election.

The next day, in *Le Devoir*, Jean-Luc Pépin challenged the claimed links between the Tremblay document and his own commission's report. Finding a 'disconcerting generality' in the Tremblay paper, he reminded Clark that Pépin-Robarts had based its conception of a renewed Canadian federalism on federalism, dualism, and regionalism – dualism here implying official bilingualism, the two original founding peoples, and similar historical realities. The idea of constitutional dualism provided a necessary counterweight to the centrifugal elements inherent in any exaggerated notion of regionalism. The Tremblay document passed over the idea of constitutional dualism in silence, Pépin noted.

Three days later, in *The Gazette*, Tremblay returned to the attack. He had been instructed to use the Pépin-Robarts report as the basis of his work; however, he was still on the third draft of the table of contents of his report. The whole project had, of course, become aleatory after the budget débâcle, and it seemed to disappear and be forgotten after the election of a new Trudeau government.[9]

2

Constitutional parameters

The Supreme Court of Canada, in December 1979, rendered three long-awaited rulings – on the Senate reform proposals in the Constitutional Amendment Bill, 1978, which had lapsed with the dissolution of Parliament in the spring of 1979; on Quebec's Bill 101, in a case argued before the Court in June 1979; and on language rights in Manitoba, in a case argued as late as October 1979. It was widely expected the Court would 'twin' the language cases, balancing Quebec against Manitoba by releasing the judgments the same day.

Fortuitous elements of internal court organization now joined with pragmatic political decisions to determine the timing of release of the Court's rulings. First, Mr Justice Yves Pratte resigned from the Court on 28 June 1979, officially for reasons of health but with some suggestions of dissatisfaction on his part with the Court's work schedule.[1] According to Court rules, Mr Justice Pratte must render judgment, in every case in which he had sat, within six months of his resignation; in order to be eligible to participate in the final decision, these judgments would have to be rendered by 28 December 1979. Second, Chief Justice Laskin had fallen ill during the summer of 1979 after participating in the hearings on the Quebec language law case and the Senate reform advisory opinions. He had been hospitalized for a number of months on the west coast, far from Ottawa and day-by-day Court politics and administration, and unable to rejoin the Court for the opening of its fall session in October or indeed until early December. Finally, Mr Justice Pigeon was due to retire at the beginning of February 1980.

It was desirable from a public educational viewpoint to have as many as possible of the Court's nine judges participating in the final decisions in such *causes célèbres* and desirable from a practical viewpoint to have as many judges as possible take part in the decision-making process, the formation of a majority consensus, and the subsequent rationalization of that consensus in the opinion-writing. A December release became imperative.

It was widely believed that Chief Justice Laskin had originally assumed the obligation of writing the Court's opinion on the Senate reform issue, *Reference re Legislative Authority of Parliament to Alter or Replace the Senate*, 102 DLR (3d) 1 (1980); see extracts in Appendix F. This plan had been interrupted by his prolonged illness. The Court presented a *per curiam* ruling, on behalf of the eight judges participating in the final holding (Chief Justice Laskin, and Justices Martland, Ritchie, Pigeon, Dickson, Estey, Pratte, and McIntyre), without any indication as to its author or authors. Mr Justice Beetz had earlier disqualified himself from participating in the Senate matter on the ground of an expert opinion that he had given to the federal government years before, and touching on the Senate; any further delay in announcing the Court's ruling might have seen a bench of as few as six judges – a political and public relations disaster if the Court had not been unanimous. Well over a year later, during the course of argument before the Court on the issue of the constitutionality of the proposed joint (Senate-House) resolution to the Queen on repatriation of the BNA Act, Chief Justice Laskin, apparently by inadvertence, identified Mr Justice Martland as the author of the Senate reform ruling.[2]

The opinion is not a particularly satisfying disposition of a great constitutional case. It is anonymous and thereby fails to expose the nuances of the issue and individual judges' thinking and their doubts or questions; it also appears to lack a summary, in clear and direct language, and succinct form, of the actual grounds of decision. In short, for a plural (mixed common-law and civil-law) tribunal, the Court's ruling seems to miss the strengths of each tradition.

The questions, as formulated by federal justice minister Otto Lang, were as follows:

1 Is it within the legislative power of the Parliament of Canada to repeal sections 21 to 36 [the Senate] of the British North America Act, 1867, as amended, and to amend other sections thereof so as to delete any reference to an Upper House or the Senate? If not, in what particular or particulars and to what extent?

2 Is it within the legislative authority of the Parliament of Canada to enact legislation altering, or providing a replacement for, the Upper House of Parliament, so as to effect any or all of the following:

- (a) to change the name of the Upper House;
- (b) to change the numbers and proportions of members by whom provinces and territories are represented in that House;
- (c) to change the qualifications of members of that House;
- (d) to change the tenure of members of that House;
- (e) to change the method by which members of that House are chosen by ...
     (iv) providing for the direct election of all or some of the members of the Upper House by the public; or
- (f) to provide that Bills approved by the House of Commons could be given assent and the force of Law after the passage of a certain period of time notwithstanding that the Upper House has not approved them?

If not, in what particular or particulars and to what extent?

One preliminary question seemed to call for an answer, namely the jurisdictional issue. According to accepted canons of judicial self-restraint, a court should not rule on a constitutional issue if the matter can be disposed of on a prior, procedural, or adjectival law question. By the time the Court was prepared to rule on the Senate reform issue, the Trudeau government had long since been defeated and replaced; the Constitutional Amendment Bill, 1978, not having been enacted by Parliament before the government's defeat, had lapsed altogether. The failure of the Supreme Court at least to canvass the preliminary, procedural issue is a weakness in the Court's opinion. The opinion purports to be dedicated to a strict and complete legalism unrelieved, on its face, by policy considerations. The Court, here as in some of the 1978 decisions already referred to, in fact has contributed to its own subsequent difficulties by rushing to judgment in cases perhaps better left to the ordinary political process for resolution. From the moment of the Trudeau government's reference of the issue to the Court in November 1978, changing the Senate had disappeared as a priority concern and a matter of public controversy.

The opening pages of the opinion were a résumé of the constitutional amending process as set out in a 1965 federal government white paper signed by Justice Minister Guy Favreau, *The Amendment of the Constitution of Canada*. The Court took note also of the amendment of section 91(1) of the BNA Act, effected by the BNA (No. 2) Act, 1949, enacted by the British Parliament at the request of the federal government. It confers upon the federal Parliament exclusive legislative authority over

the amendment from time to time of the Constitution of Canada, except as regards matters coming within the classes of subjects by this Act assigned exclusively to the

Legislatures of the provinces, or as regards rights or privileges by this or any other Constitutional Act granted or secured to the Legislature or the Government of a province.

The Court looked at the measures subsequently enacted by the federal Parliament under this power. Two amendments, in 1952 and in 1974, readjusted representation in the House of Commons; one, in 1975, increased the representation in the House of Commons of the Northwest Territories. Two amendments affected the Senate, one in 1965 providing for the compulsory retirement of senators appointed henceforth at the age of seventy-five and one in 1975 providing for representation for the Yukon Territory and the Northwest Territories by one member each. These constitutional amendments the Court now (at p 8) dismissed as 'federal "housekeeping" matters which, according to the practice existing before 1949, would have been referred to the British Parliament by way of a joint resolution of both Houses of Parliament, and without the consent of the Provinces.'

This judicial dismissal was necessary to enable the Court to proceed (at pp 8–9) to a distinguishing of the case at hand:

The legislation contemplated is of an entirely different character. While it does not directly affect federal-provincial relationships in the sense of changing federal and provincial legislative powers, it does envision the elimination of one of the two Houses of Parliament, and so would alter the structure of the federal Parliament to which the federal power to legislate is entrusted under s. 91 of the Act.

The Senate has a vital *rôle* as an institution forming part of the federal system created by the Act.

The Court took note of the fact that the Senate 'was not and is not an elected body' (9) and cited Sir John A. Macdonald's view that the Senate's role was 'to protect local interests and to prevent sectional jealousies ... To the Upper House is to be confided the protection of sectional interests ... for the purpose of defending such interests against the combinations of majorities in the Assembly' (9).

It recited, with approval, a dictum by the Lord Chancellor, Lord Sankey, in the Privy Council in 1932 (*Re Aerial Navigation, A.-G. Can.* v *A.-G. Ontario et al.*, [1932] AC 54, 70) to the effect that the BNA Act 'embodies a compromise under which the original Provinces agreed to federate ... It is important to keep in mind that the preservation of the rights of minorities was a condition on which such minorities entered into the federation' (13). And it concluded that the power conferred on Parliament by section 91 (1) of the BNA Act, as amended by the BNA (No. 2) Act, 1949, in regard to 'the amendment ... of the Constitution of Canada,' in fact meant only that the subsection 'confers a power of amendment subject to specified exceptions which ... contemplate the continued existence of both the Senate and the House of Commons. For the foregoing reasons, we would answer the first question in the negative' (15–16).

In thus overriding the ordinary meaning of the words, the Court resorts to policy considerations extrinsic to the law itself. This is an accepted role for constitutional courts which admit, frankly, to a legislative, law-making function; it is less usual for the Supreme Court of Canada. Its justification has to be, first, that the words of the constitution are not explicit or unambiguous, and that the Court must perforce move boldly to fill the gap; and, second, that the policy considerations invoked can be justified in contemporary societal terms.

It is one thing to refer to the original intention, of the Fathers of Confederation, to make the Senate the protector of regional or sectional interests. But it is surely to live in von Ihering's famous 'Heaven of juristic concepts' remote from constitutional reality for the Court to insist on viewing the Senate as fulfilling any such role today. The Court seems to make the fatal confusion between constitutional law in books and constitutional law in action. As such, the judgment represents a flawed invocation of policy as a guide to the interpretation of constitution and statute.

These criticisms seem applicable, even more, to the Court's answers to the second main question. Although invoking, with apparent enthusiasm, the BNA Act's preambular reference to a 'Constitution similar in principle to that of the United Kingdom,' the judges view with repugnance the suggestion – in question 2(f) of the reference – that 'all bills be given assent and the force of law after a certain time period notwithstanding that they had not been approved by the Upper House' (16). This reduction of an unlimited veto power to a mere suspensive veto was accomplished as early as 1911 in the United Kingdom, without disturbing the constitutional foundations of the state.

Question 2(a), (b), (c), and (d) the Court refused to answer, 'in the absence of a factual context or actual draft legislation' (16). It did seem, in its comments in passing, to disapprove of the notion of a change of name for the Senate; of any change in the numbers of senators from the different provinces and territories so as to correspond to changes in population distribution, (this could affect 'the system of regional representation in the Senate ... one of the essential features of that body when it was created. Without it, the fundamental character of the Senate as part of the Canadian federal scheme would be eliminated' [17]); and of changes in the qualifications of senators or even of their tenure (presently, under the constitution, to the age of 75).

Question 2(e) (iv), on possible direct election of all or part of the Senate, was dismissed (18) on the score that it would

involve a radical change in the nature of one of the component parts of Parliament. As already noted, the preamble to the Act referred to 'a Constitution similar in principle to that of the United Kingdom', where the Upper House is not elected. In creating the Senate in the manner provided in the Act, it is clear that the intention was to make the Senate a thoroughly independent body which could canvass dispassionately the measures of the House of Commons. This was accomplished by providing for the appointment of members of the Senate with tenure for life. To make the Senate a wholly or partially elected body would affect a fundamental feature of that body. We would answer this subquestion in the negative (17).

It is a very static view to regard British constitutionalism as wedded to the principle of purely nominated or hereditary upper houses (compare Australia's directly elected Senate). In truth, the British House of Lords and the Canadian Senate are the exceptions – the constitutional aberrations, if you wish – in Commonwealth constitutionalism, where the clear trend is either to abolish upper houses or to legitimate them by election. The 'radical change' so deplored by the Supreme Court would in fact accord with the best trends in modern liberal democratic constitutionalism.

The Supreme Court implies that direct election would impair the function of the Senate as 'a thoroughly independent body which could canvass dispassionately the measures of the House of Commons' (18). Could it be seriously contended that the Senate, filled by political patronage on an appointive basis, does that? The Court would seem not merely to have departed from its own ordinary canons of strict and literal interpretation, but to posit its conclusions upon conceptions of the function and purpose of an upper house which the constitutional historian and the political scientist alike know to be unfounded. The Court would seem to have done its best to create further clogs upon constitutional change in Canada.

In November 1980 the Lamontagne subcommittee of the Senate's Standing Committee on Legal and Constitutional Affairs (the Goldenberg committee), presented its *Report on Certain Aspects of the Canadian Constitution*. The report recommended, among other things, a redress of present imbalances in Senate representation from the different provinces. This would involve increasing the Senate from 104 to 126 members, with each of the four western provinces and Newfoundland increasing in numbers: British Columbia and Alberta each to twelve senators, Manitoba and Saskatchewan each to ten senators, and Newfoundland to eight.

The subcommittee made a well-reasoned case for retention of a Senate as a house of 'sober, second thought.' It recommended rejection of various provincial governments' proposals for converting it into a House of the Provinces, constituted by provincial (patronage) appointments. These proposals, in the sub-committee's view, stemmed from a confusion between executive and legislative power in a federal system and from often wildly inaccurate perceptions of the foreign examples they purported to study (particularly the West German *Bundesrat*). The provincial proposals could better be achieved by building upon the first ministers' conferences.

The subcommittee still recommended substantive changes in the Senate. All future appointments should be for a ten-year term only, renewable for a further five years upon the recommendation, by secret ballot, of a special committee of the Senate. Legislative power should be limited to a suspensive veto. These positive recommendations, from a particularly enlightened group of senators, would seem to be blocked by the constitutional barriers created by the Supreme Court's advisory opinion.

On 13 December 1979, the Supreme Court released its judgments on the appeals in the Quebec and the Manitoba language laws cases. Chief Justice Laskin had originally indicated that the judgments would be handed down on 21 December, but this brought an immediate protest by Premier Lévesque, who had already announced that date for the official unveiling of his 'question' for the forthcoming Quebec referendum. Lévesque told reporters he would be in touch with the Supreme Court about the clash of dates; but the Court, in announcing the new and earlier date, said that it had received no word from Quebec and had decided on its own.[3]

The judgment – 101 DLR (3d) 394 (1980) – on Quebec's Bill 101 in *Attorney-General of Quebec* v *Blaikie* arose from a 1978 decision. Chief Judge Deschênes of the Superior Court of Montreal had ruled in early 1978 – 85 DLR (3d) 252 (1978) – and had been confirmed on appeal by a unanimous seven-judge bench of the Quebec Court of Appeal in late 1978 – 95 DLR (3d) 42 (1979). The latter had been appealed by the Quebec government to the Supreme Court. The federal attorney-general had intervened before the Superior Court and also the Court of Appeal of Quebec in support of the attack on the constitutionality of Bill 101.

The suit had been launched by three Montreal lawyers on the argument that articles 7 to 13 (chapter III, the language of the legislature and the courts) were *ultra vires* the Quebec legislature because they were in direct conflict with section 133 of the BNA Act. The question, in effect, was whether the Quebec legislature could, as part of its undoubted power under section 92(1) as to the 'amendment from time to time, notwithstanding anything in this Act, of the Constitution of the Province,' amend section 133 by indirection so far as it required the use of English, as well as French, in the Quebec legislature and in the Quebec courts.

Before the Supreme Court, the federal attorney-general again intervened in behalf of the three Montreal lawyers contesting Bill 101 and was joined by the attorney-general of New Brunswick. They were also joined by the litigious Mr Forest of Manitoba, who was challenging Manitoba's language law; his late intervention was allowed by the Supreme Court – 101 DLR (3d) 394, at 396 (1980) – in a very broad definition of the minimum legal 'interest' necessary before one may challenge the constitutionality of a statute. The Quebec government was joined by the Manitoba government in its appeal.

The nub of the Supreme Court's unanimous judgment is to be found in its adoption of Chief Judge Deschênes's reasoning that section 133 is not part of the 'Constitution of the Province' within the meaning of section 92(1), but is 'rather part of the constitution of Canada and of Quebec in an indivisible sense, giving official status to French and English in the Parliament and in the Courts of Canada as well as in the Legislature and Courts of Quebec' (394, 400).

The Court then reached out for a notion foreign to Canadian constitutional jurisprudence, of 'entrenchment' beyond the possibility of amendment or repeal except by some extraordinary means. (Sections 35 and 152 of the South Africa Act allowed repeal [amendment] only by an extraordinary, two-thirds majority of the South African Parliament.) The Supreme Court of Canada did not spell out just how, and by whom, and through what processes, and with what extraordinary majorities, if any, entrenchment had been secured, and it gave no supporting citations. The conclusion rests upon the Court's own categorical assertion (at 401), in its judgment:

But s. 133 is an entrenched provision, not only forbidding modification by unilateral action of Parliament or of the Quebec Legislature but also providing a guarantee to Members of Parliament or of the Quebec Legislature and to litigants in the Courts of Canada or of Quebec that they are entitled to use either French or English in parliamentary or legislative assembly debates or in pleading (including oral argument) in the courts of Canada or of Quebec.

The Court then ventured into the administrative implications and applications of its ruling. Citing assorted general dicta from Privy Council decisions of yesteryear[4] in favour of avoiding 'overly-technical' judicial approaches and opting instead for 'broad' or 'flexible' interpretations (394, 403), it reasoned that 'the proper approach to an entrenched provision ... [is] to make it effective through the range of institutions which exercise judicial power, be they called courts or adjudicative agencies' (404).

According to section 133,

not only is the option to use either language given to any person involved in proceedings before the Courts of Quebec or its other adjudicative tribunals (and this covers both written and oral submissions) but documents emanating from such bodies or issued in their name or under their authority may be in either language, and this option extends to the issuing and publication of judgments or other orders (404).

In speculation in late 1979 it had been pointed out that every Quebec law enacted since the adoption of Bill 101 in 1977 had been adopted solely in French. Although the Quebec government continued to translate its laws, the English version, available for anglophone citizens, was not official. If the Supreme Court should uphold the complaint against Bill 101, then all these laws would become unconstitutional and would have to be voted again in the national assembly, this time in French and in English.

The Court decision struck down only sections 7 to 13; and the Lévesque government immediately brought forward its own emergency, omnibus bill, already prepared, retroactively passing in English all the laws that had been passed only in French. This omnibus bill was adopted on 14 December, following eight hours of debate through the preceding night.[5] Despite the general sigh of relief that the enormous inconveniences caused by the Supreme Court judgment could be overcome so quickly and easily, doubts remained as to the effects of the Court's ruling upon Quebec administrative law as a whole. These stemmed from a certain generality and imprecision in the formulation of the Court's opinion, a failure to spell out its practical application in any helpful detail, and the suspicion that perhaps the Court itself had not fully comprehended all the implications of its own decision at the time of announcing judgment. In the later opinion of Quebec government jurists, all laws passed only in French since the adoption of Bill 101 could be challenged constitutionally, as could all administrative regulations adopted by the Quebec government in that period and indeed all administrative regulations adopted since 1867 that were not adopted in both French and English. According to the same reasoning based on the Court's opinion, all municipal regulations and all school board regulations were also affected with the same nullity if not adopted in both languages.[6]

In the face of confusion of potentially vast dimensions the only rational solution would be to approach the judges themselves for a clarification of those questions raised, but left unanswered or obscure, in their judgment.[7]

The Quebec justice minister, citing 'anarchy and legal insecurity' for Quebec administrative agencies, municipalities, and school boards, made application to the Supreme Court in February 1980, for just such a clarification. He sought at the same time that the Court restrain its judgment so as not to apply to 'decentralised organisms' such as the municipalities and the school boards.[8]

The Supreme Court, on 6 April 1981,[9] finally accepted this argument, in part at least. It specifically exempted municipalities and school boards in Quebec (and in Manitoba also) from the obligation to enact their regulations in both French and English. The unanimous decision of the seven-man bench based this latest ruling on the fact that the municipalities and school boards were using only one language before the BNA Act took effect. Although section 133 does not refer specifically to municipalities and school boards, the Court concluded that that could not be viewed as an oversight but must be considered a 'purposeful silence' to which effect must be given if the founding fathers' intent were to be respected. The BNA Act used religious safeguards, not linguistic ones; and since it was explicit on the subject of religious safeguards with respect to education (section 93), its silence on language of school by-laws must also be deliberate. Hence section 133 should not apply to school by-laws. The Court, however, ruled at the same time that semi-public bodies, such as public utilities and professional associations, that adopt regulations requiring government approval must use both French and English in the regulations they publish. Lawyers for the Quebec government were reported, after this latest ruling, as indicating that it would not mean major changes for the way the Quebec government operated, all legislation and regulations requiring the lieutenant-governor's decision being, by now, in both French and English.[10]

On the same day as its judgment on the *Blaikie* appeal, the Supreme Court gave its ruling on appeal from the Manitoba courts in the *Forest* case, involving constitutionality of Manitoba's language laws. Once again, the decision was unanimous *Attorney-General of Manitoba* v *Forest*, 101 DLR (3d) 385 (1980). The case had arisen from a five-dollar automobile parking ticket issued in 1976, and written in English. The complainant, Forest, a private citizen and Franco-Manitoban, had sought to use that case as a device for testing the constitutionality of the Official Language Act of Manitoba (1890), making English the sole official language in the Manitoba legislature and courts. The federal Manitoba Act (1870) had expressly permitted the use of either English or French in the Manitoba legislature and courts. Thus, a constitutional question necessarily arose as to the power of the Manitoba legislature to repeal (in 1890) the language sections of the 1870 statute.

A complex set of legal manoeuvres arose. Forest had brought what is called a taxpayer's suit, seeking a declaration of the unconstitutionality of the 1890 statute. The Court of Queen's Bench of Manitoba, in a ruling by Chief Justice Dewar in mid-1978 – 90 DLR (3d) 230 (1979) – based on the preliminary, procedural question, held that Forest did not possess the necessary interest to entitle him to a declaration on the validity of the Manitoba statute. Chief Justice Dewar's holding was based on a careful review of general Commonwealth[11] and also recent Canadian[12] case law on the degree of 'interest' necessary for a plaintiff to be able to invoke the constitutional issue.

However, in 1979, the Manitoba Court of Appeal, in a unanimous decision – 98 DLR (3d) 405 (1979) – overruled the Court of Queen's Bench decision. In a judgment written by Chief Justice Freedman, it reversed the Court of Queen's Bench on the preliminary, procedural question, holding that Forest had the necessary standing for an adjudication. It held, on the merits, that the 1890 act, so far as it abrogated the right to use French in the courts of Manitoba, fell because of conflict with the paramount federal statute, the Manitoba Act of 1870, as confirmed by the BNA Act of 1871. Chief Justice Freedman pointed out that the original French-speaking citizens of Manitoba had been induced to put an end to their insurrection against the British crown during Manitoba's formative years on the basis that their rights would be ensured. The Manitoba Act, admitting Manitoba to Confederation, guaranteed Franco-Manitobans the maintenance of their linguistic rights, and it was simply not constitutionally competent for the province of Manitoba, by the later provincial statute, to take away those rights.

In the proceedings before the Manitoba courts, the federal attorney-general had intervened in behalf of the original complainant, Forest; and he was joined, in the hearings on the appeal to the Supreme Court, by the attorney-general of New Brunswick. Manitoba's Official Language Act of 1890 had instituted English-language unilingualism not merely in court proceedings in Manitoba, but in the records and journals of the legislative assembly; and it had also provided that statutes enacted by the legislature need be printed and published only in English. The conflict with the Manitoba Act was clear and direct. The province was compelled, in order to try to justify the claimed supremacy of the later, provincial statute to rely upon section 92(1) of the BNA Act and the power therein contained for the province to legislate as to 'the amendment from time to time, notwithstanding anything in this Act, of the Constitution of the Province.'

In its ruling, the Supreme Court gave a restrictive interpretation of the meaning of 'Constitution of the Province':

Although, in a certain way, the whole Manitoba Act may be said to be the Constitution of the Province, it is apparent that the amending power conferred by s. 92(1) cannot have been intended to apply to the whole of this statute any more than all the provisions of the B.N.A. Act touching upon the Constitution of the Provinces in this wide sense can be said to be subject to it. For instance, the provision respecting education, s. 93 [of the B.N.A. Act] ...
    The judgments in ... cases under s. 93 show that these provisions were considered as entrenched. (389)

It is clear – though this part of the ruling is somewhat elliptical in its reasoning – that the Court assimilated section 23 of the Manitoba Act of 1870 to section 133 of the BNA Act in terms of constitutional weight or authority. Both, in the Court's view, were constitutionally entrenched and therefore beyond the powers respectively of the Manitoba legislature and the Quebec legislature to amend by provincial legislation passed under section 92(1) of the BNA Act.

I shall leave to one side the general issue whether such a concept as entrenchment is not anachronistic in relation to the BNA Act and also whether it is not inconsonant with the sovereignty of Parliament, which dictates that, within their respective law-making competences under sections 91 and 92, the federal and the provincial governments have plenary, unlimited law-making powers.

One yet wonders why the Court did not apply the normal principle of constitutional construction of deciding on a lesser, non-constitutional ground, where it is available. On ordinary principles of federal supremacy, the Manitoba Act of 1870, as expressly recognized and assimilated by the BNA Act of 1871, would, as both constitutional law and also federal law enacted within federal law-making competence, rank as superior to provincial statute law. In avoiding the simplest and most obviously direct and economical route to decision, the Supreme Court was clearly seeking to render an object lesson on language rights in a broader, pan-Canadian context, and in effect to 'balance' Quebec and Manitoba together. There may be political advantage in this, of course, but it has to be balanced against the general skimpiness of the legal reasoning and argumentation in the Manitoba ruling.

Even the advantage in balancing Quebec and Manitoba did not, however, go unchallenged. *Le Devoir* commented that the apparent equality between the two decisions remained abstract and theoretical. As Premier Lévesque had remarked, it had needed hardly two years to re-establish in Quebec an equilibrium between English and French that Quebec's Bill 101 of 1977 had broken. In Manitoba, in contrast, the Court's current judgment could not efface a century of injustice to Franco-Manitobans: it could not bring back to life a francophone community largely eaten up by assimilation into the anglophone majority.[13] As the *Fédération des francophones hors Québec* also commented, restoring to French its status of an official language in Manitoba would change nothing as to the loss of control by Franco-Manitobans over their education, their economy, and all the institutions of their collectivity.[14] The conscious joining of the two decisions by the Supreme Court thus was viewed as somewhat arch and overly calculating and may have been counter-productive.

The other major criticism advanced against the *Forest* ruling echoes the criticisms made by the Quebec government against the *Blaikie* ruling, though with even more intensity. Manitoba's attorney-general, Mr Mercier, estimated that all provincial laws enacted since 1890 would now have to be translated into French, a task which he thought might cost $15 million.[15] He indicated that the provincial government would indeed move to re-establish services in the two official languages, in the legislative assembly and in the courts. It would vote $500,000 over the next fourteen months to translate laws and regulations into French and would provide free translators in the courts, since only three or four magistrates were sufficiently bilingual to act in French. Mercier, a French-Canadian by origin but speaking no French, conceded that if the provincial law of 1890 had not been adopted 'you would have had a bilingual Attorney-General.'[16]

The Supreme Court was buffetted by more than its fair share of misfortunes and unable to maintain a continuing collegial presence throughout the stages of consensus formation in these three important cases. We see a bench of fluctuating membership, forced to stretch its own practice to muster a persuasive number of voices for any final decision. Some of those decisions give the appearance of having been hastily put together, as to both substance as well as form, behind the public facade of unanimity.

The Court sometimes seems overly eager to engage itself in political battles. Perhaps it should apply the principle and lessons of judicial self-restraint – insist upon a valid and sufficient constitutional 'interest'; resolve cases, wherever possible, on preliminary issues; decide on lesser grounds before ruling on issues of constitutionality. Such an approach might spare the Court some disappointments and some embarrassments, without any loss to the cause of community problem-solving in general.

3

The Quebec referendum

Premier Lévesque, in his 1976 election campaign, had promised a referendum on separation before any future Parti québécois government would try to take Quebec out of Confederation. This promise was thought to have been a crucial factor in his electoral victory. After the elections, Lévesque seemed determined to try to make an ally of time and to launch a massive public educational campaign to build up to a majority from the estimated less than 20 per cent of Québécois who were thought to be supporters of separatism. This was undoubtedly the key factor in the repeated postponements of the referendum; though some observers, noting the often uneasy balance within the ministry of social democrats and nationalists, began to speculate about the government's seriousness about the referendum.

The government sought the most attractive question[1] and chose a 'soft' question rather than a 'hard' one, one with generalities and abstractions as a deliberate device for reducing opposition. The government sidestepped some incidental constitutional questions – whether a province might validly legislate to hold its own referendum on separation from the national whole, and whether the question should not be subjected to due process tests of 'vagueness' and required to meet at least minimum criteria of clarity and comprehensibility. The federal government, for political reasons presumably and not for constitutional ones, decided not to challenge the holding of the referendum or the formulation of the question. And so the campaign was free to proceed on a high plane, free from incidental complications.

The question, released in December 1979, was long and editorializing in tone and content, if not indeed argumentative or tendentious:

THE QUESTION:

The government of Quebec has made public its proposal to negotiate a new agreement with the rest of Canada, based on the equality of nations.

This agreement would enable Quebec to acquire the exclusive power to make its laws, administer its taxes and establish relations abroad – in other words, sovereignty – and at the same time, to maintain with Canada an economic association including a common currency.

Any change in political status resulting from these negotiations will be submitted to the people through a referendum.

On these terms, do you agree to give the government the mandate to negotiate the proposed agreement between Quebec and Canada?

YES ☐
NO ☐

The question was watered down to coax reluctant supporters who might rally to the government's social democratic ideas but not to its separatist cause. Its third paragraph promised yet another referendum before Quebec could leave Confederation, if only Quebec voters would vote yes this time. A yes vote now would give nothing more than a mandate to negotiate with the federal government, and on 'sovereignty-association,' not outright separation. The complex sovereignty-association concept had been the subject of a special Quebec government white paper, *La nouvelle entente Québec-Canada. Proposition du gouvernement du Québec pour une entente d'égal à égal: la souveraineté-association*, issued about the time of the early announcement of the referendum question; but it remained a highly, perhaps deliberately ambiguous, proposal. It seemed capable of facing both ways at once – towards independence under a smokescreen juridical formula, and towards Quebec's remaining within Confederation with powers, as set out in the referendum question itself, not necessarily substantially surpassing those already existing. 'Camouflage and evasion,' said Quebec Opposition Leader Claude Ryan in replying to Lévesque's first announcement of the referendum question; 'manoeuvring and deceitful, it reflects the opportunism and intellectual confusion of the government, it drowns the desired objective in the means for achieving it.'[2] Did the referendum question conform to Quebec's own referendum law, the law on popular consultation (Bill 92 of 1978)? Opinions had been given by Quebec jurist and Liberal deputy Herbert Marx to the effect that the question as actually posed was illegal under the Quebec law,[3] but Ryan decided not to contest the legality and to fight the referendum campaign on the political merits.

The campaign focused on fundamental issues of Canadian federalism and Quebec's role in it, and on the differing conceptions of the three main leaders, Lévesque and Ryan of course, but also necessarily Prime Minister

Trudeau. It was a debate between French-Canadians; interventions by Anglo-Canadians seemed largely irrelevant and designed perhaps more for home audiences than with any serious expectation of influencing the outcome. The debate turned as much on Ryan's philosophy of federalism as on Lévesque's. Ryan had been the publisher and principal editorialist of *Le Devoir* for a decade and a half prior to his entry into politics and his election as Liberal leader in April 1978. He had a fully developed and self-consistent body of constitutional ideas. His signed articles over the years covered most aspects of federal-provincial relations, Quebec's own special constitutional claims, and the vexed language question both at the federal and national level and within Quebec itself. His editorials had strongly influenced Quebec's rejection of the so-called Victoria Charter of 1971 on which there had been a full federal and provincial consensus, and also the final shape of Bill 22 of 1974, which made French the official language of Quebec. It may be queried whether he had any pressing need now to essay a definition of his constitutional thinking.

Overriding the normal counsels of prudence that an opposition should confine itself to attacking a government's program and keep it on the defensive, Ryan set up a commission to advise on constitutional questions. Commencing work in June 1978, it presented a 145-page book (*Livre beige*) in January 1980 – *Une Nouvelle Fédération canadienne*. Composed principally of young lawyers, and with a large panel of consultants, the commission undertook twenty separate and distinct studies, on cultural affairs, communications, the economy, manpower and immigration and labour, industry and commerce, the financial and banking system, and related matters. The reach was thus vast, and its time was limited by the forthcoming referendum and election.

The problem was compounded by the commission's decision not to limit itself, as every Quebec government since the opening of the Quiet Revolution had done, to identifying Quebec's special cultural, social, and economic conditions and needs and the adjustments flowing therefrom, but to attempt a more comprehensive outlook and to develop a constitutional plan of which Quebec's claims would simply be part. This was courageous and magnanimous, but it ran two risks: the chance of error as to what the rest of Canada might want, and also the possibility of diluting Quebec's special constitutional needs and claims in the quest for a genuinely 'Canadian' constitutional program.

There was no time for sociological studies of conditions in English-speaking Canada, and the commission was dependent upon whatever data and evaluations of public concerns in English Canada could be filtered through heavily right-of-centre provincial administrations. Most of these had only rudimentary conceptions of constitutional change. Quebec leaders of the 1960s had recognized that the federal government and the other provinces were not prepared to accept a decentralization or weakening of the federal system. Quebec's case for a 'special' or 'particular' constitutional status had therefore supposed that Canada would remain centralized, along post-Keynesian lines, for all the other provinces.

The *Livre beige* owed obvious intellectual debts to the Pépin-Robarts report published twelve months before. A number of the Pépin-Robarts research staff spilled over into the Liberal commission and the wider ranks of its specialist consultants. The *Livre beige* displayed much of the philosophical sweep and grandeur of the Pépin-Robarts original, and also some of its more manifest weaknesses – the attempt to assume the functions of a constituent assembly and to produce a detailed constitutional blueprint. The blueprint, because of its very detail, could become very quickly dated in the light of subsequent events and remain a straight-jacket for the party leader.

The *Livre beige* was admirable in its clear identification of key concepts and its ability to move from high-level, abstract principles to intermediate or secondary principles that might be more immediately useful in problem-solving. This, in the early part of the work, was thought to owe most to Ryan and in terms of its style and rigorous reasoning bore the stamp of his years at *Le Devoir*. The later, detailed constitutional prescriptions were the work of the commission members and consultants without too much direct input from Ryan who, as a busy party leader, could hardly engage himself in day-by-day debates and exchanges. The *leitmotif* of Pépin-Robarts had been federalism, dualism, and regionalism and an equilibrium or balance of constitutional forces between them at any time. This conception is not repeated here. The equality of the 'two founding peoples' is affirmed, along with the need to 'grant to Quebec guarantees appropriate to facilitate the protection and affirmation of its distinct personality ... guarantees which should not be narrowly confined to the sole field of cultural policy' (22, my translation). But, such guarantees ought not to 'contradict the principle according to which *all* the partners [in the federal system] should be fundamentally equal within the federation' (22).

Dualism thus seemed subordinated to regionalism, and Quebec's particularity to a general provincial rights stance. Quebec would try to bargain with Ottawa for a general decentralization in favour of *all* the provinces. Quebec would benefit, but the commitment of the other provinces to decentralization would still have to be demonstrated. This apparent downgrading of Quebec's special role was a principal source of the manifest lack of enthusiasm with which the paper was greeted by intellectual elements in French Canada. Almost without exception, Quebec intellectual leaders, from Léon Dion and Gérard Bergeron on, criticized these aspects of the paper.

The paper was often *avant-garde* in constitutional terms:

> It supported an entrenched Bill of Rights which would recognise French and English as the official languages of federal institutions, extend to Ontario and New Brunswick the obligations already imposed on Quebec and on Manitoba by section 133 of the B.N.A. Act and by section 23 of the Manitoba Act respectively, and give to every individual of the French or English language the right to require that his children receive primary or secondary education, in their maternal language, in the Province in which they were resident. (32–3)

Further

> It provided for a constitutionally explicit status for the Native Peoples of Canada, with a specific guarantee of their rights and their cultural and linguistic traditions, and with the Native Peoples to be represented and consulted in any discussions on the adoption of a new constitution. (85–6)

Its stipulation as to language of education was far broader in the rights accorded to non-French persons than those in either Bill 22 or Bill 101, and so the criticisms of the loopholes in both those bills would apply even more to the *Livre beige* – a point of attack for commentators. On the related cultural issue of control over cable television, it broke with post-Quiet Revolution positions in stipulating that while the allocation of frequencies and technical norms should belong to the federal government, there should be no specific allocation of competence as to the content of radio, TV, or cable TV broadcasts. On this point, former Liberal minister Jean-Paul L'Allier broke with Ryan and came out in favour of a yes vote in the referendum campaign.

Among English-language commentators, and also among federal Liberals in Ottawa, a principal source of challenge came in the proposals for institutional change. Mainstream thinking since the Quiet Revolution would have seen the Senate converted into a 'deux nations' chamber, with its members drawn equally from Quebec and English Canada and retaining the existing rights of veto of federal legislation. The *Livre beige* opted for the abolition of the Senate and for its replacement by a new body – a *Conseil fédéral* – which would 'concretise the interdependence of the two orders of government.' It would be composed of delegations named by the provincial governments, would act on the mandate and instructions of those governments, and vote *en bloc* according to those instructions. Delegations were to be proportional to population, with Quebec to have a minimum of 25 per cent of the total.

The new federal council was to have drastic powers in relation to the federal government and federal instrumentalities, its agreement (ratification) being required for all of the following:

the exercise of the federal Emergency power;
the exercise of the federal spending power in areas of provincial competence;
every delegation of legislative competence between governments;
treaties concluded by the federal government in areas of provincial competence;
international and interprovincial plans for the marketing of agricultural products;
the nominations of the chief justice and the justices of the Supreme Court of Canada, and their removal from office;
the nominations of the presidents and directors of federal crown corporations and similar federal institutions.

The council was also to have the right to be consulted and to give its opinions on the monetary policies and the budget and fiscal policies of the federal government, on the mechanisms and rules for application of financial equalization throughout Canada, and on every federal initiative that it judged to have an important regional or provincial effect.

Finally, it would have a permanent committee, composed 50 per cent of French-language persons, to pass on (and ratify) federal government initiatives on language and related cultural matters within federal competence and also to ensure that the federal civil service reflect at all levels the French-English dualism.

In sum, the new federal council would have been able to exercise a stranglehold over major areas of federal activity by either refusing its assent or else applying its right to be consulted and to give its opinions in such a way as to obstruct federal decision-making. This caused dismay among strong federalists, leading to the recurrent suggestion that Liberals in Ottawa were less than happy with it. Ryan's supporters insisted that the federal council was a new body, separate and distinct from the existing Senate, which was to be abolished. There were some links to the existing first ministers' conferences. Yet by and large the federal council seems to have been directly borrowed – without any independent research – from the *Bundesrat* proposal that had been circulating among various private interest groups and foundations for several years. It had been taken up most recently by the Pépin-Robarts commission. The federalists saw attenuation of federal decision-making power – a 'House of Obstruction' – and Quebec nationalists saw the abandonment of Quebec's special historical claims. Hence the *Livre beige* neither received the intellectual support nor exercised the political influence that the quality of its authors and their research warranted. In the long run, it forced Ryan to go on the defensive, particularly on language of education, and may thus have contributed to his eventual defeat in the 1981 election. Such issues were not so predominant in the referendum campaign and in any case were balanced there by Trudeau and various English-speaking premiers' promises for a renewal of the federal system after any no vote on sovereignty-association.

The vote result of the referendum was clear-cut and decisive, 59½ per cent no and 40½ per cent yes; 80 per cent of Quebec's 4.4 million voters cast their ballots. What did the substantial majority voting no opt for? Was it for Ryan and the *Livre beige*? Was it for Prime Minister Trudeau's constitutional changes? Was it for the vision of a new federal system projected by those English-speaking Premiers who ventured in person into the latter stages of the campaign? Or was it simply an expression of a conviction that self-determination could best be achieved – and to a very considerable extent already had been achieved – within Canadian federalism? The host of variables and actors in the campaign compounds the problem of deciding just what mandate can be extracted from it.

The role of the English-speaking premiers was, even on the most favourable appraisal, of only marginal significance, but had an importance for the post-referendum period when Trudeau endeavoured to engage them in a renewal of federalism. Of the four premiers who chose to intervene, Premier Davis comes through most clearly, although even he tended perhaps to speak too much in terms of generalities. He did announce that the Ontario government would refuse to negotiate sovereignty-association, in whatever form, in the event of a yes vote; he refused to comment publicly on the *Livre beige* and its constitutional proposals. But he did engage Ontario to undertake the task of constitutional reform after the referendum vote; and he also promised a renewed federation in which the French fact – in Quebec and in the provinces with French-speaking minorities (principally Ontario) – would be promoted.[4]

Perhaps the last word on the referendum should belong to a Québécois. In his book *Le Québec et le Canada. Les voies de l'avenir* (1980), Professor Léon Dion quotes an answer he gave – in Edmonton – to the question 'What does Quebec want?': 'I am a tired federalist.' His book is a form of personal odyssey; unwilling to embrace the separatist program of the Parti québécois, yet unhappy with the classical federalism of Trudeau, he is gravely disappointed by what he characterizes as the lack of intellectual rigour and of respect for all the lessons of Quebec history in the *Livre beige*. Dion was finally led to conclude that he must vote yes, while waiting, vainly, for constitutional reform that will be something of a third way between the Lévesque and Ryan positions.

Dion is at his best as a critic, for he draws upon his formidable skills as both a sociologist and a political scientist. The lack of an adequate attention to societal facts has made so many constitutional reform projects essentially exercises in logic and not in life and thus largely irrelevant. Dion uses sociological tools to clarify and identify the alternative constitutional premises for a renewed federal system, and then, and only then, applies his Cartesian discipline to explore all the logical consequences of each possible basis for a new system. He rejects the notion of constitutional decentralization of all the provinces, and the alternative notion of five regions. Both run counter to all the historical trends of liberal, post-industrial societies and also misunderstand the true character of Canadian society. If Quebec is a distinct society within the Canadian political society as a whole, so is anglophone Canada which (regrettably, in Dion's view) doesn't yet see itself that way. The conclusion is clear, however, that while there are deux nations, there are certainly not dix nations.

After a decade and a half of sound arguments for 'special' or 'particular' status for Quebec, and just when many people in English Canada seemed prepared to accept such a condition, some key Quebec leaders chose to abandon it in favour of an exaggerated provincial rights campaign anchored as much, or more, in the ambitions of certain natural resources-rich, English-speaking provinces, as in Quebec itself. Such an unholy alliance contained perils for Quebec unless the new western allies could count, like successive Quebec governments, on continuing public support for their special demands – a condition yet to be demonstrated. This seems Dion's major objection to the *Livre beige*.

The Pépin-Robarts report seems to come closest to meeting Dion's rigorous standards. It also perhaps accepted more at face value than it should have the degree of popular backing for provincial rights, but it did make significant openings towards the notion of asymmetrical constitutional arrangements which would make possible some sort of special status for Quebec. Dion was one of those 'three wise men' called in by the Pépin-Robarts commission, half-way through its labours, as a guide for the choice of the commission's main policy options, and these sections of the report, at least, owe a good deal to Dion's constitutional thinking.

Indications, once again, that timely administrative pragmatism may be the most useful solvent for Canadian federal problems had been given in the aftermath to the decisions (of the Federal Court in 1977 and the Federal Court of Appeal in 1978) in the dispute between the francophone and anglophone air traffic controllers in Quebec (*Association des Gens de l'Air du Québec* v *Lang*).[5] A federal commission of enquiry composed of three judges (Judges Chouinard, Heald, and Sinclair) unanimously recommended, in the summer of 1979, that Quebec skies should become bilingual for air traffic control, and the federal government promptly decided, in August 1979, to authorize the use of French in aerial communications in Quebec.

The decision, perhaps predictably, was assailed by the anglophone Canadian Air Traffic Controllers Association (CATCA), as endangering security in the air, but the commission and the federal government were impressed by all the empirical evidence of the safe operation of bilingualism in air traffic control even within the crowded air corridors of western Europe.[6] Michel Roy in *Le Devoir* noted (6 April 1979) the delay involved in applying in 1979 a decision for which all the rational justification was known and available three years earlier, when the dispute had first arisen, and also the recourse to a commission of enquiry. He speculated that the federal government saw the need to conquer, by gradualist means, resistance by English Canada to the introduction of French into Quebec skies. It wouldn't have sufficed simply to say that bilingualism presents no risks in aviation: it was necessary to prove it carefully, making an ally of time to do so.

Executive pragmatism has had its place, too, in the area of language policy, rendering at least tolerable divergent and often seemingly incompatible federal and provincial policies. I have suggested that the most significant legal heritage of the Quiet Revolution has been the two language laws, Bill 22 of 1974 and Bill 101 of 1977. The ties between the two are clear, in spite of party differences. These bills have enabled a social and economic revolution to be effected within Quebec in the guise of a linguistic reform. The French-as-language-of-work stipulations have been rather more important in their impact than the French-as-official-language sections. They opened the way to access, at long last, and on some equitable basis, by the French-Canadian majority in Quebec, to economic decision-making power in the province.

There was a time when we seemed, in Canada, to be mounting two radically different and mutually irreconcilable language policies – federal official bilingualism policies, expressed in the Official Languages Act of 1969 and resting on the 'personality' principle; and Quebec government policies which effectively 'territorialized' the French fact within the province of Quebec. A collision course seemed more or less inevitable, but has been avoided. The federal government refrained from frontal assaults, in the courts, to both Quebec language laws. Such complaints as emerged came from individuals or pressure groups within the anglophone community of Quebec.

Though the federal government might intervene in such private litigation, as in the *Blaikie* case, the litigation was usually on subsidiary or peripheral issues, so that even if successful, as in *Blaikie*, it would not threaten the major sections of the bill. Ottawa's legal interventions, though no doubt designed with some degree of mischief in regard to the Lévesque government, seemed also directed as much or more to the anglophone community outside Quebec – to indicate that the federal government was indeed actively fighting Quebec's language policies. Such interventions were deliberately modest and low key and never pejorative.

This seeming self-restraint was balanced, increasingly, by increasing flexibility, common sense, and humanity in Quebec's application of its own language-of-work stipulations. Pragmatic adjustments and compromises such as these, on both sides, have facilitated coexistence of federal and Quebec language policies, with distinct and separate, but not conflicting, zones of application for each. The two language policies may conceivably emerge as complementary and mutually supportive.

Are we seeing – have we in fact already seen – the emergence of a new and fundamental compromise involving accommodation of the two different language policies, federal and Quebec? One of the rare qualities of the BNA Act, and one of the key reasons for the survival of the constitutional system it established, is its very open-endedness; this has enabled its accommodation, without significant textual changes, to a rapidly evolving society. While it has remained virtually intact, it has undergone significant changes in its *meta*-legal, political premises. There have been several such significant changes since 1867, without any corresponding change in the constitutional text. Issues of ultimate political philosophy, those 'inarticulate major premises,' become vital at certain times, as Donald Smiley has reminded us.[7] It is tempting to try to explain the sovereignty-association vote, as being, at least in part, due to a sophisticated recognition of this new and basic fact, and of its important practical consequences for the survival and extension of the French fact within Quebec and Canada as a whole. If such a basic compromise has emerged, it would be at least as important as the rewriting of the superstructure – the BNA Act.

4

Federal-provincial diplomacy summer 1980

The defeat of sovereignty-association in the Quebec referendum brought a certain mood of relief and gratitude – almost of public thanksgiving – in English Canada. It brought also a flood of premature, and as it turned out inaccurate, predictions that the Parti québécois was finished and a new 'federalist' government would soon be installed. Mr Ryan himself argued that Premier Lévesque should heed the referendum verdict and immediately dissolve the national assembly and call fresh elections.[1] Lévesque, however, chose to bide his time and waited a further eleven months. In the mean time he continued to attend first ministers' conferences and to take part in intergovernmental discussions both on the ordinary housekeeping business of the federal system and also on proposals for its renewal or reform.[2] Neither Prime Minister Trudeau nor any of the English-speaking premiers challenged his right to do so; and some of the bitterest English-speaking foes of Trudeau and of the federal government (and the most recalcitrant opponents of both the French fact in Quebec and of official bilingualism) soon embraced Lévesque as a worthy and active ally in a common cause against Ottawa. The intellectual inconsistency of such a complete *volte-face* seems not to have bothered or even to have occurred to these premiers. Lévesque, for his part, together with his minister for inter-governmental affairs, Claude Morin, reacted to this strange political turn-around with wry good humour, participating elegantly, even jovially, in the premiers' desperate attempts to remake Confederation in their own image by wresting more and more power from Ottawa, while at the same time officially maintaining his public commitment to eventual secession from Canada.[3]

In English Canada there was a desire to do something, as yet undefined, as payment of one's debt of gratitude to Quebec. The federal government, aware from experience that moods of public euphoria tend to be short-lived, decided to profit from this fleeting moment and to move on the constitutional front.[4] But in what direction, and with what specific formulae? The problem was to define the mandate deriving from the referendum vote. The four English-speaking premiers who had intervened in the campaign had been halting and unspecific, and whatever commitment they had to recognition of the French fact in Quebec dissipated very quickly after the votes had been counted.

The remaining premiers immediately demonstrated that the new constitutional opportunity, for them, had nothing to do with Quebec but solely with promoting their own provincial interests; and this not even on a unified basis, which might at least have facilitated some balancing with French interests, but on an every-man-for-himself basis. The only common point was opposition to Ottawa in every form.[5] An important opportunity for timely constitutional change when there seemed to be a consensus or at least willingness in English Canada to do something for Quebec may have been lost thereby.

Prime Minister Trudeau had his own problems in defining the mandate from the Quebec referendum campaign. He had actively intervened and campaigned with a generally recognized substantial impact on the final result. He had himself promised substantial, but unspecified change in the federal constitution *after* a no vote. His eleven years as prime minister, and concrete measures such as the Official Languages Act and projected measures such as the Constitutional Amendment Bill, 1978, presaged the direction, if not the intensity of commitment, of federal initiatives.

There were significant differences in philosophy, and also of a programmatic character, between the federal Liberals and Claude Ryan's provincial Liberals, which became patent during the referendum campaign. Ryan, strongly influenced by the Pépin-Robarts report, had come out in favour of a generalized decentralization of the federal system, at the expense of the federal government and in favour of all of the provinces. But as opposition leader he had no standing as participant in any constitutional processes and therefore no forum outside Quebec in which to air his views. Trudeau, while never repudiating the Ryan program, had been noticeably silent about it during the referendum campaign, as he had earlier been publicly cool to the Pépin-Robarts report and its main proposals. And Lévesque, committed to separation, had no apparent interest in developing a more workable, 'renewed' federalism based on Ryan's or any other proposals. His role thereafter was that of an amiable 'spoiler,' establishing friendly relations with those English-speaking premiers most fiercely opposed to Ottawa, lobbying in London against the federal proposals for change, but offering nothing positive to try to improve the federal system or ease its internal tensions.

For Trudeau, the decision to act quickly, to try to seize the maximum momentum from the Quebec vote, was clear. The next decision, the choice of the arenas and processes of constitutional change and by implication the participants or players, seemed clear. But it was fraught with predictable consequences and was, it may be suggested, the worst of all possible options. Taking note of fifty-three more or less continuing years, from 1927, of first ministers' conferences trying to achieve constitutional amending machinery for the BNA Act, Trudeau resolved to convoke another constitutional conference. If, of course, he had chosen some other, more promising arena, he would have left himself open to the charge of violating federal comity, if not indeed breaching a constitutional custom or convention.

But the choice of the arena, once made, foreclosed other choices. It locked the whole constitutional reform process into a cast of players – the provincial premiers – who had a vested interest in the constitutional status quo. That excluded interesting new players such as the municipalities, mere creatures of the provinces in the largely rural, agrarian Canadian society of 1867, but increasingly displacing the provinces as key arenas for community problem-solving. It also excluded the Indian and native peoples who, according to legal conceptions of 1867, had been mere subject peoples and hence legal non-persons and not entitled to come to the conference table. Imaginative new projects, involving the recasting of the old provincial boundaries so as to break up existing provinces into new ones or to combine several of them into a single province in accord with contemporary social or economic needs, seemed doomed to failure, granted the bias of the existing provinces for maintaining their vested interests.[6] Other federal systems have not been afraid to change territorial boundaries, recognizing that in fundamental constitutional change nothing can or should be sacred and beyond critical examination.

Trudeau felt himself the prisoner of fifty-three years of practice as to constitutional change: could he have handled the opportunity better? After the Quebec referendum, he could have deliberately limited the agenda of his constitutional conference to responding to the French fact in Quebec and enshrining it in the federal constitution, and with the weight of English-speaking public opinion behind him, he might have shamed the English-speaking premiers into full acquiescence.

The prime minister had displayed magnanimity to the defeated sovereignty-association forces in Quebec. This self-restraint, the more remarkable because Trudeau is not normally given public credit for the quieter virtues, could, and perhaps should, have been balanced by affirmative action. Proposals could have been made, for example, to abolish section 133 of the BNA Act so far as it required bilingualism in the legislature and the courts of Quebec but not of any other provinces, or to extend section 133's obligations also to other provinces with significant francophone minorities such as New Brunswick and Ontario. Either way, this would have required a formal constitutional amendment to the BNA Act.

But in other areas of concern to all Quebec governments since the Quiet Revolution, for example, regulation of the nature and character of immigration into the province, and control of cable television within the province, Quebec's constitutional claims could probably have been met by administrative agreements and accords between Quebec and Ottawa. The necessary patterns and precedents for this had already been established by the earlier highly successful understanding on immigration, effected between Lévesque's government and Ottawa at the height of their public quarrels on larger issues.[7]

In still other areas, namely the application and development of Quebec's language policies, the same result of a federal deference to Quebec interests could be achieved by simple federal self-restraint. This would have involved refraining from direct assaults on Quebec's language laws, in the Supreme Court or elsewhere, and from intervening before the courts in behalf of private interest groups and other pressure groups within Quebec who had turned to the courts in a guerrilla war.[8]

Trudeau perhaps overestimated the power of the more reluctant English-speaking premiers to stonewall Quebec-only constitutional concessions in language and culture and therefore overestimated the need to buy their support by offering them deals of their own. He made the fatal decision not to limit himself to constitutional satisfaction of Quebec's special historical claims, but to open up the constitutional debate more generally. In doing this, he not only opened a Pandora's box of competing provincial special interests but also lengthened the time dimension, so that the advantages of speed and of profiting from public support began to be lost as the days began to pass.

The first ministers' conference on the constitution began within three weeks of the referendum, on 9 June 1980. The federal government text setting out the proposed agenda spoke of the time having come to draft a new Canadian constitution. It then hedged its bets by suggesting that that task was impossible to achieve in a single blow and that to demonstrate tangible progress intensive negotiations should start on a series of subjects already accepted by the Canadian public and by the various governments as important.

Two main categories were identified euphemistically as the 'People's List' and the 'Governments' List.'[9] In the first were a statement of general principles (presumably a new constitutional preamble); a charter of rights (including language rights); an undertaking to respect the principle of equalization and the reduction of regional disparities; the repatriation (henceforward designated as 'patriation') of the constitution to Canada. In the second were resource ownership and interprovincial trade; offshore resources; powers affecting the economy; communications, including broadcasting; family law; a new upper house, 'involving the provinces'; the Supreme Court, 'for the people and for governments'; and fisheries.

The draft statement of principles invoked the 'help of God' in proclaiming Canada a 'free and self-governing people, born of a meeting of the English and French presence on North American soil which had long been the home of our Native Peoples, and enriched by the contribution of millions of new Canadians from the four corners of the Earth.'[10]

This is heady stuff and leads on to a definition of the state, in equally rhetorical terms, as 'one sovereign country, a true federation, conceived as a constitutional monarchy and founded on democratic principles.'[11]

Perhaps generalities were needed to veil the hard bargaining necessary to resolve the basic contradictions inherent in placing side by side the 'official status of the French and English languages in Canada' and the 'diversity of culture within Canadian society'; the 'authority of Parliament' and the 'authority of the legislative Assemblies of our several Provinces'; and, not least, the 'authority' of the provinces and the 'rights of our Native Peoples.'[12]

Finally, the paper set out a calendar involving an intensive series of organizational meetings, study sessions, and actual negotiations, by heads of government, ministers, and civil servants, through the summer. At a wind-up session, in Ottawa from 8 to 12 September, a federal-provincial entente on a new constitutional charter covering all the matters in the people's list and the governments' list would be signed. Trudeau would obtain a new constitutional consensus in under four months from the Quebec referendum.[13] Successful European constitution-making in situations of public euphoria similar to the post-referendum mood in Canada might have been quicker, but Canada might still profit from English-Canadian enthusiasm and openness to the French fact.

The conference had no sooner opened than it was apparent that any consensus on the people's list and the governments' list would be very, very difficult to attain.[14] The fault lay in part in the agenda, which blended the low-level and the sublime. But it was now not simply a matter of reaching consensus between Ottawa and Quebec. Premier Lévesque, sensing perhaps the political ambiguity of his own position, was not the 'spoiler' in the renewed debate. He and other Quebec representatives were invariably courteous and low-key in public discussions, looking with humorous detachment on the angry attacks on Ottawa by less experienced or less sophisticated premiers. And it was not a matter of reaching consensus between Ottawa and the provinces *en bloc*.[15] Such an easy solution, if it had ever been possible, quickly disappeared when it became apparent that the English-speaking premiers too often had very little in common, in terms either of intellect, training, and personalities or of the basic interests they represented.

The problem of achieving a consensus in the summer-long negotiations became one of trying to build through mini-accords on each of the subjects in the detailed lists. This meant that success could be attained only by an enormous display of co-operation, goodwill, and generosity all-round, in the interests of Canada as a whole, or else by enormous hard work and application to low-level exchanges and bartering and political 'horse-trading' in the worst sense. The post-referendum noble sentiments were soon dissipated, and the absence of interpersonal harmony was exacerbated by the abrasive negotiating style and at times gratuitous rudeness of several of the English-speaking delegations.

The provinces were interested in different things and normally would not transcend their own narrow interests unless offered a substantial *quid pro quo* in return.[16] Only Premier Hatfield of New Brunswick seemed interested in a genuine extension of French-language rights to inhabitants of his province. Premier Davis of Ontario made polite comments, though offering nothing very tangible to his province's large French-speaking minority. The other premiers seemed either indifferent to the French language or else downright hostile to the French fact within their own provincial jurisdiction.[17] Some premiers were clearly one-issue people.[18] Premier Peckford would speak only of Newfoundland control over offshore oil, which became his provinces' prime demand and the key to his co-operation on any other subject in the agenda.[19] Trudeau said Peckford was trying to trade human rights (here, language rights) in return for economic rights (here, offshore oil). Premier Bennett of British Columbia might easily, with a little more finesse, have emerged with full tax jurisdiction over natural gas in interprovincial or international trade (his prime objective); he missed that opportunity by insisting on Senate reform, which everyone else had quickly dismissed as of low priority and an irritating distraction to other, much more important issues.

Premier Lougheed of Alberta wanted provincial jurisdiction over taxation of natural resources, both *intra*provincially and extraprovincially, thereby in effect reversing the major Supreme Court decisions in this area in recent years. Also, and not perhaps unreasonably in view of his province's special economic base, he wanted Canada to move as quickly as possible to world market prices for oil. Just as understandably, Premier Davis, leader of a province relying very heavily on its secondary industries and without major energy resources, wanted maintenance of an artificially low price for Canadian oil, well below world levels.[20] Premier Blakeney of Saskatchewan had his own natural resources, had been particularly angered by the recent Supreme Court decisions against his government, and tended, on economic grounds, to side with Lougheed. But he deferred at the same time to his official NDP philosophy which had always stressed the need for a strong central government and maintenance of the larger, national interest against the interests of the provinces.

The result, after three months of negotiations, was a failure to achieve consensus.[21] At the final September meeting the main preoccupation of the players, before the television cameras, was with mutual recrimination, and with offering self-justification to one's electorate and to the subsequent verdict of history.

Any plan of producing a limited constitutional consensus on Quebec in the shortest time possible had been put aside at the start. It was almost inevitable, then, that no new consensus on comprehensive constitutional change would be reached.[22] The most, realistically, to have hoped for would have been a lowest-common-denominator consensus on a very few subjects or else a largely vacuous, cosmetic overall plan. A genuine breakthrough, going beyond the limited Quebec issues, would require new players, new arenas, and new processes.

Some critics of the federal government were inclined to suggest that Trudeau had planned it that way, correctly anticipating that the premiers would be unable to agree even among themselves. He could then, justifiably, attempt a much more ambitious constitutional project, using all the devices of participatory democracy – constituent assembly and/or popular referendum – to achieve his goal. Though he subsequently made much of 'fifty-three years of failure,' his follow-up to the conference breakdown was relatively modest in its search for an alternative arena and process and eschewed the participatory route altogether. He opted instead for action by Parliament on an all-party basis and for an agenda which involved issues not just of concern to Quebec but fell far short of the sweeping proposals advanced by the federal government in June.

5

Unilateral federal action

It is understood that the decision *not* to profit from the breakdown of negotiations by going directly to the people through a referendum[1] was prompted
by the justice ministry's reading of the advisory opinion on Senate reform.
This, in the ministry's view, established the British route to amending the
BNA Act as still applicable and obligatory.[2] That is, of course, arguable as an
interpretation of a ruling that will hardly rank as among the Supreme Court's
most lucid or persuasive. Constituent power is, in Kelsen's terms, a pre-
legal, or meta-legal, political act.

In an era of constitutional democracy, constituent power comes from the
people, and there is little reason to believe that had Prime Minister Trudeau
proceeded boldly by going directly to the people with a new constitutional
project, the courts or any other authority would have stood in the way of any
resounding endorsement. A legally unimpeachable, popular source of sovereignty would thus have been established (in place of or as a supplement to
the older imperial basis, now presumably fallen into constitutional disuse),
just as it had been in the United States and in France. The indispensable
condition would be a clear popular mandate, and the necessity of obtaining
this would itself have constrained and controlled the content of what subsequently became the 'patriation project.' Trudeau, in a public interview in
Vancouver, indicated that he had rejected such an approach on strictly legal
grounds; it would represent a 'revolutionary' step, involving too sharp a
break with the original British basis of Canada's constitutional system. The
answer reveals a side of Trudeau's character well known to perceptive stu-
dents of law though not perhaps to the general public. Trudeau tends to be
ultra-positivistic, emphasizing continuity in historical development rather
than natural law-style sudden change and insisting on dotting the 'i's' and
crossing the 't's.' Perhaps as a consequence, the whole patriation project has
a conservative, even dull quality, lacking elegance and sparkle, or any

novelty in legal terms, in spite of the intellectual gifts that the prime minister could have brought to bear.

The decision to act through Westminster had, therefore, certain important consequences. It undoubtedly affected the content of the proposed changes. Given more than half a century of full juridical sovereignty and independence, and the rapidly declining proportion of English-speaking Canadians, it would be both constitutionally inelegant and politically impracticable to retain a made-in-Britain amending machinery. This dictated, paradoxically, that the constitutional package, while deliberately choosing the British route for its formal enactment, must ensure that this would be the last British constitutional change for Canada.

The starting point must therefore be the termination of the British juridical connection. The BNA Act, as amended, would be sent to Canada. This process was immediately referred to, somewhat euphemistically, as 'repatriation' or 'patriation,' forgetting or conveniently overlooking the fact that more than a century of constitutional practice had given the original charter of 1867 a Canadian character and style all of its own, separate and distinct from its original roots. Terminating the British connection would (according to positivistic legal views) leave the BNA Act without any possibility of further amendment, since it lacked any constitutional amending machinery within itself, apart from the limited amending competences established under sections 91(1) and 92(1) of the act, as amended.

Some form of amending machinery would have to be added. The expectation in 1927 had been that this task would be achieved within Canada economically and expeditiously, and that this last British footnote would have been removed by the mid-1930s. More important problems, plus the effective operation of other, informal modes of constitutional change (developing constitutional custom and convention, judicial legislation) postponed the realization of this quest till the late 1940s; thereafter inter-governmental negotiations proceeded without any sense of urgency until the Quiet Revolution and the rise of the Parti québécois.[3] Half a century of frustration would be brought to an end now. The successive draft proposals advanced by the federal government did not differ materially from those first advanced in the late 1920s, which suggests either that the underlying sociological realities dictate the positive law responses in this area, or else that the subject is not important and that the constitution will continue to change, if it must, by other, informal modes as in the past.

The most controversial element in the constitutional package was the constitutionally entrenched bill of rights.[4] And yet a bill of rights – at least in its language and cultural aspects – was the main thing for which a constitutional mandate could be justified by the Quebec referendum. There would, of course, still be room for argument as to whether or not the mandate should be limited to Quebec's own special claims in this area (Bill 22 and Bill 101)[5] plus some related concessions such as acceptance of an increased Quebec control over communications and an augmented Quebec representation on the Supreme Court and in the Senate. Constitutional recognition of the French fact within Quebec could be supplemented or replaced by a bolder and much more comprehensive federal approach to official bilingualism *throughout* Canada. That institutionalized bilingualism now required by section 133 of the BNA Act for the Quebec legislature and Quebec courts could be applied to all the provinces or certainly to those such as New Brunswick and Ontario having substantial French-speaking populations.

An entrenched bill of rights that would go beyond language questions and take in the common law legal rights – due process, freedom of speech and the press, and related rights – would no doubt derive from Trudeau's 1980 election mandate to undertake more sweeping constitutional changes. Such changes had been envisaged in the Constitutional Amendment Bill, 1978, and other federal constitutional documents and white papers published since 1968.

To go beyond this into new categories of constitutional rights not previously raised – aboriginal and native peoples' rights, for example – would be to try to profit from a favourable opportunity to achieve desirable objectives that might otherwise require years of public education and frustrating political compromises to achieve.

With the general outline of the repatriation package established, and the British route decided upon, a choice still had to be made as to the preliminary, Canadian part of the process. Only the federal government had juridical personality and could legally represent Canada vis-à-vis Great Britain, but it would obviously add to the authority of the repatriation package and also confer on it legitimacy in strictly Canadian terms if it could have an unimpeachable Canadian legal source and origin.

Hence the decision, to use Parliament. The mechanism selected was an all-party, Senate-House special joint committee on the constitution. The cabinet would first prepare a draft resolution containing the repatriation package; the joint committee would consider the draft resolution and, if it thought it necessary, amend or extend it; the amended draft would then be submitted to each house separately for approval; and finally, the joint resolution, as voted out by the two houses, would be transmitted by the federal government to the British government for formal submission to, and formal adoption by, the British Parliament by way of British statute applicable to Canada.

The joint committee seemed to offer a speedy end to the constituent process, and the federal government had concluded that it must act quickly or lose a rare opportunity for worthwhile constitutional change. The date originally set for completion of the committee's consideration of the federal government's draft – the beginning of December 1980 – reflected this urgency. Since the draft was not unveiled until 2 October 1980, there would be, with the time taken to organize the committee, only six weeks for its work; this was later extended by two months less the Christmas vacation period. For quick passage at Westminster, Prime Minister Thatcher needed to have the repatriation package ready before the Christmas 1980 parliamentary recess; otherwise it would become embroiled in her own budget debate and so become delayed in passage through no fault of its own. The ultimate objective was passage by the British Parliament with a comfortable margin of safety before Canada Day, 1 July 1981.

The joint committee (the Hays-Joyal committee after its two co-chairmen) had twenty-five members, drawn from the two houses and the three parties. It was far too large to function effectively as a committee of the whole or as a legislative drafting committee, yet not large enough to create subcommittees to which it could delegate its main functions. Not all the members seemed able to be present at any one time, since the committee's work coincided exactly with the heaviest schedule of House of Commons debates. It might perhaps have overcome these handicaps with self-restraint and the best use of its limited time. The wealth of source material and analysis already assembled by commissions of enquiry remained seemingly unread – presumably for lack of time – by the committee. The Hays-Joyal committee was the fifth federal commission of enquiry on the constitution in two years. There had been two excellent, if somewhat unobtrusive Senate committee reports on the constitution (see above, 3 and 7); the outstanding Lamontagne-MacGuigan joint committee which had reported in October 1978 (see 3); and the Pépin-Robarts report (see 8–11). The Lamontagne-MacGuigan committee had been, in terms of membership, perhaps the richest of all Canadian parliamentary commissions of enquiry on the constitution; it numbered three former premiers (Henry Hicks, Duff Roblin, and George Smith), former Opposition Leader Robert Stanfield, and a wealth of House talent. There was no reason for passing over the Pépin-Robarts and Lamontagne-MacGuigan reports in silence, when they had laid all the necessary groundwork for substantial constitutional changes.

It was also a major error to try to retrace all the ground already covered by those two commissions by entering on extended public hearings, before the television cameras. Only well-organized and well-financed pressure groups could afford to travel to Ottawa to appear before the committee. The public advertisements inviting testimony brought a heavy response, and this meant a high degree of selectiveness and potential bias in the final choices of witnesses. The committee prided itself on having sat for 267 hours and three minutes and having heard ninety-five groups and five individuals designated by the three parties as 'party expert witnesses.'

On looking through the committee's list, it is difficult to avoid the conclusion that it was heavily weighted in favour of the more aggressive, vocal, and unrestrained, and also the best financed, of our burgeoning army of national pressure groups and special interests lobbies. There was an observable absence of balance – ethnic and cultural, religious, political and ideological, and above all linguistic and regional – in the list. Various interest groups and governments, in Quebec and in the west, decided to boycott or at least stay away from the committee's hearings.

But if you strip away the veil from various purportedly 'national' pressure groups or lobbies with high-sounding, pan-Canadian names you find that there was all too often no consultation with rank-and-file members and that the brief was in fact the creation of a small, permanent Toronto- or Ottawa-based executive.

The committee's soundings were not fully representative in either a cultural and linguistic or a regional sense. Its report reflected too much the golden triangle of Canadian political life – Toronto, Ottawa, and English Montreal – and failed therefore to produce a proper balancing of the conflicting forces within Canada today. These doubts are compounded when one observes duplication of testimony (some witnesses turned up more than once under different group names and sponsorship – were some of those 'groups' not hastily organized for the purpose?) There was also what Professor Georges Scelle of the University of Paris used to call the '*dédoublement fonctionnel*,' where someone already employed by or under contract to a government testifies in his other capacity as, say, university professor or independent specialist, in favour of a governmental measure under political attack. Scelle's doubt was not as to the scientific validity of the evidence being offered in that other, 'expert' capacity, but as to the degree of authority that should be accorded to it, under those circumstances.

Some bright new faces did, indeed, testify before the committee – the Indian nations and the other native communities,[6] the municipalities – and it was a breakthrough to have them appear in public and state their constitutional case. But it must be concluded that the committee's pursuit of that elusive national constitutional consensus involved a flawed dialectical process, in which all the main competing interests were not adequately represented or canvassed. The end product was not a satisfactory synthesis of what the country wanted or needed. One wonders if the committee would not have done better to pass up all the political attractions of publicly televised hearings in favour of quiet study and reflection and give-and-take on the formidable body of research and findings already assembled by its immediate predecessors.

The actual mode of operation of the committee was the classical political method of party 'horse-trading' and bargaining, relieved only by the casual element of the lobbyist and special interest groups appearing with their own particular claims to peddle. Some of these pressure groups had by now graduated to the class of 'professional' witnesses. In such a situation, the most vocal group is king, and it requires skilled counsel work, through preliminary examination of witnesses on the *voir dire*, to demonstrate just how representative or unrepresentative such groups really are.

6

The patriation package

On 2 October 1980 Prime Minister Trudeau announced a Proposed Resolution for a Joint Address to the Queen respecting the Constitution of Canada (see Appendix A). It involved 1) a preamble, containing a formal request for enactment by the British Parliament of both 2) the Canada Act (which would be the last statute to be passed by the British Parliament in relation to Canada) and 3) the Constitution Act, 1980, comprising the substantive content of the patriation package (Charter of Rights, amending procedure, and other matters). According to section 1 of the Canada Act, the Constitution Act would thereby be 'enacted for and shall have the force of law in Canada and shall come into force as provided in that Act.'

When the Canada Act should have been enacted by the British Parliament, the Constitution Act would then be assimilated and integrated with the BNA Act of 1867, as amended. The new, consolidated act would be designated (section 59 of the proposed resolution) the Constitution Acts, 1867 to 1980. A special schedule 1 to the Constitution Act, 1980, entitled 'Modernisation of the Constitution,' set out the means for achieving this and, incidentally, tidying up the BNA Act generally by repealing various 'spent' provisions that had become dated.

The Charter of Rights and Freedoms (part I, or sections 1–30) broke down its catalogue of rights into various categories and sub-categories. Section 2, on fundamental freedoms, guarantees freedom of conscience and religion; freedom of thought, belief, opinion, and expression, including freedom of the press and other media; freedom of peaceful assembly and of association. Democratic rights, sections 3–5, are the right to vote and stand for office; plus the limiting of the federal Parliament to a five-year maximum term, and the requiring of the federal Parliament and the provincial legislatures to meet at least once a year). Section 6, mobility rights, guarantees the right to move and take up residence in any province, and to pursue the gaining of a livelihood in any province).

Legal rights, sections 7–14, are defined as the 'right to life, liberty and security of the person and the right not to be deprived thereof except in accordance with the principles of fundamental justice,' – section 7. Sections 8–14 seemed designed to reproduce a good deal of the American constitutional jurisprudence (case law) on due process and the limitation of the state police power. Non-discrimination rights (section 15) are defined as the 'right to equality before the law and to the equal protection of the law without discrimination because of race, national or ethnic origin, colour, religion, age or sex,' (15[1]), but as not 'preclud[ing] any law, program or activity that has as its object the amelioration of conditions of disadvantaged persons or groups' (15[2]).

Official languages of Canada (sections 16–22) and minority language educational rights (section 23) tried to tread through the language minefield. Undeclared rights and freedoms (section 24) were inserted, it is understood, at the last minute in response to Indian and native peoples' lobbyists, and rank as a 'saving' clause preserving existing rights and freedoms, such as they might be, and specifically 'any rights or freedoms that pertain to the native peoples of Canada.' The remaining sections (25–30) were of a general character only, the most important being the 'primacy' clause (section 25) which established as a rule of interpretation that 'any law that is inconsistent with the provisions of this Charter is, to the extent of such inconsistency, inoperative and of no force and effect.'

The remainder of the repatriation package (parts II to VI), was devoted as follows: part II to affirming commitment to the constitutional principle of economic equalization and the correction of regional disparities of an economic character within Canada (section 31); part III to institutionalizing the federal-provincial inter-governmental conferences (section 32); parts IV and V to devising rules for interim constitutional amending procedures (IV: sections 33–40) and for permanent amending procedures (V: sections 41–51); and part VI to general dispositive provisions (sections 52–9).

Only those sections, in parts IV and V, dealing with amendment procedures need concern us now. The patriation package proposed an interim, two-year period during which the federal and provincial governments would try to achieve unanimity on an amending formula. If they succeeded, the constitution would be amended to incorporate that formula. If eight or more provinces, representing at least 80 per cent of the total population of all the provinces, agreed within two years on an amending procedure, then that formula and a formula similar to the Victoria formula (approved in 1971 by the federal government and all the provinces except Quebec) would be submitted to the electorate in a referendum within four years after patriation. If, however, the provinces did not present an alternative amending formula, then a formula similar in principle to the Victoria formula would automatically come into effect two years after patriation.

The Victoria formula was based on the principle that amendments to certain parts of the constitution should require, in effect, a double consensus – a consensus in each 'region' of the country as well as a general, nation-wide consensus. The Victoria formula had required that this consensus be expressed through provincial legislatures and the federal Parliament. The formula in the proposed resolution would allow that consensus to be expressed also through a national referendum, the initiation of such a referendum resting with Parliament. In general, the formula would require constitutional amendments to be approved by Parliament and by either the provincial legislatures or (in a national referendum) by a majority of voters in a majority of the provinces, including, however, every province now having, or having once had, at least 25 per cent of the population of Canada; at least two Atlantic provinces amounting together to at least 50 per cent of the population of the Atlantic provinces combined; and at least two western provinces amounting together to at least 50 per cent of the population of the western provinces combined.

It all sounds very complicated, and, of course, it was complicated. The proposed procedures resulted from half a century of bartering and compromises, that were themselves the product of a somewhat confused mishmash of American, Australian, and Swiss amending procedures. The difficulties in comprehending just what was really intended by these detailed, often alternative, amending procedures hurt the rest of the patriation package by denying it that instant public understanding and sympathy necessary to carry the whole package through to adoption.

Sometimes, the very complexity of the alternative arrangements raised criticisms and public fears presumably not intended by the drafters. For example, the requirement that amendments be approved by every province that either now had, or once had had, at least 25 per cent of the population was interpreted (correctly, of course) as giving a permanent veto to either Quebec or Ontario. The new amending procedures, because of their very complexity, were hardly likely to work, producing in fact a rigid constitution; this fact was hardly sufficient to outweigh these other charges, since the critics concentrated on the law as actually written and not on how it was likely to operate.

The amending procedures were an abstract, technical draft little directed, in either content or language and style, to the general public but seemed to have been prepared by one group of civil service functionaries for another. Similar criticisms apply also to the rest of the patriation package, and not least to the Charter of Rights and Freedoms. Here we are in to what the great Harvard jurist Thomas Reed Powell called the vagaries and varieties of constitutional drafting. Do you aim for an exhaustive, social planner's blueprint that leaves nothing to chance? Or do you produce a short and succinct charter with a generality that enables its continuing adaptation to rapidly changing conditions? This latter approach characterizes both the American Bill of Rights that accompanied the constitution of 1787, and that has survived successfully to this day and the French Declaration of the Rights of Man and the Citizen of 1789, that was put into force again by the constitutions of both the fourth and also the present fifth French Republic. But it was not the approach adopted by Prime Minister Trudeau's legal advisers in the elaboration of the patriation package.

There is a heavy, wooden quality to the language and style, and it is written in technical, lawyer's language that is often difficult for the layman to understand or sympathize with. It is far too long. It does advance general principles, as in section 15(1): 'equality before the law' and 'equal protection of the law,' both of which have a well-accepted connotation and a breadth and generality of application in comparative constitutional law. But it promptly cuts them down by enumerating specific cases, putting to one side the legal maxim that to define something by way of example is promptly to exclude everything not so mentioned. The temptation to keep adding to the list of examples became most marked during committee hearings. Those pressure groups that did manage to be heard in the limited time available demanded their own express inclusion in the list. It is not difficult to predict that this particular section of the charter, if and when adopted, would have a far more limited operation and range of protection than the plain, direct, and unqualified guarantee of the 'equal protection of the laws' contained in the fourteenth amendment to the American Constitution.

The Charter of Rights broke no significant new ground in comparison to the classical bills of rights such as those of the United States and France. Perhaps political and ideological factors kept out the newer, more rhetorically styled rights – the right to work or to guaranteed employment – of a social democratic character. But for a government officially committed to liberal ideas in political, social and economic life the mobility rights (section

6) are but a pale, weak imitation of those in the Treaty of Rome of 1957 (preamble and articles 2, 3, and 7), which instituted the European Economic Community and constitutes the basic charter of the European community.

What is worst in the Canadian charter, however, is the presence, too often, of what Judge Jerome Frank used to characterize as 'weasel-word' exceptions. Provisions accompany the statement of a right and qualify or take it away in the same breath that it is proclaimed. Thus, section 1 'guarantees the rights and freedoms set out in it *subject only to such reasonable limits as are generally accepted in a free and democratic society with a parliamentary system of government*' (my italics). That would make no less than five weasel-word exceptions in the single qualifying clause, and one wonders why it was thought necessary to introduce them at all. If it was to avoid the possibility of absolutistic, un-fact-oriented decisions on application of the charter in extreme situations, then we might note that it is a truism of Western constitutionalism that constitutional rights are not to be interpreted in the abstract but, instead, have to be balanced against other, countervailing social interests in concrete situations. The great Mr Justice Oliver Wendell Holmes pointed out that the right of free speech, unqualified as it is in the American Bill of Rights, would not justify a man's shouting 'Fire!' in a crowded theatre. Pragmatism and ordinary common sense can surely be relied upon as much in Canadian, as in American, constitutional jurisprudence without the need to hedge with potentially debilitating express verbal limitations.

The same consciously contrived legal antithesis can be seen in the drafting of the more detailed, applied sections of the Canadian charter. Thus the basic guarantee of procedural due process (section 7) can indeed be taken away 'in accordance with the principles of fundamental justice'; and the guarantee against search and seizure is qualified by the exception of 'grounds, and ... procedures, established by law' (section 8), as also is the guarantee against detention and imprisonment (section 9). The federal government's timidity, or apparently overly solicitous desire to protect the administration of justice, no doubt stemmed in measure from the dominant role of technocrats and bureaucrats generally in the actual drafting (poets and philosopher-statesmen were influential in the elaboration of the American and French charters). But it was also due, it is clear, to the defensive posture that the federal government felt compelled to adopt in response to the violent partisan criticisms launched against its whole repatriation package following its decision to act unilaterally.

The federal Progressive Conservative party was the heir to John Diefenbaker's 'Tory radicalism' and his statutory Bill of Rights. It might confidently have taken over the whole project for an entrenched bill of rights and tried to rewrite its contents in conservative terms, and it must assume a large part of the responsibility for the failure of the charter to achieve the inspiration and grandeur of the American and French charters and other more contemporary ones. Internal leadership quarrels among the Conservatives seem to have brought the decision to fight the *process* of repatriation, at the expense of remaking or refining its contents. Hence, the absence of a right of property, conservative-style or otherwise.

The federal New Democratic Party, making the key policy decision to back the patriation project, was certainly able to influence the character and development of the charter during committee stages. But the influence was technical rather than philosophical, having regard to the differences in Liberal and NDP ideology and so marginal at best, the NDP having limited political weight in Ottawa. In addition NDP leader Ed Broadbent was unable to deliver the support of his key party colleague, Premier Blakeney of Saskatchewan.

CONSOLIDATED RESOLUTION

It is remarkable how little substantive change occurred in the patriation package between 2 October 1980 and early February 1981. Extensive direct oral and written testimony from various pressure groups, special interests associations, and lobbyist organizations had little impact. The final, consolidated resolution – as tabled by the minister of justice, Mr Chrétien, in the House of Commons on 13 February 1981, together with amendments approved by the House of Commons on 23 April 1981 and by the Senate on 24 April 1981 – has cosmetic changes that do not change the basic philosophy or organization or style (see Appendix B). The Charter of Rights and Freedoms is now endowed with a preamble, and with God, who finally appears in that preamble, accompanied by 'the rule of law' which is not, however, further defined.

God, though not present at the creation or otherwise mentioned in the first public draft, had been sponsored by the Conservative members of the Hays-Joyal committee (together with the dignity of the family and respect for moral and spiritual values),[1] at the resumption of the committee hearings in January 1981. He made it through to the final draft approved by the House and Senate, unencumbered by family dignity or moral and spiritual values, but in lock-step with the rule of law and consigned, as a pleasing generality, to the preliminary, preambular part of the Charter of Rights and Freedoms: 'Whereas Canada is founded upon principles that recognize the supremacy of God and the rule of law.'

In the end, the Conservative members of the joint committee, deciding that 'a little God' was not enough, voted against the Liberal members' amendment including God in the charter. Prime Minister Trudeau commented that the Conservatives had 'played rather political games and they deserved to be caught in their game,' the debate over whether or not God should be included in the constitution being, in his view, 'inspired more by fear of the electorate than of God, and that is not very flattering to God.' He said it was strange, so long after the middle ages, that some politicians felt obliged to mention God in a constitution, which is, after all, a secular and not a spiritual document; though it was his own personal preference to include a mention of God in the preamble.[2]

Another initiative of the Conservative members was to try to annex the 'enjoyment of property and the right not to be deprived thereof except in accordance with the principles of natural justice' to the guarantee of the right to life, liberty, and the security of the person contained in section 7 of the first draft.[3] This was vigorously opposed by the NDP members[4] as 'opening the door to large multinational corporations while tying up progressive zoning or expropriation legislation in the courts.'[5] Worse still for the Conservatives, they had forgotten or else chose to ignore that three Conservative provincial governments (Prince Edward Island, Nova Scotia, and Newfoundland) had opposed the sanctioning of a constitutional right of property, during the abortive summer of 1980 negotiations, on the score that that would limit their ability to control the growing foreign and absentee ownership of scarce farmland.[6] The federal government, looking for allies in repatriation, had seemed prepared to accept both God and private property in the interests of forming a larger alliance[7]; it was encouraged by this developing resistance to renege on its early undertaking to the Conservative members,[8] and the right of private property did not figure in the final consolidated resolution.

It was in the non-discrimination rights (section 15) – restyled 'Equality Rights' (section 15) in the final version – that the opportunity for pressure group and special interest lobbying activity was at its greatest. Women's rights, as the product of aggressive and articulate public pressure groups, did well in the original draft of October 1980, and even better in the final draft of April 1981, capturing an additional section (28) under the general clauses. Homosexuals and the poor, neither as well organised nor as publicly persuasive, failed to be included in either the first or the final draft.[9] Senior citizens, a rapidly increasing voting bloc, made both the first and the final draft with the outlawing of discrimination on account of 'age.' The handicapped didn't make the first draft, but lobbied hard in the interim and profited from a favourable press and public opinion and entered the final draft under the rubric of discrimination on account of 'mental or physical disability.' In the view of the committee majority, enough was enough and there must be some end to the definition by way of countless enumeration: a Conservative amendment to guarantee the right of deaf people to the assistance of an interpreter in court (as if the courts either in civil law Quebec or in the common law provinces would attempt to try a deaf person without one) failed to make it.[10]

The opening section of the charter, in response to criticisms, was redrafted as to its qualifying clause. The rights and freedoms set out in the whole charter are now to be subject to 'such reasonable limits prescribed by law as can be demonstrably justified in a free and democratic society,' the five weasel-word exceptions of the first draft having now been reduced to four. This is no doubt an advance, although the ambiguity that characterized the first draft still remains. The legal rights (due process) affirmed in sections 8 and 9 of the original draft, which seemed to have been directly borrowed from recent foreign (Indian, Japanese) constitutional terminology, have now been rephrased so as to guarantee simply (and more conventionally, it may be suggested) against 'unreasonable search and seizure' (section 8) and against 'arbitrary' detention or imprisonment (section 9).

The non-discrimination, now 'equality' rights (section 15), the well-known guarantees of 'equality before the law' and 'equal protection of the law,' have been restated as equality 'before and under the law' and as 'equal protection and equal benefit of the law,' though whether or not with the intention of excluding automatic application in Canadian courts of the, on the whole, beneficent foreign 'equal protection' precedents is not clear. The first draft banned discrimination on the basis of 'race, national or ethnic origin, colour, religion, age or sex,' the second mentions 'race, national or ethnic origin, colour, religion, sex, age or mental or physical disability.'

As a result of the welcome initiative of Premier Hatfield of New Brunswick, a Conservative leader supporting the patriation package, English and French became, in the final draft, official languages of New Brunswick (section 16[2]). There were changes in the statement of minority language educational rights (section 23), which did not, however, remove the points on which Premier Lévesque contended that there was a direct conflict with Quebec's Bill 101 and with Quebec provincial competences generally. Section 24 of the first draft, saving 'rights or freedoms that pertain to the native peoples of Canada,' was renumbered section 25 in the final draft and re-phrased so as to 'save,' now,

aboriginal, treaty or other rights or freedoms that pertain to the aboriginal peoples of
Canada including
(*a*) any rights or freedoms that have been recognized by the Royal Proclamation of
October 7, 1763; and
(*b*) any rights or freedoms that may be acquired by the aboriginal peoples of Canada
by way of land claims settlement.

This is, it is true, more specific than the first draft, but it may be doubted
whether it creates any additional legal protection. It does not, in any case,
meet the full Indian and native claims for recognition of their historic claims
arising under general, customary international law from the fact of the original British and French colonization. A new part II, section 34 (Rights of the
Aboriginal Peoples of Canada), seems designed, somewhat imperfectly, to
fill the gap by declaring that the 'aboriginal and treaty rights of the aboriginal
peoples of Canada' are 'recognized and affirmed' (section 34[1]), and by
then stipulating that '"aboriginal peoples of Canada" includes the Indian,
Inuit and Métis peoples of Canada' (section 34[2]).

There is a new section 28 declaring, presumably to make assurance doubly
sure, that the charter's rights and freedoms are 'guaranteed equally to male
and female persons'; and one wonders, again, whether that was necessary for
any other than rhetorical purposes, granted the explicit language of section
15(1) (equality rights). There is also a new section 29 saving existing rights
or privileges guaranteed under the constitution in respect of 'denominational, separate or dissentient schools' (for example, section 93 of the BNA
Act, though it is not, in fact, specified). This express insertion came at the
instigation of religious pressure groups, though whether in reaction to the
section 15 open society-style guarantee against discrimination based on religion or to the new preambular, rather more closed society proclamation of
the 'supremacy of God' is not clear. There is even, in the final draft, a pious
genuflection in the direction of multiculturalism, with the injunction that the
charter is to be 'interpreted in a manner consistent with the preservation and
enhancement of the multicultural heritage of Canadians' (section 27).

If the final product in April 1981 seemed somewhat disappointing and lacking in romance and poetry, some small part of the burden must also be
assigned to the bureaucratic advisers of the joint committee. They produced,
as the first public draft; in October 1980, a heavy, Germanic text that had
none of the clarity and succinctness of either the American Bill of Rights or
the Declaration of the Rights of Man. It was a complex lawyer's text that
needed professional advice for its understanding.

No doubt Ed Broadbent was intent on defending his own unqualified support for the package when he characterized the final draft as 'the best Bill of Rights in the Western world.' Equally euphoric comments by federal government officials or salaried consultants, summoned as expert witnesses, that the charter represented a 'real breakthrough' can no doubt be taken as manifestations of Scelle's *dédoublement fonctionnel*. Prime Minister Trudeau himself admitted the political dilemma of satisfying the various pressure groups each peddling its own particular wares, and the constitutional and legal problems that could follow if one did yield to them: 'In an effort to get everyone on board we negotiated. We put a lot of water in the wine and we weakened the bill of rights.'[11]

Too much political timidity also blunted the message of the new Charter of Rights and weakened its popular appeal. Except for the mobility rights (section 6), there was no opening at all to the new economic rights that interest contemporary constitution-makers, no attempt to break significant new ground in constitutional drafting terms.[12]

The cries of Hosanna with which the new version of section 1 was greeted by several federal government advisers,[13] and the enthusiastic accolade accorded by Broadbent,[14] both seem exaggerated. But there appears absolutely no warrant for the cries of doom and the complaints of a taking away of provincial or human rights launched by right-wing critics of the whole principle of a constitutionally entrenched bill of rights. These later-day intransigents rejected any notion of a constitutional bill of rights on the 'English' argument that such matters as protection of the individual against administrative intolerance or the arbitrary caprices of changing majorities in the legislature are better left, 'as in Great Britain,' to the self-restraint and wisdom of the government of the day.

They conveniently forgot, of course, that Britain is bound, today, by the European Convention on Human Rights and is sometimes haled before the European Commission and the European Court for alleged violation of the convention's norms, for example in regard to handling of the Irish problem. Britain is also bound by the Treaty of Rome and subject to enforcement of its provisions before the High Court of Justice of the European Communities in Luxembourg. Of course, with Canada an 'immigrant' country with its original 'English' component steadily dwindling in proportion to the rest of the population, the argument from history – here 'English' history – loses a good deal of its authority. And that is to say nothing of its technical limitations in terms of constitutional teachings today. More and more, constitutional bills of rights are being accepted as a necessary institutional element in the limiting and 'legitimating' of constitutional power; and it would be surprising if

Canada, with its strong French civil law influences, were to be immune to those general intellectual trends.

There were some concealed traps, of course, in the Charter of Rights and Freedoms, no doubt understood and intended as such by the bureaucrats who drafted them but perhaps not fully comprehended by the political leaders sponsoring the charter and by the rank-and-file members of the joint committee. Not the least important was the seeming direct opening to 'reverse discrimination' or 'affirmative action'[15] contained in section 15(2) of both drafts. This could, with sympathetic interpretation and application by the Supreme Court, on patterns established in cognate cases by the US and Indian supreme courts, open the door to a wave of Court-based activism aimed at redressing social and economic inequities. The spectre of judicial legislation was invoked not merely by right-wing opponents, but also by some left-of-centre critics such as Premier Blakeney, who was angered by the Supreme Court's 1978 decisions denying provincial taxation of natural resources in extraprovincial trade.[16]

The new section 24(1) ('Enforcement') of the final version seemed to encourage speculation as to massive new opportunities for judicial legislation and litigation. It introduced a direct right of access by any person to the courts in furtherance of the new rights and freedoms. Was this intended simply to repeat Dicey's traditional common law constitutional proposition that constitutional rights could always be raised in the course of ordinary litigation before the ordinary courts? Or did it envisage a new federal civil rights court or else a new original jurisdiction for the existing Supreme Court, along the lines of the West German federal constitutional court? The issue is not clear.

The changes in regard to the proposed new amending procedures seemed designed to soften somewhat the requirements for provincial assent. Thus section 43(1), formerly section 38(1), reduces the number of provincial legislatures required to introduce a new amendment formula from eight to seven, though still retaining the requirement of at least 80 per cent of the population of all the provinces. Section 46(1), formerly section 41(1) reduces the difficulty of assent of provincial legislatures by striking out the requirement that the necessary two Atlantic provinces and the necessary two western provinces must have a combined population of at least 50 per cent of the population of the region. The constitution, with the new amending procedures, will still prove rigid in practice and incapable of change under normal circumstances.

One last major change was the addition of a new section 92A to the original Act of 1867, as amended (now renamed the Constitution Act, 1867), granting to each province the exclusive law-making competence over exploration for non-renewable natural resources; the development, conservation, and management of non-renewable natural resources and forestry resources in the province; and the development, conservation, and management of sites and facilities for the generation and production of electrical energy. The same section also gives the provincial legislatures concurrent powers with the federal Parliament (with the federal law to prevail over provincial law in the event of conflict), in relation to the export from the province to another part of Canada of the primary production from non-renewable natural resources and forestry resources and the production from facilities for the generation of electrical energy.

The new section also gives provincial legislatures the competence to make laws in relation to the raising of money by any mode or system of taxation in respect of non-renewable natural resources and forestry resources and the primary production therefrom, and sites and facilities for the generation of electrical energy and the production therefrom. This is the case whether or not such production is exported from the province, but with the proviso that there must be no differentiation in such provincial taxation as between production exported to another part of Canada and production not exported from the province.

The new section was directed to the natural resources-based western provinces and designed to remove one of their principal sources of grievance under the BNA Act, namely the limitation of the provincial tax power to 'direct taxation within the Province.' In 1978 the Supreme Court struck down both Saskatchewan's tax on windfall profits accruing to the oil companies as a result of OPEC's massive increase in world oil prices in 1973 and its potash pro-rationing scheme that it had applied since 1969 to regulate its potash industry.[17] These decisions had angered Premier Blakeney and section 92A was a last bid to win him over to Ed Broadbent's support of the repatriation package. (Alberta and British Columbia also had natural resources that they wished to tax in export in interprovincial trade.) However, Blakeney and his western colleagues remained opposed to the package.

By agreement between the federal parties, and aided by Liberal control of both houses of Parliament, the patriation package, was consolidated, together with amendments approved on 23–4 April 1981. It awaited only the final determination of its constitutionality by the Supreme Court, now agreed to, however reluctantly, by the prime minister. If the Court should rule it unconstitutional as a whole, the project would presumably lapse. If the Court should uphold it, either in whole or in part, it should then be immediately voted upon and adopted as a formal joint resolution to the Queen by both houses of Parliament, and then immediately transmitted to Westminster.

7

Cutting the imperial
Gordian knot

The 'British connection' to the Canadian constitution arose innocently enough from a long-past error or oversight. The British parliamentary draughtsman of 1867 failed to include in the BNA Act any internal amending machinery. In constitutional and legal terms this was a major blunder and undoubtedly stemmed from the ignorance of British constitutional lawyers with the problems of wrtten constitutions and the practical necessity of having amendment formulae built in. Canada's was the first federal constitution in the British Empire, and British lawyers, as we know from Dicey's later strictures,[1] disdained to study American federal forms and practice and were incapable of crossing the linguistic frontier to comprehend Swiss federalism. Even if they had been comparative lawyers, however, the sovereignty of Parliament could hardly have accommodated easily the notion of constitutional checks and balances. Thereafter, however, every 'made-in-Britain' constitutional charter was given an autonomous amending process, beginning with Australia in 1900 and South Africa in 1909. Because of this original gap in the BNA Act, the many formal amendments made after 1867 were all effectuated by statutes of the British Parliament initiated at the request of, and in accord with texts submitted by, the Canadian government.

Some of the provincial premiers in Canada, during the debate over Prime Minister Trudeau's repatriation package, argued that there existed a convention (custom) requiring that the Canadian government should consult with the provincial governments about and obtain their consent to any amending statute. This argument was posited upon the premises that there was such a custom in existence, properly evidenced by past practice and (more importantly) that it was juridically normative and enforceable by the courts as such. This was later to form the basis of the dissident premiers' campaign, before three carefully selected provincial courts of appeal, to try to block adoption of the package and its transmission to London. The legal merits of the argument are canvassed in detail below.

Practice indicates there is no absolute custom of Ottawa's consulting the provincial governments and obtaining their consent prior to any approach to the British government. On the dozen amendments to the BNA Act made between 1867 and 1930, there is evidence of consultation with the provincial administrations in only one case, in 1907. With the substantially lesser number of amendments since 1930 the record is more mixed, but it is worth noting that the provincial administrations were not consulted at all on the constitutional amendments of 1943 and 1946 or on the two major amendments of 1949 (the one admitting Newfoundland to Confederation, and the other establishing the Canadian Parliament's power to amend the BNA Act by its own legislation in respect to federal matters). It is difficult to see how one can argue for the existence of such a constitutional convention when so many examples – in fact, the overwhelming majority – point the other way.

As a matter of imperial and Commonwealth history, the British government has consistently applied the principle of acting upon the request of the Canadian government, and in the form requested by it. The amending statute has been drafted in Canada and adopted by the British Parliament in that form. An earlier disposition by the British to cavil on some purely verbal questions seems to have been peacefully resolved long ago in a storm in a teacup over a transposed comma, with the British government thereafter going along even with bad syntax in the interest of imperial relations.

Relations between Britain and Canada are no longer governed by imperial legal norms but are subject to supranational law – whether inter-Commonwealth law or international law. It was therefore a little surprising to find, in January 1981, a committee of the British House of Commons[2] advancing legal claims over Canada and its constitution in language that seemed better suited to the era of General Gordon of Khartoum.[3] The Kershaw committee asserted, variously, that Britain today is the 'constitutional guardian' of Canada; that Britain has special rights, of a 'quasi-treaty' character, or of 'customary international law as it has specially evolved between the two states,' in relation to the Canadian constitution; that the British Parliament is legally established today as 'guardian of the rights of the (Canadian) Provinces'; and that the British Parliament has a legally based 'duty or responsibility to the Canadian people or community as a federally-structured community which has left its ultimate legal constituent powers in the hands of the UK legislature.'[4]

We may, I think, dispose fairly quickly and easily of the international law argument; a 'quasi-treaty' is a non-concept, devoid of legal meaning or consequences, and quite incapable of creating any positive law rights of Britain and its Parliament in relation to Canada and its Parliament.

One wishes one could be more optimistic about the pretensions to be some sort of 'guardian' of the Canadian constitution. The committee was probably harking back to the rather odd and short-lived plan brought forward by the Colonial Office in the mid-1960s to enable Britain to extract itself as painlessly as possible from the Rhodesian imbroglio. It conceded the political fait accompli of independence for the white minority régime while rendering lip-service to the principle of black majority self-determination, by making Britain in effect 'trustee' of black majority rights after such white-dominated independence.

In the 1930s Hitler's régime claimed the legal right, as *parens patriae* of German minorities in neighbouring states, legally to intervene at will in those states' internal affairs. Suffice it to say that the claim was rejected at the time by most western European governments as incompatible with the principle of state sovereignty.

There is not a word in the Statute of Westminster of 1931, or in the two imperial conferences (of 1926 and 1930) that preceded it, or in the subsequent declaration of commonwealth prime ministers of April 1949 about a legal 'guardian' status for Britain vis-à-vis Canada or its constitution. Sir Ivor Jennings insisted (correctly, it is submitted), that the Statute of Westminster was no more than a legal declaration of fundamental changes in the legal relations of Britain and the dominions that had already long since occurred.[5]

The Judicial Committee of the Privy Council, a worldly wise and richly experienced tribunal, displayed a remarkable capacity to adjust gracefully, even elegantly, to great historical trends, and it acquiesced easily and in timely fashion to the 'winds of change' in the empire between the wars with its judgment in *Moore* v *Attorney General for the Irish Free State* in 1935.[6] And twelve years later it accepted the full legal power of the old dominions to move to abolish, by their own legislation, the erstwhile legal right of appeal that had existed from their own courts to the Privy Council.[7] Canada responded by legislating in 1949 to sweep away the appeal to the Privy Council and to establish the Supreme Court of Canada as the final court of and for Canadians. Kershaw and his committee members would seem to be trying to turn the clock back more than half a century.

The committee next invoked the international law doctrine of 'state succession' to try to dismiss the claims – potentially in the range of billions of dollars – advanced by the Indian and native peoples of Canada against the British Crown. The 'new' international law is rapidly challenging more traditional, 'classical' international law, in respect to the spoliation of Indian lands and their resources. Sir Anthony's committee cannot have it both ways.[8] If Canada should be less than sovereign in relation to Britain, there could, of course, be absolutely no question of a legal succession from Britain to Canada of Britain's legal obligations vis-à-vis the Indian and other native peoples of Canada.

In fairness to Prime Minister Thatcher and her government, it should be noted that the eleven-member Kershaw committee was not an official organ of the British government. Its members were not selected by Mrs Thatcher; she did not ask them to investigate the Canadian constitution; its report and its conclusions were in no way binding on her or on the British Parliament. The members of the committee were not specialists or authorities on constitutional law or on things Canadian. Its members were, in fact, largely unknown back-benchers who, in the case of the Conservatives, had not managed to make it into the cabinet. The chairman, Sir Anthony Kershaw, had briefly been a junior minister in Edward Heath's Conservative government, but had been passed over by Mrs Thatcher for her administration.

Why did the committee rush to embrace Canadian constitutional problems when there were so many more immediate and pressing issues closer at home – Northern Ireland and racial disturbances in suburban London? Perhaps more distant problems seem blander and at least they are far away from home. A Labour member of the committee, in a debate before the British-Canadian Studies Association in Oxford, in April 1981, suggested that the initiative had flowed from a concerted anti-federal government letter-writing campaign to British MPs, initiated by various provincial premiers and their parties in the late summer of 1980 when the first ministers' conferences were obviously about to break down. By venturing 'prematurely' into issues of Canadian and inter-Commonwealth constitutional law, before any formal request from the Canadian government should have reached London, Sir Anthony and his colleagues violated one of the prime principles of constitutional law: self-restraint in regard to great political issues. Chief Justice Samuel Freedman of the Manitoba Court of Appeals invoked this principle in the decision of early February 1981 rejecting arguments against the repatriation package.[9]

Prime Minister Thatcher, in an answer given in early February 1981 in the British House, applied the same canon of constitutional self-restraint. She refused to respond to hypothetical questions until she received a formal request from the government and Parliament of Canada. At that time, she told the House, 'we have to deal with it as expeditiously as possible in accordance with precedents and the law.'[10]

In her answers to questions in the House, she had been quite clear in her recognition that the legal subordination of the Canadian Parliament to the British Parliament had disappeared.[11] It would be quite improper for the British government to attempt to deal directly with any one or more of the provincial governments within Canada, without the prior leave or authority of the Canadian government (as it would have been in the 1960s for the French government to try to deal directly with Quebec and bypass Ottawa in the process). Canada being *one* person at international law, the Canadian government is its only legitimate spokesman abroad and its only official channel of communication with foreign countries. Mrs Thatcher's approach to the Canadian constitutional question had, in this respect, been one of studied correctness and strict observance of protocol, in contrast to that of the Kershaw committee. Provincial premiers and their subordinates seeking to meet with the British government on official business have been required by the British government, politely but firmly, to be officially sponsored and accompanied by officials of the Canadian high commission in London as the only proper delegates of the Canadian government.

Mrs Thatcher reflected her full awareness of and respect for these basic principles of international law in her replies during question period on 9 December 1980: :'On 14 previous occasions this House has been asked to deal with a request from the federally elected Parliament of Canada. It has done so in accordance with well established precedent, bearing in mind that we are an elected Parliament and that the Federal Parliament of Canada is a similarly elected Parliament.' The reply she gave the same day to a Conservative back-bencher, Robin Maxwell-Hyslop, was even more categorical:

Mr. Robin Maxwell Hyslop:
The only elected body that can make representations on behalf of the Canadian people to another Commonwealth government, such as our own, is the Federal Government of Canada.

Provincial administrations cannot have any *locus standi* vis-à-vis the Government or Parliament of the United Kingdom.

Mrs. Thatcher:
I believe we can only receive a request under the relevant statute from the Federal Parliament of Canada.[12]

The Second Legal Adviser to the British Foreign and Commonwealth Ministry, J.R. Freeland, in direct testimony to the Kershaw committee in November and December 1980, had expressed identical legal opinions to those of the prime minister, in an exhaustive review of the constitutional precedents.[13] However, the Kershaw committee chose to avoid the issue. It summoned its own expert witnesses – all British. It avoided the conventions of inter-Commonwealth law and plunged into purely internal Canadian questions. It was here that its tactics were most open to criticism and censure. Its three British expert witnesses, while distinguished in their own particular specialist fields, had no claims to expertise in Canadian constitutional law. Two of them had been retained by the Quebec government to advise on general constitutional questions. This need not have affected the intellectual quality of their testimony, but it did raise the question whether Sir Anthony and his committee, if they should wish their report to be viewed as impartial, might not have had an obligation to consult also expert witnesses chosen by other interested parties.

The Canadian government, in a white paper issued in March 1981, under the authority of the minister of justice, Mr Chrétien, quite rightly castigated the Kershaw committee on this point.[14] The signal omission to attempt to hear both sides was, to say the least, incomprehensible in a parliamentary committee at least some of whose members had legal training. The Chrétien white paper, with classic understatement, suggested that the submissions to the Kershaw committee by the three British legal scholars, 'two of whom indicated that, though expressing personal views, they had been consulted by provincial governments,and none of whom claimed expert knowledge about the Canadian Constitution ... did not present, in total, a balanced view of the question ... Many of the submissions suffered from illogicality and errors of fact.'[15]

A subsequent official reply published in April 1981 by the Kershaw committee[16] to the white paper was, understandably ènough, quite defensive in relation to the Canadian government's criticisms of its basic method and legal reasoning. How could it be otherwise? But it offered no satisfactory explanation – other than a plaintive footnote[17] – of its failure to observe the elementary legal principle of hearing the other side, and to at least try to balance the testimony by other expert witnesses, not yet parti pris in the whole affair and, ideally, from Canada itself.

A purely informal committee of back-benchers of the British House of Commons, headed by Jonathan Aitken[18] seemed, perhaps because of the lack of parliamentary seniority of its members, to bring together a much more varied, interesting, and certainly larger group of members of both houses.

Mr Aitken had a family background in Canada. Bruce George was a Labour MP and professional sociologist with a long-standing interest in the legal status and condition of aboriginal peoples in the Commonwealth. Mr George saw the patriation issue, quite frankly and openly, as an opportunity to compel full respect for and honouring of the original legal obligations of the British Crown to the Indian, Inuit, and other native peoples of Canada arising from the original Indian treaties signed by the British Crown and from the original British acts of conquest or colonization.[19] George Foulkes was particularly interested in regionalism and devolution within Britain itself, especially as it might affect Scotland, and viewed the Canadian issue as an opportunity also to discuss such specifically British issues before the House of Commons. In consequence of this diversity of approach, the Aitken committee had a certain intellectual vivacity and also a sense of humour and freedom from cant lacking in the approach of the Kershaw committee.

On the whole, however, as the second report of the Kershaw committee, in April 1981, finally admitted, the fact of the litigation now finally before the Supreme Court of Canada on the constitutionality of the whole repatriation package was 'bound to weigh heavily' with the British House of Commons.[20] The provincial premiers, who had chosen to fight the package not on its political merits but through a guerrilla war of litigation, were now hoist by their own petard. For in insisting that the repatriation package was 'unconstitutional,' rather than demonstrating that it was politically unwise or unreasonable, they necessarily equated constitutionality with political wisdom. A favourable Supreme Court decision on constitutionality should thus foreclose any further room for political manoeuvre within and outside Canada. Having chosen the rules of the repatriation game themselves, the premiers must now live with them or accept the political burden of the charge of being ungracious losers. Their over-hasty and perhaps also over-confident decision to resort to litigation may thus, paradoxically, have speeded up what Prime Minister Trudeau had been calling the cutting of the imperial Gordian knot.[21]

8

The premiers in court

The breakdown of constitutional negotiations in September 1980 brought an angry response by most of the provincial premiers and a search for any means, political or legal, for blocking unilateral initiatives. With Ottawa's decision to refrain from a referendum, London seemed a profitable arena for provincial blocking action. The emphasis was to be on lobbying the cabinet, officials of the Foreign and Commonwealth Ministry, and rank-and-file members of Parliament in the hope that they might enter into delaying tactics and harass or frustrate the passage of the British legislation formally enacting the Canadian constitutional changes. A concerted public letter-writing campaign was launched by several, principally western-based pressure groups and lobbyist organizations opposed to the federal government's proposals, British immigrants or British-descended families in Canada were to write to their relatives in Britain or directly to British members of Parliament urging the rejection of repatriation and any accompanying changes to the Canadian constitution. Constitutionally inelegant as it may have been for Canadian citizens or Canadian organizations to ask parliamentarians of a foreign country to mount action against the Canadian government, there is no doubt that the campaign was a success, though individual MPs complained of the occasionally stridently racist, 'anti-French' character of the correspondence.

Mrs Thatcher made it clear that she would deal only with the Canadian government, the premiers and their officials being legal non-persons except in so far as they might be officially sponsored and accompanied by officials of the Canadian high commission. Provincial premiers visiting London would, of course, continue to be treated politely, given a cup of tea, and shown the rose garden; but anything beyond that would violate Commonwealth protocol and so would not be extended to them.

After the first humiliating rebuffs in London, the premiers seem to have turned their attention from the firmly closed doors of British government offices to the parliamentary lobbies. Left this time mainly to lower-level, permanently resident provincial officials in London, the attempt to use the 'British connection' was concentrated on rank-and-file parliamentarians, with a systematic campaign of wining and dining as many of these as possible in the hope of influencing their votes. A separatist Quebec government was now seeking British support against the Canadian government, and it seems acknowledged that the 'battle of the dining-rooms' mounted by Quebec's agent-general, Mr Loiselle, was the most impressive from the viewpoint of cuisine. Other provinces followed, at considerable expense, to the point where it was guessed that perhaps two-thirds of the 635 members of the British Commons had been entertained by one or more provincial governments, some of them many times.

The Canadian Indian and native peoples' position, in strict legal terms, was much stronger than that of the provincial governments. They were, unlike the provinces, no mere internal subdivision of Canada, but could lay claim to direct treaty relations with the British Crown. They now decided to follow the provinces' example by setting up their own permanent mission in London to lobby the British government and British parliamentarians – the Office of the First Nations of Canada. The Indian peoples reached a new political constituency in Britain, separate and distinct from that of the provincial governments. Indeed, satisfaction of Indian historical claims to land and to mineral and related property rights, and also of the further claims about spoliation of their original territories, must occur mainly at the expense of the provinces. Some interesting and active British MPs who had hardly succumbed to provincial pressures seemed genuinely moved by the contention that the British government remained bound under international law to recognize and preserve the Indian nations' historic claims.

The Indian and native peoples of Canada, as a plural society with many distinct and different nations, had many different points of view on the best legal way to achieve national self-determination, inside or outside Confederation. They had difficulty in producing and maintaining any firm political consensus on long-range objectives or on short-range tactics. Not everyone within these communities necessarily agreed on the political and legal merits of trying to use the 'British connection' to advance Indian claims. This tended to impair the clarity of the Indian message to British parliamentarians and thus to compromise its effectiveness in a politically fluid situation in London.

The provinces, however, realized at last that any direct approach to Mrs Thatcher to block repatriation was doomed to failure, given her firm refusal to deal with them, and recognized that action through parliamentarians would require a good deal of time as well as money and was quite unpredictable in its results. They therefore resolved on other action – this time, through the courts. The federal government was, understandably, not disposed to co-operate with the recalcitrant premiers in referring its own repatriation package to the Supreme Court of Canada for advisory opinion as to constitutionality. The possibility of a case-controversy challenge to the package was legally foreclosed until such time as it should be enacted by the British Parliament and applied in Canada. The premiers resolved to approach the matter indirectly by way of application for declaratory judgment by the respective provincial courts of appeal. A delaying action before the courts, even if it could not legally constrain the federal government from going ahead with its plans, might embarrass it on the chance of at least one adverse verdict being given. The Supreme Court of Canada might take the matter on appeal from the various provincial courts of appeal; or the federal government, facing one or more adverse court of appeal decisions, might then move to resolve the political embarrassment by seeking a final, definitive ruling from the Supreme Court on appeal.

The court strategy was to launch common actions, accompanied by multiple, mutually supportive interventions, choosing only those courts thought to be favourable to the dissident premiers' viewpoint. Harassment could backfire in the event of court rejections of the provinces' arguments. The courts selected as being most sympathetic were Manitoba, Newfoundland, and Quebec – a representative sample in regional, cultural and linguistic, and legal (civil law, common law) terms, though not inevitably pro-provincial.

The Manitoba case was argued in early December 1980, with decision rendered at the beginning of February 1981[1]; see Appendix G1. It arose, procedurally, as a reference to the Court of Appeal of Manitoba by the lieutenant-governor of that province, under provincial law, of three questions concerning the federal government's Proposed Resolution for a Joint Address to Her Majesty the Queen respecting the Constitution of Canada:

First, would the Proposed Resolution, if enacted, affect federal-Provincial relationships or the powers, rights or privileges granted or secured by the Constitution of Canada to the Provinces, their legislatures or governments; and if so, in what respects?

Second, was it a Constitutional Convention that the Canadian Parliament would not request the British Parliament to enact legislation amending the Constitution of Canada affecting federal-provincial relationships or the powers, rights or privileges granted or secured by the Constitution of Canada to the Provinces, their legislatures or governments, without first obtaining the agreement of the provinces?

Third, was the agreement of the Provinces constitutionally required for amendment to the Constitution of Canada where such amendment affected federal-Provincial relationships or altered the powers, rights or privileges granted or secured by the Constitution of Canada to the Provinces, their legislatures or governments?

There were legal interventions by Quebec, British Columbia, Prince Edward Island, Alberta, and Newfoundland in support of the Manitoba government, as well as by the Four Nations (Indian) Confederacy. The two other dissident provinces, Saskatchewan and Nova Scotia, did not appear.

The court rejected all of the Manitoba government's legal arguments. Though the actual decision was rendered by a three-to-two vote, the key majority opinion was written by Chief Justice Samuel Freedman, one of Canada's most distinguished jurists. On the first question, Chief Justice Freedman's opinion is a classical exercise in the principle of judicial self-restraint:

I deem it useful to define the boundaries within which our enquiry should be conducted ... And clearly what does not fall within their scope is the political wisdom or unwisdom of what is contained in the Joint Address. The attempt by the federal power to patriate the constitution unilaterally may be an act of high statesmanship or of political folly. This is not a determination that we are called upon to make ... we are concerned not with the wisdom or policy of the Proposed Resolution but only with its constitutional legality. We continue to function on this Reference as a court of law.

Chief Justice Freedman found the proposed resolution subject to the real likelihood of amendments and thus to being altered, deleted, or supplanted before it should be deemed ready for transmission to Britain. To answer questions, now, as to its constitutionality would thus be to leave the court 'exposed to the risk of such an adventure in futility.' He therefore declined to answer the first question in view of the 'tentative nature of the contents of the proposed Resolution,' concluding that such an answer now would be 'speculative and premature.'

On the second question, Chief Justice Freedman's answer was negative, based on an exhaustive and painstaking examination of all the past practice as to 'made-in-Britain' amendments to the Canadian constitution since 1867.

While the historical practice did, certainly, indicate consultation by the federal government with the provinces on a number of occasions, such examples as there were were not 'appropriate to the existence of a convention full-blown, vigorous, and operative. A convention should be certain and consistent; what we have is uncertain and variable.'

As to the final question, Chief Justice Freedman had little difficulty in concluding, from his answer to the preceding question, that the answer must also be in the negative: 'No convention, no rule of law. The matter is as simple as that.' But the chief justice did take the opportunity of categorically rejecting what an earlier writer had called the 'constitutional formula or legend which has come to be known as the compact theory of Confederation,' supposedly resting on the principle that any change in the nature of the federal system required the consent of all the provinces, 'otherwise there would be a breach of the compact (or contract, or treaty) which was the basis of Confederation.' In the Chief Justice's view, the compact theory, as sought to be applied to the Canadian constitution, was 'supported neither by history nor by subsequent usage.'

If the Manitoba Court of Appeal was a bad guess for the premiers, they could draw some comfort from the unanimous ruling of the Newfoundland Court of Appeal, given at the end of March 1981,[2] on the same three questions plus an additional, strictly Newfoundland question; see the extracts in Appendix G2. This fourth question referred to part V (procedure for amending the Constitution) of the proposed resolution. It asked whether, if that were enacted and proclaimed, the terms of union of Newfoundland with Canada in 1949, and also the provisions of section 3 of the BNA Act of 1871 (allowing alteration of provincial boundaries by federal legislation enacted with the consent of the provincial legislatures concerned), could be amended, directly or indirectly, without the consent of the government or legislature or a majority of the people of Newfoundland voting in a referendum held pursuant to such part V. The decision of the three-man bench was rendered in one, fairly brief opinion. In contrast to the opinions filed in the Manitoba case, it is light in its citation of authority, perhaps because the court concentrated so very fully on the heady stuff of constitutional convention which has never, in the past, lent itself easily to express identification. Once again, six of the eight dissident premiers (Saskatchewan and Nova Scotia excepted once again) were represented on the same side against the federal government.

The court, while admitting, at the outset, that 'as a broad generalisation, questions that are speculative and premature, and those that are purely political in nature, are not appropriate for judicial response,' nevertheless disagreed with the characterization made by the Manitoba court of the proposed resolution, and proceeded to answered that 'without getting into specifics, it is clear that a "Charter of Rights and Freedoms" must infringe upon the powers of the Provinces to legislate in respect to property and civil rights, as granted by s. 92 of the Act of 1867.'

This is an interesting conclusion, of course, but the process of reasoning by which it is reached is somewhat elliptical. Surely it is only by getting into the specifics of concrete problem-situations that the existence of a conflict between the proposed Charter of Rights and the BNA Act can be demonstrated?

The same essentially elliptical reasoning seeming to rest on the court's own *ipse dixit*, may be seen in an equally intriguing statement by the court:

The constitutional status of the Provinces of Canada as autonomous communities was confirmed and perfected by (a) the Statute of Westminster giving effect to the constitutional principle declared by the Imperial Conference that both the United Kingdom and the Dominions are autonomous communities equal in status, in no way subordinate one to another in any aspect of their domestic or external affairs; (b) the recognition by that Conference of the division of power among the constituent parts that make up the Dominion of Canada by which each is autonomous, in no way subordinate one to another; and (c) the surrender by the Imperial Parliament to the Provinces of its legislative sovereignty, over matters declared by the British North America Act to be within the exclusive legislative competence of the Provinces.

This is, to put it mildly, a rather specialized, latter day view of the Statute of Westminster. A glance at the text of the statute will confirm that there is nothing in it, in terms, supporting the court's contention of a constitutional recognition of the 'autonomy' of the provinces. The provinces, purely internal subdivisions of Canada, were not dealt with in the Statute of Westminster or party to the 1926 and 1930 imperial conferences, among self-governing nations, which led to it.

The conclusions of the Newfoundland court, being unsupportable by the text or the legislative history of the Statute of Westminster, must stand or fall on other legal arguments. The court itself cited with approval a dictum by Lord Denning, given, however, forty years after the Statute of Westminster was adopted and in a British case that had no connection with Canada or Canadian law. Lord Denning, by way of indicating the practical limits to the principle of the sovereignty of Parliament, had suggested that the British Parliament could not and would not reverse the Statute of Westminster. This is very, very true; but what is its legal relevance to the claims of the provinces against the repatriation package? The gaps between claimed legal authority and normative conclusion are too great to be filled by a judicial *ipse dixit* alone.

On questions 2 and 3, about a constitutional convention requiring the prior agreement of the provinces to any constitutional amendment affecting provincial powers, the court, considering the same source materials as the Manitoba court, reached the directly opposite result and found in favour of the provinces. On the last question, related to part V (amending procedure) of the proposed resolution, the court's conclusion was that the terms of the union could not, as they now stood, be changed without the consent of the Newfoundland legislature; but that this could be obviated by use of the amending procedures set out in part V (sections 41 and 42).

The last of the three provincial courts to rule on the repatriation package, the Quebec Court of Appeal, gave judgment in mid-April 1981 – see the extracts in Appendix G3 – and by a four-to-one vote it upheld the federal government's arguments.[3] The questions referred to it were the same basic questions as those in Manitoba and Newfoundland. Once again, there were interventions in favour of Quebec by five other dissident provinces (Saskatchewan and Nova Scotia again not choosing to rally publicly to the common legal cause). The Quebec Court of Appeal, apparently unexpectedly for the dissident provinces, had no difficulty in concluding that – in the terms of Chief Justice Crête – 'speaking always on the juridical level, the federal government project, even if it was unilateral in character, was founded in legality.' Two of the judges, Justices Turgeon and Owen, were quite categorical in rejecting the dissident provinces' argument that Confederation was a compact between the provinces, with the contended juridical consequence that the federal system could not be changed without their consent. As Mr Justice Turgeon remarked – 'The compact theory is a purely political argument which hasn't any juridical base.' Mr Justice Owen, in agreeing with Mr Justice Turgeon on this point, also adopted the remarks of Chief Justice Freedman, that the compact theory was supported neither by history nor by subsequent usage or judicial practice; and he expressly noted that the three provinces – Canada, Nova Scotia, and New Brunswick – which were united in 1867 under the BNA Act were 'not sovereign states which by agreement formed a federation. In my opinion the Compact Theory of Confederation is unfounded.'

Mr Justice Bélanger, suggesting that the compact theory was one advanced by anglophone, rather than francophone, authors on the constitution, insisted that even if it had existed in 1867, there could not be deduced therefrom the conclusion that the constitution was incapable of amendment without the assent of each one of the provinces, for the power of amendment at that time rested uniquely with the British Parliament. This was the position essentially taken by Chief Justice Crête in his opinion: whether or not one accepted the compact theory, the BNA Act could be modified or abrogated only by another law emanating from the British Parliament. These four majority opinions, joined with that of Chief Justice Freedman, would thus seem to have given the legal quietus to a theory of Confederation popular in former times with French civil lawyers and suddenly discovered and taken up by English common law spokesmen for the dissident Premiers.

Even before the announcement of the Quebec decision, and perhaps in over-reaction to the Newfoundland ruling which appeared more and more an odd-man-out decision without the full doctrinal legal base or authority of the Manitoba and Quebec decisions, Prime Minister Trudeau announced his intention to allow the repatriation package to go to the Supreme Court for ruling, before sending it to Westminster.[4] It was a calculated political risk. If he should lose before the Supreme Court, he would certainly have to drop his repatriation package in its present form and either re-present it later conformably to any Court criticisms of its substance or process or else abandon it altogether. If he should win, however, he would effectively have beaten the dissident premiers at their own game. For their main tactical objection to the repatriation package had been that it was 'unconstitutional'; and they had chosen to justify their actions in court and in London on this ground.

9

The Supreme Court ruling

On 28 September 1981, the Supreme Court of Canada handed down its decision in the matter of the appeals from the rulings of the three provincial courts of appeal upon the references concerning the constitutionality of the federal government's patriation project.[1] The ruling (see Appendix H) is complex and baffling and technically unsatisfactory. American commentators would characterize it as a 'no-clear-majority' decision; and the American-born English jurisprudent A.L. Goodhart[2] would rightly castigate it as one whose principle of decision (*ratio decidendi*) was obscure. Supreme courts, as tribunals, do have a duty – part of their public educational function and as a guide to lower courts, to legal practitioners, and even to themselves – to set out the grounds on which they have decided a case. For Goodhart, the principle of decision would be a compound of the rule or rules of law adopted by the court concerned from past decisions, plus the material facts cited by the court in its opinion.

The doctrine of precedent, to which the Supreme Court of Canada, like other English common law-descended tribunals, professes itself to be bound, rests upon rendering the principle of any case (in Jeremy Bentham's term) 'cognoscible.' The problem is compounded in the case of a multi-member tribunal, and even more so where the court is closely divided and when the individual judges feel free to file separate opinions, whether majority (concurring) or minority (dissenting). In its 'golden age' the 1950s, the Supreme Court of Canada was dominated by a liberal activist bare majority led by the great Mr Justice Ivan C. Rand; its decisions, often five-to-four in vote, were characterized by a plethora of separate opinions, concurring and dissenting. It was very difficult and sometimes impossible to extract any lowest common denominator of agreement among the majority judges as a possible guide for the future and indication for what, if anything, the decision could stand as a precedent.

In the Supreme Court's patriation project decision there are only four opinions, which is quite modest in comparison to the great Court of the 1950s; but there is evidence of minimum consultation and co-ordination among the nine judges and of their inability or unwillingness to co-operate in trying to produce one common, majority, opinion. The decision reveals itself to be two separate and parallel decisions that never meet and that have, in fact, no intellectual bridge between them. There was a polarization between liberal and conservative wings (as to judicial method) and perhaps also, and more significantly, between the philosophical liberal and conservative wings (as to judicial ideology and basic values).

For the Court splits decisively between a trio of its philosophically more liberal members, Chief Justice Laskin and Justices Estey and McIntyre, and a pair of its philosophically more conservative members, Justices Martland and Ritchie (appointed by John Diefenbaker). What we have is a majority opinion on the legality of the patriation project, signed by seven of the nine members (Chief Justice Laskin, and Justices Dickson, Beetz, Estey, McIntyre, Chouinard, and Lamer), though without, in the usual way, indicating the author or at least its *rapporteur*, and confirming the legality of the federal government's action. A dissenting opinion on legality is signed by Justices Martland and Ritchie.

But there is a second majority opinion filed in the case, going to the issue of the 'conventionality' of the project and signed by six (Justices Martland, Ritchie, Dickson, Beetz, Chouinard, Lamer), though without, in the usual way, indicating the author or *rapporteur*, and declaring the federal government's action unconventional. The dissenting opinion here is signed by Justices Laskin, Estey, and McIntyre. There are no other opinions filed, and nothing by way of an opinion of court to try to bridge the two different majority opinions, with their differing personnel.

One's sense of bafflement is deepened when one analyses the patterns of voting and discovers that the majorities are constituted by the same four judges – Justice Dickson and the three Quebec judges (Justices Beetz, Chouinard, and Lamer – who simply cross over from one side of the Court to the other, to join with the liberal wing for the legality opinion and with the conservative wing for the conventionality opinion. It does not take too much detective work to recognize certain basic similarities of writing style as between, on the one hand, the majority opinion on legality and the dissenting opinion on conventionality, and, on the other hand, the majority opinion on conventionality and the dissenting opinion on legality. If Chief Justice Laskin, with his clearly identifiable drafting style, is undoubtedly the principal author of the first pair of opinions, Justices Martland and Ritchie's ties to the second pair also seem apparent.

The intriguing thought remains that the majorities in the two opinions may have been made by a group of four judges on roller-skates who did not father either of the two majority opinions. This group could have followed the normal practice in split-majority opinions of filing a separate opinion explaining just how they felt they could reconcile their own votes within the two parallel majority opinions. Not to do so would seem a breach of the Court's educational obligations. Chief Justice Charles Evans Hughes of the US Supreme Court once quipped, when criticized for an evident ellipsis in an obvious compromise opinion of the court in a tightly divided court, that his first obligation as a chief justice was to build a majority – he would leave it to the law professors and the law schools to try to rationalize what the decision actually meant.

Two of the 'silent four,' Justices Chouinard and Lamer, both from Quebec, had just been appointed; and Justice Beetz, one of the intellectually most distinguished members of the Court, has a reputation for not making up his mind quickly or rushing into opinion-writing. There were, of course, enormous political and public pressures to decide the patriation issue quickly – pressures which the Court seemed to resist, as best it could, with good humour. But, in the end, a decision rendered less than five months after the end of oral argument constitutes something of a record for the Court in a major case; and it is not unfair to suggest that the comparative haste with which the Court decided the case shows up in the imperfections in the opinion-writing and the lack of internal discipline in the rationalization of the grounds of decision-making in the case.

One has least difficulty with the seven-man majority opinion upholding the legality of the federal government's action. For the legal objections to the project had all centred upon the argument that it violated a convention (custom) of the constitution. Such provincial legal objections hardly needed three provincial court of appeal hearings, a Supreme Court appeal, plus the batteries of lawyers and the many hundreds of thousands of dollars in actual legal costs, to receive their final legal quietus. A.V. Dicey,[3] in first developing the concept of constitutional conventions in 1885, recognized that constitutional conventions, even if they could be proved to have arisen in particular cases, were not enforceable by courts of law. For remedy for their alleged abuse, the recourse must be to the ordinary political processes and not to the courts. Chief Justice Laskin and his colleagues, in the majority opinion on legality, mercifully administered the legal *coup de grâce* to the assertion that a constitutional convention (assuming it existed in the first place) has the force of law and should be enforced by the courts: 'What is desirable as a political limitation does not translate into a legal limitation, without expression in imperative constitutional text or statute.'

To the argument that the Canadian federal system is a compact, with the consequence that amendments to the constitution could be made only with the consent of all the provinces, the majority opinion responded:

Theories, whether of a full compact theory (which, even factually, cannot be sustained, having regard to federal power to create new Provinces out of federal territories, which was exercised in the creation of Alberta and Saskatchewan) or of a modified compact theory, as urged by some of the Provinces, operate in the political realm, in political science studies. They do not engage the law.

And the opinion concluded:

The one constant since the enactment of the British North America Act in 1867 has been the legal authority of the United Kingdom Parliament to amend it. The law knows nothing of any requirement of provincial consent, either to a resolution of the federal Houses or as a condition of the exercise of United Kingdom legislative power ...

What is central here is the untrammelled authority at law of the two federal Houses to proceed as they wish in the management of their own procedures and hence to adopt the Resolution which is intended for submission to Her Majesty for action thereon by the United Kingdom Parliament. The British North America Act does not, either in terms or by implication, control this authority or require that it be subordinated to provincial assent. Nor does the Statute of Westminster interpose any requirement of such assent. If anything, it leaves the position as it was before its enactment. Developments subsequent thereto do not affect the legal position.

Having thus, with devastating judicial logic and a masterly survey of constitutional history, disposed of the objection that the patriation project was illegal, it might normally have been concluded that the Court's work was finished. Not the least paradox in the decision, however, is that the more policy-oriented judges are the ones to apply – very impressively, as it turns out – a strict-construction approach to the legality issue; whereas the conservative or 'black-letter law' judges, whose opinions are normally marked by a respect for law *stricto sensu* and a deliberate eschewing of policy considerations, launch themselves into high policy discussions, untethered by past precedent, in going on to decide that the federal government's actions are indeed unconventional (whether or not they are legal). The six-man majority on conventionality never, however, seems very comfortable in its new 'policy' role: and for two, at least – Justices Martland and Ritchie – it seems out of character.

One might normally have expected the majority to rule that the issue of conventionality was not a legal issue and therefore not one on which the Supreme Court could, or should, deign to rule. The doctrine of 'political questions,' as outlined earlier by Chief Justice Freedman, provided a perfect justification for judicial self-restraint and for returning the issue of whether or not there was a convention to the ordinary political processes (general elections and the like) for decision. Instead, the six-man majority opinion on conventionality ventured into what must be characterized as an extended *obiter dictum* on general constitutional morality. One might be tempted to draw comparisons with Chief Justice Marshall's celebrated decision in *Marbury* v *Madison*. In the opinion that first established judicial review as a constitutional institution, he both decided the case on a narrow technical ground and also took the opportunity of reading an extended lecture on proper governmental conduct to his erstwhile political enemies, the incoming Jefferson administration. Chief Justice Marshall was clearly conscious, at all times, of what he was doing; the Supreme Court of Canada, because of the nature of the 'no-clear-majority' holding and the two parallel, but different, majority opinions, seems to have acted without any overall design.

Collectively, the message from the Court amounted to the statement that the project was legal, but not conventional. A distinction known to continental European civil law constitutionalism but not, heretofore, to Anglo-Saxon common law constitutionalism would thus seem perforce to have been introduced into Canadian constitutional law. The judges, however, left it to the legal commentators to try to explain its concrete implications, if any, in Canadian constitutional jurisprudence. The other (seven-man) majority opinion proclaimed that a convention is not law and will not be enforced by courts. What is it then, and from where does it obtain its sanction, if any; and who, if anyone, will enforce it? From the technical-legal viewpoint, it is not a very satisfactory decision. It has, however, been greeted as a politically rather wise decision, even if not directly intended as such – some form of compromise, Canadian-style, which, in seeming to give something to all sides, facilitated the political compromise which followed the decision by a little more than a month.

The six-man majority opinion (Justices Martland, Ritchie, Dickson, Beetz, Chouinard, and Lamer) on the issue of the conventionality of the patriation project starts out with an excursus on the nature of constitutional conventions. It makes a basic distinction between 'conventions' and the 'law of the

Constitution' – the constitutional charter; imperial statutes still legally in force in Canada, federal parliamentary statutes, provincial legislative enactments, certain imperial orders in council of relevance to Canada, and also rules of the common law developed in judicial decisions. Citing Dicey, the six-man opinion describes conventions as

the principles and rules of responsible government, several of which ... regulate the relations between the Crown, the Prime Minister, the Cabinet and the two Houses of Parliament. These rules developed in Great Britain by way of custom and precedent during the nineteenth century and were exported to such British colonies as were granted self-government.

The opinion suggests that

A federal constitution provides for the distribution of powers between various legislatures and governments and may also constitute a fertile ground for the growth of constitutional conventions between those legislatures and governments. It is conceivable for instance that usage and practice might give birth to conventions in Canada relating to the holding of federal-provincial conferences, the appointment of lieutenant-governors, the reservation and disallowance of provincial legislation ... The main purpose of constitutional conventions is to ensure that the legal framework of the Constitution will be operated in accordance with the prevailing constitutional values or principles of the period.

Further:

In contradistinction to the laws of the Constitution, [conventions] are not enforced by the courts. One reason for this situation is that, unlike common law rules, conventions are not judge-made rules. They are not based on judicial precedents but on precedents established by the institutions of government themselves ... To enforce them would mean to administer some formal sanction when they are breached. But the legal system from which they are distinct does not contemplate formal sanctions for their breach.
  Perhaps the main reason why conventional rules cannot be enforced by the courts is that they are generally in conflict with the legal rules which they postulate and the courts are bound to enforce the legal rules ...
  This conflict between convention and law which prevents the courts from enforcing conventions also prevents conventions from crystallising into laws, unless it be by statutory adoption.

Conventions are not law; they will not be enforced by the courts; there are no legal sanctions for their breach. These are conclusions with which the other, seven-man majority opinion, and the three-man (Laskin, Estey, McIntyre) dissent to the six-man majority opinion, would have no difficulty. Why continue further? Invoking the preamble to the BNA Act of 1867 – 'federally united ... with a Constitution similar in principle to that of the United Kingdom' – the opinion suggests that that is why it is 'perfectly appropriate to say that to violate a convention is to do something which is unconstitutional although it entails no direct legal consequence ... The foregoing may perhaps be summarised in an equation: constitutional conventions plus constitutional law equal the total Constitution of the country.'

Next comes a more difficult question. Does the question whether or not there exists a convention requiring consent of the provincial governments to proposed amendments raise an issue appropriate for determination by a court? 'It was contended that the issue whether a particular convention exists or not is a purely political one. The existence of a definite convention is always unclear and a matter of debate. Furthermore conventions are flexible, somewhat imprecise and unsuitable for judicial determination.'

The opinion responded to this argument by suggesting that the question was

not confined to an issue of pure legality but it has to do with a fundamental issue of constitutionality and legitimacy. [The governments of Manitoba, Newfoundland, and Quebec] ... are in our view entitled to an answer to a question of this type ... Nor are we asked to enforce a convention. We are asked to recognise it if it exists. Courts have done this very thing many times in England and the Commonwealth to provide aid for and background to constitutional or statutory construction.'

The opinion cited seven cases, including one from Australia in 1925 and two from pre-Biafran civil war Nigeria. The most important, *Liversidge* v *Anderson*, was a 1942 British decision[4] on the scope of wartime emergency powers; it hardly seemed *à propos* since its reasoning involved statutory construction grounds. Relying on these decisions, however, the opinion concluded that it was proper for it to proceed to answer the conventionality question:

In so recognising conventional rules, the Courts have described them, sometimes commented upon them and given them such precision as is derived from the written form of a judgment. They did not shrink from doing so on account of the political aspects of conventions, nor because of their supposed vagueness; uncertainty or flexibility.

In our view, we should not, in a constitutional reference, decline to accomplish a type of exercise that courts have been doing of their own motion for years.

The opinion concluded that there was a convention requiring that the federal government consult with the provinces and obtain their consent prior to approaching the British government. Such practice was neither continuing nor unbroken over a period of years, as normally required to prove the existence of a convention. How to explain all the exceptions, in the twenty-two amendments to the BNA Act since 1867, to the claimed convention? The only possible way out is to be found in the statement that 'these precedents must be considered selectively' and in the proceeding to pick and choose among them. Five, those of 1930, 1940, 1951, and 1964, plus the Statute of Westminster itself, seemed appropriate for such 'selective consideration,' as being amendments that 'directly affected federal-provincial relationships in the sense of changing provincial legislative powers':

These five amendments are the only ones which can be viewed as positive precedents whereby federal-provincial relationships were directly affected in the sense of changing legislative powers.

Every one of these five amendments was agreed upon by each province whose legislative authority was affected.

In negative terms, no amendment changing provincial legislative powers has been made since Confederation when agreement of a province whose legislative powers would have been changed was withheld.

There are no exceptions.

The courts below it 'fell into error' or had been otherwise 'misled' in 'failing to differentiate between various types of constitutional amendments':

The Quebec Court of Appeal put all or practically all constitutional amendments since 1867 on the same footing and, as could then be expected, concluded not only that the convention requiring provincial consent did not exist but that there even appeared to be a convention to the contrary ... The Manitoba Court of Appeal was similarly misled, in our respectful opinion, but to a lesser extent.

All five amendments were from the last half-century of Confederation; what of the first sixty-three years? Would the five be enough to constitute that continuing and unbroken practice necessary for the formation of a convention? The group of six was silent on this point.

As to how many provinces must give consent, the opinion was determinedly coy: 'We have reached the conclusion that the agreement of the provinces of Canada, no views being expressed as to its quantification, is constitutionally required.'

Why so? Having ventured, where legal positivist angels normally fear to tread, the group of six promptly 'passed the buck' back to the political arms of government:

It would not be appropriate for the Court to devise in the abstract a specific formula which would indicate in positive terms what measure of provincial agreement is required for the convention to be complied with. Conventions by their nature develop in the political field and it will be for the political actors, not this Court, to determine the degree of provincial consent required.

It is sufficient for the Court to decide that at least a substantial measure of provincial consent is required.

It is necessary to distinguish the decision on the patriation project as a technical judgment from its consequences for the constituent process in Canada. The decision fails in its primary responsibility of providing a clear and logically reasoned judicial argument as an authoritative statement to the parties actually before the Court, and also as an educational guide to lower courts, the legal profession, and the general public. The absence of a formal opinion of court that would bridge the two separate and parallel majority opinions on legality and conventionality is the most serious gap in this respect. The four judges who crossed back and forth between the seven-man and the six-man majority opinions had some obligations to their judicial colleagues, to the legal profession, and to the general public to set out publicly how, if at all, they felt able to reconcile their positions. The decision is not a good example of collegiality in decision-making on a multi-member tribunal, and it compares most unfavourably with similar decisions of the US Supreme Court which exercises an admirable self-discipline and produces, even with narrowly divided votes, a clear basis of reasoning.

However, the decision allowed everyone to snatch something from the judgment, often by highly selective quotation from the two majority opinions. All the main protagonists were able to retreat without intolerable loss of face, even though the federal government had clearly won on the only relevant issue for a court of law – the issue of legality – and the dissident provincial governments clearly lost. It is tempting to think that the Supreme Court planned it that way from the very beginning: to give the federal government the victory it could not, on all the precedents, be denied on the law, but at the same time to read a public lecture, to all sides, on federal good manners (in German theory, *Bundestreue*). To reach this result it had to get into high political, policy questions transcending the strict legalism on which it has normally insisted.

One of the main arguments from the Quiet Revolution was that judicial review of the constitution is inherently political in character; rather than deny that elemental truth, it would be better to mandate the judge – by legislative election as in West Germany, or by Senate confirmation as in the United States – to arbitrate such issues. The case for a special constitutional court seems rather more persuasive in Canada after the decision on patriation. The only other logical alternative for a court wishing to preserve its independence in an era of political change is judicial self-restraint and a prudent refusal to be drawn into great political questions more appropriate for other branches of government.

10

The Guy Fawkes Day compromise

The Supreme Court decision on the patriation project was followed by a period of considerable confusion. Federal Justice Minister Jean Chrétien, beseiged by media representatives who demanded a public comment immediately, correctly claimed that the federal government had won its case and would proceed, promptly, to have Parliament adopt the joint resolution. Prime Minister Trudeau, absent in South Korea on a state visit, announced he would only comment on the decision after he had slept overnight. With the delay, and presumably some interim briefings from his staff in Ottawa, he showed himself conciliatory and apparently open to further talks with the provincial governments, though affirming his intention to press ahead with parliamentary adoption of the resolution. He indicated that the condition of further talks would be that the provinces give up their demands for unanimous provincial consent and accept patriation and a charter of rights.[1] He flew on to the Commonwealth prime ministers' conference in Australia, where he consulted again with Prime Minister Thatcher. She repeated her earlier undertaking that the British government would act on a formal request from the Canadian government, but hinted that there might be difficulties with timing and staging such legislation – some refractory backbenchers had indicated that they might try to delay or frustrate the measure at the behest of various provincial governments and some native and Indian groups.

The eight dissenting provincial premiers took what public profit they could from 'unconventionality.' Claiming that the decision was a *legal* stand-off – which hardly seems true – they took advantage of the *political* stand-off resulting from public understanding of the ruling. All signs pointed to yet another, and presumably the last, first ministers' meeting before the final vote in Parliament. Such renewed negotiations, even if they should prove futile, as appeared likely, would serve to show the Canadian public and Mrs Thatcher and any of her refractory back-benchers that the federal Government was exhausting all possibilities before going to London. The dissident premiers had indeed lost decisively. Now they ran the risk, while facing re-election in several cases, of having any further delays perceived as simple obstructionism. All the public opinion polls indicated that patriation and an entrenched charter of rights had support. In the public confusion over the Court's 'no-clear-majority' opinion, the premiers might yet be able to retreat without too much loss of face.

There were also signs that the hitherto seemingly solid front of the eight provincial premiers opposed to patriation was beginning to crack. Premier Lougheed had always viewed constitutional change as an instrument for achieving non-constitutional (essentially economic) goals; he had already achieved his oil pricing agreement, on essentially his own terms, in direct, bilateral negotiations with Ottawa at the opening of September. Premiers Bennett and Peckford were the two provincial leaders most committed to confrontation with the federal government as, seemingly, a political end in itself. Lougheed had negotiated with the federal government only for himself and his own province and left other provinces with similar claims out in the cold; Bennett and Peckford, after their initial shock, tried to open up their own negotiations with Ottawa. Why had they not adopted a similar tactic several years earlier, when it would have been politically more timely and likely, therefore, to yield a rather more generous federal response? But negotiate they now did, on economic issues. Would there now be a breaking of ranks by other members of the gang of eight?

Premier Lyon of Manitoba was identified in the public mind as on the far, far right of the political spectrum, intransigent on the subject of an entrenched charter of rights, and therefore quite intractable as to any change of front. Premier Blakeney of Saskatchewan had been trying to distance himself from the federal NDP (which was committed to supporting the patriation project) and found himself allied with six conservative premiers in a bitter opposition to a constitutional bill of rights. That basic contradiction and the comments of his own party colleagues were beginning to catch up with him. The premiers of Nova Scotia and of Prince Edward Island were considered, even though conservative, to be more moderate and pragmatic than their colleagues and therefore more disposed to compromise.

That left only Premier Lévesque, perhaps the intellectual leader of the gang of eight. Rebounding from defeat in the referendum, he had returned to full participation in first ministers' conferences on renewal of Canadian

Confederation. He did not seem to see any contradiction in such a role, and neither Prime Minister Trudeau nor the other premiers raised any objection. Lévesque had delivered himself, energetically and jovially, to a very expensive campaign of lobbying British members of Parliament to reject the patriation project. While the other premiers mounted similar campaigns, none was as sophisticated or as generously financed as the Quebec government's. However, one or more of the English-speaking premiers might come to conclude that the Lévesque campaign was mischievous in motive and execution and that there were risks of being seen to be politically naïve and to be used by Quebec separatists for their own ends.

Lévesque had broken with the constitutional strategy developed and practised by all Quebec premiers since the early 1960s. As Léon Dion had noted, they had all emphasized, successfully, Quebec's particularity – that it was not a province 'comme les autres.'[2] Implicit was the larger premise of Canada as a state composed of two founding nations. Quebec's special case was by now amply recognized if not necessarily accepted in English Canada. New demands, largely to do with control of tax revenues from exploitation of natural resources, were being advanced by the English-speaking provinces, and especially those in the west. By merging his campaign with theirs, Lévesque necessarily gave up Quebec's claims to distinctiveness. He also passed up the long-standing *entente cordiale* between Quebec and Ontario developed by Jean Lesage and John Robarts in the early 1960s and continued until 1976.

The gang of eight seemed an unholy alliance of mutually incompatible personalities, with quite disparate political, social, and economic interests and linked only by a common dislike of Prime Minister Trudeau. Could Lévesque really believe that he could reach an accommodation with the four western premiers on, for example, language of education, more easily than he could with his natural allies in this area of policy, Ontario and New Brunswick, or for that matter with the federal government? There was a certain gambler's recklessness in his decision to throw in his own lot and Quebec's with the gang of eight, and there was a certain political naïveté in his trusting in the pledge that he extracted from the other seven premiers that they would maintain solidarity and that none would make a separate deal with the federal government without the full assent of all the rest.

The Guy Fawkes Day compromise of 5 November 1981, between the nine English-speaking premiers and Ottawa, finally broke the constitutional logjam. Lévesque reproached his co-premiers for 'behaving like carpet salesmen' with their wheeling and dealing political trade-offs, and complained bitterly of being isolated. But, in truth, he had been overly clever and had succeeded in isolating himself (though not necessarily his province). In negotiations with the rest of the gang of eight in the spring of 1981, he had been prepared to give up the right Quebec had always claimed and succeeded in maintaining of a right of veto over all constitutional amendment proposals touching on provincial powers.[3] When he sought to revive this claim after the Guy Fawkes Day compromise, Jean Chrétien gently reminded him that it was too late to do so.[4]

On the day before the compromise, Lévesque had nibbled at the bait thrown to him by Prime Minister Trudeau and agreed to accept an offer to break the constitutional deadlock by holding a nation-wide referendum to settle once and for all the constitutional amending formula and the proposed Charter of Rights.[5] As a proponent of the constitutional referendum and having himself applied it, Lévesque would have found it difficult publicly to turn down the proposal. But he must have known that it would be anathema to his English-speaking colleagues, for all the public opinion polls indicated that they would be turned down by any referendum on patriation and the Charter of Rights. In breaking ranks on this referendum issue, Lévesque was hardly in a position to object when they all broke ranks with him and made their own deal the very same evening. He perhaps was entitled to complain of a certain lack of common courtesy and civility on their part in that they did not consult with him about their separate deal until the moment of its public announcement the next day.[6] Angry comments, could not veil the fact that alliances of convenience invite double-dealing and the political double-cross.

That a deal of some sort would be reached had been apparent by the time the first ministers' conference on the constitution opened in Ottawa on 2 November 1981. Public impatience over the very real economic problems of inflation and high unemployment grew steadily worse, and it would be a brave premier or prime minister who would appear responsible for any further delay in the constitutional talks. The only real question was which premier would be the first to break ranks and whether it would have a snowball effect. Advance speculation centred on Bennett, who had just concluded a handsome bilateral deal on natural gas with Ottawa and was thought to be chafing at his enforced subordinate role to Lougheed, and on Blakeney, who seemed to be embarrassed by his earlier fierce opposition to a constitutional bill of rights, the academic and public criticisms having by now caught up with him.

In the end, seven of the gang of eight joined with the two staunch federal allies, the premiers of Ontario and New Brunswick, in reaching a deal with Prime Minister Trudeau (see Appendix C) that involved acceptance of the patriation package – patriation itself, plus a modified amending formula and a modified Charter of Rights. It is generally agreed that the key movers in building the new alliance were Lougheed, Blakeney, and Davis. The latter overcame his erstwhile unpopularity (as the federal government's staunch ally) with the other premiers to fulfil the crucial function of intermediary between the premiers and Trudeau.

Lyon might have been an obstacle to the last; but had to return home to fight in the provincial election, then seeming dangerously close for his government. A surprise was Peckford, who came into the conference with the reputation and the record of a bitter enemy of Ottawa and of a man who mistook noisy verbal confrontation for quiet diplomacy. He not merely reversed his position but did so with public gusto and some humour and thus established himself, in the public mind at least if not that of his colleagues, as the author of the final draft of the compromise agreement and as one of the great successes of the whole conference.

The price of the compromise agreement was, however, a considerable degree of give-and-take on all sides. If the seven premiers who quit the gang of eight may, on many views, be seen as finally bowing to the inevitable, Prime Minister Trudeau had to accept significant changes in the constitutional amending machinery and some substantial modification of the terms and also the practical application of his cherished Charter of Rights.

As to the constitutional amending machinery, the most significant change was the deletion of the provision for consultation of the general public by way of referendum, in case of future deadlock. This meant giving up on 'participatory' or direct democracy to which the prime minister and the Liberal party were officially wedded. Since the prime minister had seemed curiously diffident to using public consultation as a method of building public support for the patriation project, perhaps the loss was more notional than real.

The other significant change in the amending machinery was the deletion of the effective Ontario and Quebec right of veto, which had been strongly objected to by the leaders of the rapidly growing western provinces. Ontario volunteered to give up its right of veto as a gesture to all the other Provinces; Quebec had agreed to give up the right of veto in April 1981 and was not now consulted. Henceforth constitutional amendments would require majorities in both federal houses of Parliament, plus majorities in the legislatures of at least two-thirds of the provinces having at least 50 per cent of the population of all of the provinces. This would mean majorities in the legislatures of *seven* out of the *ten* provinces, and, according to present population distribution, would mean that either Quebec or Ontario (though not necessarily both) would have to be among those seven. Except for Quebec, no one at either the federal or the provincial level seemed too unhappy at these changes. There seemed to be a growing conviction that the constitution would anyway become rigid and prove resistant to change.

Prime Minister Trudeau had the greatest difficulty in accepting changes to his Charter of Rights. He had scornfully rejected a deal whereby the premiers would accept patriation plus a constitutional amending machinery only, in return for his giving up on the Charter of Rights. But some compromises as to its content and application he did have to accept if he wanted to persuade some at least of the gang of eight to join him. Initial speculation centred upon the so-called 'opting in/opting out' proposals advanced by the Pépin-Robarts report. Among the ideas floated were a *total* opting in/opting out as to the whole of the Charter of Rights, at the choice of any one or more provinces; or a *partial* opting in/opting out as to selected chapters or sections of the charter, again at the choice of any one or more provinces.

The distinction between opting in and opting out lay in the relative political and psychological ease or difficulty of the two. A recalcitrant province would find it relatively easy to lose any opting in resolution in the proceduralisms of its legislative process and so escape the obligations of the charter without having to risk a negative vote in the legislature. An opting out procedure could, however, force a recalcitrant province to go on record as being against political and other rights for its citizens. It was obviously to the federal government's interest, if it conceded an opting in/opting out formula, to restrict the formula to opting out, while recalcitrant provinces would sensibly prefer opting in.

If he had to concede any such opting formula to the provinces, Trudeau made it clear, it could not extend to language rights. He considered these the key to the whole Charter of Rights, as they had, indeed, been the leitmotif of his public career. He could not be seen as abandoning language rights without, in effect, negating the whole philosophy of official bilingualism throughout Canada.

Some adjustments and modifications on language policy would remain possible, of course. The federal government had accepted the coexistence of bilingualism throughout Canada in federal government institutions and programs, and monolingualism in provincial institutions and programs in Quebec. Granted such coexistence, which the new Charter of Rights did nothing to challenge, the points of potential friction as to language were neither extensive nor incapable of diplomatic solution at the administrative level.

The main point would be what had been called the 'Canada Clause' at the St Andrews, New Brunswick, conference of 1978. It posited the right of Canadian parents moving from one province to another in the course of their business to have their children educated in their maternal language, provided it be either French or English. This had been balanced by the so-called 'Quebec Clause,' whereby Quebec, under Bill 101 of 1977, limited the right of education in English, within Quebec, in effect, to children whose father or mother had received his or her elementary education in English in Quebec, or to those whose father or mother, domiciled in Quebec on the date Bill 101 came into force in 1977, had received his or her elementary education in English outside Quebec.

Premier Lévesque had indicated at St Andrews that he would accept the 'Canada Clause,' on a basis of reciprocity – that is, that the other, English-speaking Provinces would do the same; but the St Andrews compromise had lapsed when these other provinces reneged. In effect, the new Charter of Rights would require *all* provinces, henceforward, to accept the St Andrews compromise. Even without the operation of the St Andrews compromise, however, the conflict between Bill 101 and federal objectives over minority language of education was more notional than real. Successive Quebec ministers of education since 1977 had almost uniformly granted certificates of exemption from the bill's minority-language stipulations to anglophone parents, being Canadian citizens, coming to Quebec from other provinces. The principal architect of Bill 101, Dr Camille Laurin, had himself indicated in recent months that the Quebec government might voluntarily abandon the 'Quebec Clause' in favour of the 'Canada Clause' – and this unilaterally and without demanding reciprocity from other provinces – as a gesture of confidence and goodwill at a certain point in time, perhaps several years ahead, when the general objectives of Bill 101 and the French fact within Quebec should have become consolidated and assured.

The Guy Fawkes Day compromise involved the following key changes as to the Charter of Rights. First, with respect to mobility rights, there was to be an express inclusion of the right of a province to undertake affirmative action programs for socially and economically disadvantaged individuals as long as that province's employment rate was below the national average. In effect, this would exempt a province from compliance with the mobility rights requirements and allow it, for example, to give preferential treatment to its own residents in regard to employment and contracts within the province, so long as it could demonstrate that the province fell within the 'economically depressed' category.

Second, the federal charter was to be made subject to a 'notwithstanding' clause covering those sections dealing with fundamental freedoms, legal rights, and equality rights. In effect, this allowed any province to opt out of any section within those three categories, the only legal limitation being that such opting out must be re-enacted by that province not less frequently than once every five years in order to maintain continuing validity. It raised the possibility that Prime Minister Trudeau had always dreaded in public, of a 'checkerboard quilt' of human rights throughout Canada in which some rights might be in force, at any one time, in one province but not in another. The legal spectre thus emerged of the condition described by Voltaire in his depiction of eighteenth-century France: one changed one's law every time one changed one's horse in travelling from one part of the country to another.

However, the dangers, again, seemed more notional than real. Trudeau had reduced the gang of eight's demands to an opting-out right, rather than the much more facultative opting-in formula. The possibilities of any premier's risking being characterized as a political 'red-neck' by moving to opt out of the charter, or parts of it, seemed exaggerated and worth the prime minister's gamble. This part of the constitutional deal might also operate affirmatively and educationally in terms of participatory democracy, by encouraging individuals and political action groups to get into the provincial political processes to make sure that their province should not bear the public shame of being the only province to reject a Charter of Rights and human rights for its citizens.

The opting-out right was expressly stated to extend to fundamental freedoms, legal rights, and equality rights in the federal charter. It did *not* apply, therefore, to the other categories of rights under the charter – democratic rights; mobility rights (except in so far as already mentioned above); official languages rights; and minority language educational rights. Indeed, as far as the last were concerned, there was an express stipulation that the parties had agreed that this particular section should apply to their provinces. There being thus no opting-out exception for this particular right, Premier Lévesque would henceforward be bound, whether he liked it or not. Though he had earlier seemed to find no particular problem in accepting the principle of just such an arrangement, he reacted most angrily to the compulsory application of this section (23) to Quebec. This was no doubt, however, simply part of his more general sense of frustration.

A more mysterious question concerned the effects of the compromise upon part II of the charter (section 34, rights of the aboriginal peoples) and upon

Indian and native rights generally. Indian and native rights had not been included in the first draft of the resolution, but had been inserted just in time for the public unveiling of the resolution project in October 1980. The last-minute inclusion had occurred in response to private representations from the more moderate and pragmatic Indian leadership (principally from the Treaty Nations of Alberta).

The original draft had not touched on Indian and native rights, for two obvious reasons. There was no clear majority consensus among Indian and native leaders as to these rights, and, in consequence, no federal government policy in response. The effect of the absence of any express mention would be to leave the pre-existing legal situation, such as it might be under international and constitutional law, unchanged. At the very last minute, the prime minister included a new section 24: 'The guarantee in this Charter of certain rights and freedoms shall not be construed as denying the existence of any other rights or freedoms ... that pertain to the native peoples of Canada.'

This is a type of clause inserted for greater certainty or to make assurance doubly sure. It preserves the legal status quo as to Indian and native rights, though without defining them and is, in fact, unnecessary so far as the legal continuance of those rights is concerned.

As a result of the lengthy representations and testimony and also the parliamentary debates, the original draft resolution was amended with the result of adding several more sections on Indian rights and rewording and expanding the original section 24 (now section 25). In addition to section 25, there were now sections 34 and 36.

The constitutional deal of 5 November 1981 was recorded in a text (Appendix C) setting out, very briefly, five general principles. These would still have to be drafted in technical legal language and incorporated into a new revision (Appendix D) of the consolidated resolution of 24 April 1981 (Appendix B). These five general principles would be refined, clarified, and extended. This would be the obvious time – probably the only time remaining – at which changes could still be made. Such changes obviously could not negate or otherwise vary the substance of the accord without first going back to the nine premiers, and any proposals for change would also (sensibly, if they were to have the hope of being accepted) have to be brief and to concentrate on essentials.

The only part of the accord touching on Indian and native rights was that contained in the fifth principle, and this, in effect, repeated an undertaking contained in section 36(2) of the consolidated resolution and did not mention any other sections. This fifth principle stipulated that the final resolution should provide for a constitutional conference that would identify and define the rights of the aboriginal peoples for inclusion in the constitution, and that the prime minister should invite representatives of the aboriginal peoples to participate in the discussion. Though nothing in the text of the accord either confirmed or disproved this, various Indian and native leaders claimed that section 25 of the consolidated resolution was to be retained in addition to section 36(2), but that section 34 was now to be deleted.

The search went on for the villains in the piece. It seemed that the four western premiers, as a bloc, had been most determined to exclude aboriginal rights. Their provinces would bear the main economic losses from rectification of the original Indian treaties and re-writing of land claims on some more nearly equitable basis. All nine anglophone premiers must share responsibility for the exclusion, however, if it was really intended and not arrived at unintentionally in the confusion of the deal. Premier Lougheed announced, after public outcry arose, that he would oppose the reinsertion of section 34 of the consolidated resolution, in any new and renegotiated compromise between the nine premiers and Ottawa.

Prime Minister Trudeau seemed genuinely surprised at the public outcry, confirming the thesis that the exclusion occurred unintentionally. Part of the responsibility perhaps rests with Indian and native leaders themselves. Their communities do not represent one monolithic society, but are as plural and diverse as, say, the ten provinces. There were obvious moments in the period of constitutional negotiations between the Quebec referendum and the 5 November deal when Indian and native political support for Ottawa could have made them effective power-brokers and ensured their participation in the benefits of the final arrangements. Internecine conflicts frustrated any ability to form a common front.

The more pragmatic Indian leaders found their diplomatic initiatives defeated by more radical elements that insisted on confrontational tactics more suited to the United States of the Vietnam War era. The crucial first week of November 1981 found the more radical British Columbia Indian leadership and 100 supporters away on a Constitution Train in West Germany, France, Belgium, and The Netherlands, ostensibly to 'try to rally Continental European public opinion' against Ottawa's constitutional plans. The next week saw a further fifty BC Indian leaders fly to London to lobby the British government and British parliamentary back-benchers once more.

The more radical leadership often seemed confused as to the tactical choice of allies and friends, seeming to prefer to link with the gang of eight, though Indian and native claims could hardly be satisfied except with considerable cost to the premiers, and especially the western premiers. Their errors of tactics and failure to develop a strategy do not of course excuse any blatant ignoring of their claims; but their inability to deliver their political support when it was timely and to profit from the constitutional deals remains one of the sadder 'might-have-beens' of the whole process.

Even if section 34 in the consolidated resolution were to be deleted as a result of the existence of some secret understanding, it could not change the existing status quo. The effects would be political and psychological and not legal.

One could understand the concern of the Métis that the apparent elimina- · tion of section 34(2) of the consolidated resolution might prejudice their inclusion within the constitutional category of 'aboriginal peoples.' However, the Supreme Court should normally have little difficulty in reaching a genuinely inclusive definition of aboriginal peoples, as a matter of ordinary legal interpretation and construction. And no deletion of section 34(1), if it were to result from any secret protocol, could legally derogate from the much more comprehensive definition of rights contained in section 25.

A rather more substantial question was whether the opting-out right now conferred on provinces could be used by individual provinces to derogate from Indian and native rights – either those expressly recognized by the charter or those existing under international and constitutional law. The opting-out right could not confer a greater substantive law-making competence than the provinces may already have. Section 91(24) of the BNA Act establishes the exclusive law-making competence of the federal Parliament as to 'Indians, and Lands reserved for the Indians.' There is no other head of law-making power in that area and, self-evidently, no provincial power to make laws in that area.

After the conclusion of the compromise deal, the inevitable question arose of who had won and who had lost. Certainly, the prime minister had succeeded in bringing to an end fifty-four years of negotiations over constitutional amending machinery, he had achieved the symbolic step of cutting the last vestigial constitutional link with Britain, and, finally, he had obtained what he had fought for throughout his political life in Ottawa, a constitutional entrenchment of bilingualism and a more ample and comprehensive constitutional bill of rights. Trudeau would probably emerge as the main victor in the patriation battle; but the victory, though by no means Pyrrhic, was at a certain price in terms of sacrifice of key elements of the principle and application of the Charter of Rights.

The Premiers of Ontario and New Brunswick had, with the prime minister's evident degree of success, themselves been vindicated in similar measure. As for the gang of eight, or those seven who chose to make a deal with Trudeau at the eleventh hour, they had presumably gained time – seventeen and a half months, as it turned out; but time to do what? The lack of any philosophy of constitutional change or of constitutionalism generally is one of the most disappointing features of their attempt at a common front. Purely negative attitudes – political dislike of the prime minister, for example, or even the asserted opposition to the federal government's constitutional process (for process, after all, should in the end serve substantive ideas) – could not be an adequate substitute for a reasoned, principled approach to the renewal of Canadian federalism. Of the ten premiers only Lévesque would seem to have lost absolutely, but it was a personal political loss rather than a loss for his province as a whole. It was brought on as much by Lévesque's own tactical misjudgments and his lack of any positive philosophy of federalism, as by any gratuitous malice on the part of the gang of eight or of the federal government. Even his loss was not irrevocable, but seemed eminently capable of being redeemed[7] if only he would apply himself afresh to quiet diplomacy.[8]

A retrospective assessment of the patriation battle might suggest the response given the child in Southey's 'Battle of Blenheim':

'What good came of it all?'
'Why that I cannot tell,' said he,
'But 'twas a famous victory.'

11

New players, new people's power

No sooner had the Guy Fawkes Day accord been concluded than something rather strange began to happen. There was an immediate angry reaction from public pressure groups, such as women's rights activists, who saw themselves as now excluded by an all-male cabal (the nine premiers) from the express constitutional recognition that they thought they had won in the parliamentary hearings of a year before. Assorted Indian and native leaders protested the announced deletion of section 34 of the consolidated resolution; the Indian leaders contended that this exclusion meant the effective end of Indian and native, aboriginal rights.

Premier Lévesque's bitterness was perhaps understandable. He had been out-smarted in a game that he had played with more dexterity and cynical amusement than anyone else and had, along the way, abandoned Quebec's traditional veto on constitutional change. Other, perhaps more disinterested observers, such as former Liberal Senator Eugene Forsey, one of the great Canadian constitutionalists, were sad about the seeming emasculation of the prime minister's original Charter of Rights and Freedoms. As Dr Forsey suggested, in a moving public statement: 'The Provinces have shot it full of holes: great, big, gaping holes ... [The Charter] is now being disembowelled ... The accord has poisoned the charter. If I were still in the Senate, I should have no choice but to speak and vote against the whole package.'[1]

The unexpected, however, now occurred: the genuine involvement, for the first time, of the general public. This time, it was not factitious ad hoc pressure groups and special interest lobbying that had accompanied the parliamentary hearings, though some of that, of course, continued. Rather it was a seemingly quite spontaneous and at first quite unco-ordinated public reaction, which was communicated directly and pressingly to the premiers and their supporters. While public reaction was not always based on thorough analysis of the accord, there could be no doubt of the degree of indignation over the apparent determination of seven of the premiers to exclude women's rights and aboriginal rights from any constitutional protection. There was perhaps a casual, 'trendy' aspect to this movement – why women's and aboriginal rights, but not Quebec rights? – but there was no doubt about its momentum.

Most immediately came the election defeat of the ultra-conservative Sterling Lyon, the most intransigent opponent of a constitutionally entrenched charter of rights and of court-based protection of political and civil rights in general. Rightly or wrongly, his defeat was attributed, in considerable part, to his opposition to constitutional rights and his failure to assess the opinion of his ethnically mixed electorate on these issues.[2] If he could have persistently misread his own electorate's opinion on constitutional issues, why not also the rest of the gang of eight?

The collapse of the gang of eight, evidenced already in the accord, began to take on all the semblance of a rout. Opposition Leader Joe Clark, who had previously distinguished himself as champion of provincial rights and of opposition to repatriation and the Charter of Rights unless it should have unanimous provincial support, now tried to disengage himself. He chastised the prime minister for agreeing to the deletion of women's and aboriginal rights at the behest of the provincial premiers, though Trudeau had done this in pursuit of that unanimous provincial support that Mr Clark had previously demanded as a condition of any constitutional change. Clark's *volte-face*, without so much as a by-your-leave, involved the argument that Trudeau should go directly to London *without* the consent of the provincial premiers, if need be. Clark's switch had come far too late and was largely irrelevant to the process now unfolding. It did, however, spur intransigents among the premiers to make their own rush to the lifeboats.

One was left with the unedifying spectacle of premiers falling over themselves in public to suggest that others among them were responsible for the deletion or watering down, variously, of women's rights and native rights. With Lyon's defeat, it became even more difficult for individual premiers to avoid the pointing finger of public reproach. Detective-style investigation soon narrowed the list of the intransigents to three names.

Blakeney seemed open-minded in public but rather more complex in private and ended up by offering to bargain his own acceptance of women's rights against an acceptance by the other premiers of aboriginal rights.[3] Lougheed suggested that he was not opposed to aboriginal rights, as such, but would want them to be defined before they should be included in the constitution.[4] Bennett said, *originally*, that aboriginal rights had been excluded from the charter as a conscious decision of all nine premiers and the prime minister, *next*, that he had never discussed aboriginal rights with any other premier or had it discussed with him, and, *finally*, that he would accept aboriginal rights' being included in the charter provided that the federal government picked up the bill for Indian and native land and other claims and that it cost the provincial government nothing.[5]

It was an ill-disguised provincial retreat. The federal government quickly indicated that it would not be prepared to meet the total bill of Indian and native land claims. Premier Davis's constitutional reputation had previously been unsullied. Correspondence between his attorney-general and Jean Chrétien was now leaked to the press by Indian leaders,[6] and showed Davis opposed to entrenchment of aboriginal rights because of the 'uncertain effect' it could have on property rights in the province and because it could lead to 'unfairness, disruption, uncertainty and divisions in Canadian society.' This, added to the ambiguity of Blakeney's public and private profile, suggested that even as a matter of simple, legal-textual construction it might make very little legal difference whether section 34 remained deleted or went in again. The very fact that the premiers wanted it out meant that the Indian and native leaders were right in insisting upon its express re-inclusion.

Premier Lougheed was right in his opinion that no one – the federal government, the provincial governments, and not least the various, not always united, Indian and native leaders – knew what exactly was meant by section 34. The same argument would apply to the 'aboriginal, treaty or other rights or freedoms that pertain to the aboriginal peoples' set out in the now included section 25. If premiers such as Lougheed and Bennett now felt that they were being asked to buy a 'pig in a poke,' perhaps the enormous legal fees poured down the drain in the court battle over the legality of the patriation project might more sensibly and usefully have been devoted to clarifying these very points.

As it was, Lougheed and Bennett gave way and reversed their earlier opposition to entrenchment of aboriginal rights, against a stormy background of public argument and confrontation with Indian leaders and their peoples. Alberta Indians had marched *en masse* on the Alberta legislature and Lougheed had addressed them from the front steps. The far more militant BC Indians has invaded the Social Credit party's annual convention in Vancouver, successfully demanding the right to address the convention and also meeting with key cabinet ministers. The retreat by Bennett and Lougheed was hedged in by conditions: the demand by Bennett that the federal government assume the full financial burden of satisfying Indian and native claims, which Prime Minister Trudeau promptly and firmly refused[7]; and the more subtle insistence by Lougheed that the entrenchment of aboriginal rights should be limited to 'existing' rights, a condition that Trudeau accepted.[8] But the premiers' retreat and *volte-face* were indeed made, under fire, in response to the pressure of Indian activists.

If public opinion finally made itself felt in the constitutional process, two very intriguing questions seem to arise in retrospect. Could Prime Minister Trudeau and the federal forces have successfully mobilized public opinion, much earlier, in behalf of their cause? Could such mobilization have led to a better Charter of Rights and Freedoms – something of which Trudeau would not have to say apologetically, even in wry jest: 'And you're asking me now whether I consider it a success. No. I consider it an abject failure.'[9]

The answer must be that, once Trudeau decided to leave the drafting and elaboration of his charter to the 'rude mechanicals,' the highly skilled professional civil service advisers, the opportunities for public involvement were probably foreclosed. If he could have taken only a few hours to produce a one or two-page text, it might have been otherwise. As it was, however, it wasn't really until the tampering with women's and aboriginal rights that public opinion began to be directly exercised.

As a corollary of the absence of any great appeal in the project itself and as a direct consequence of his legal conservatism, the prime minister never reached the idea of participatory democracy until the very last moment, when the cause was almost lost. The idea of a simple declaratory act of Parliament, followed by a national referendum, was quickly put aside as revolutionary and in violation of the conventions. A plebiscite endorsing patriation and the Charter of Rights could have ended, once and for all, any threat of a back-benchers' revolt in the British Parliament.

The retreat of the recalcitrant premiers after the first angry reaction to the apparent exclusion of women's and aboriginal rights, and Sterling Lyon's defeat, showed that a plebiscite vote (even non-binding) in support of patriation and the charter might have put those premiers to flight a full twelve months before. Perhaps the prime minister had concluded, by the time a plebiscite became useful, that the draft charter his advisers had saddled him with was not saleable and not worth risking a vote over. Or perhaps he had lost his faith (unwarrantedly, as events turned out) in the public's ability to engage constructively in building a renewed federation in Canada.

When the storm arose after the publication of the accord of 5 November, Trudeau maintained, somewhat archly, that the agreement having been made it could be changed or varied only with the assent of all nine premiers. He indicated, again with professed sadness, that be regretted the changes, but suggested that those organizations or private citizens who objected should address themselves to the premiers and try to get them to reverse their positions. Although the accord and the prior negotiations remained secret, it was not too difficult to identify the main villains in the piece; and judicious leaks from the federal government and from premiers now won over to its cause helped public pressures for a reversal of the more contested parts. The amended resolution (Appendix D) deposed by the federal government in Parliament on 18 November 1981, was then revised once more so as to accord a little more closely again to the consolidated resolution of 24 April (Appendix B). This final version (Appendix E) was submitted to Parliament on 18 December. The fiercest battles, as already noted, were over women's and aboriginal rights. On women's rights, the federal government had agreed to subject fundamental rights (section 2), legal rights (sections 7–14) and equality rights (section 15) to a legal power of any or all of the provinces to opt out of any or all of those parts by simple resolution of the legislature (the new section 33[1]).

Section 15 (equality rights) of the final version contains the principle of 'equal protection and equal benefits of the law without discrimination,' accompanied by a listing of specific categories of constitutionally prohibited discriminations including 'discrimination based on ... sex.' At the committee hearings women's groups had secured the inclusion of a further (legally redundant) section, 28, in the consolidated resolution: 'Notwithstanding anything in this Charter, the rights and freedoms referred to in it are guaranteed equally to male and female persons.'

In the negotiations that produced the accord, certain premiers had had added to section 28 a clause specifically subjecting it to the new provincial power to opt out. Thus, in the amended consolidated resolution (18 November), equality of the sexes was subjected, in sections 15 and 28, to the opting out power in the new section 33(1). When the premiers retreated before the fury of the campaign of the women's rights organizations, and when Premier Blakeney, the last hold-out, also gave way (presumably because his demanded barter of women's rights for aboriginal rights had now been conceded), the clause subjecting equality of the sexes to opting out was deleted from sections 28 and 33(1). However, apparently from oversight, the general subjection of equality, including equality of the sexes, to opting out by the provinces was allowed to remain, creating thereby a potential ambiguity which the courts would have to decide. Inter-governmental diplomacy conducted by telex creates its own special problems.

As for aboriginal rights, the battle centred around one section only – 34 – of the three main sections, 25, 34, and 36, which had dealt with them in the consolidated resolution. Section 25 had guaranteed 'aboriginal, treaty or other rights or freedoms that pertain to the aboriginal peoples of Canada,' and had then specifically listed the proclamation of 1763 and also 'any rights or freedoms that may be acquired by the aboriginal peoples of Canada by way of land claims settlement.' Section 36(2) had provided, simply, for the convening of a future constitutional conference, including representatives of the aboriginal peoples invited to 'participate', to discuss 'constitutional matters that directly affect the aboriginal peoples of Canada, including the identification and definition of the rights of those peoples to be included in the Constitution of Canada.'

The major focus of the premiers – of the four westerners in particular – was upon section 34, however. Section 34(1) 'recognized and affirmed' what it called 'the aboriginal and treaty rights of the aboriginal peoples of Canada.' Section 34(2) defined 'aboriginal peoples of Canada' as including 'the Indian, Inuit and Métis peoples of Canada.' It was speculated that Alberta and British Columbia considered that the deletion would strengthen their legal ability to resist rectification of land claims of Indian and native groups within their boundaries and that Manitoba and Saskatchewan, with large Métis (mixed blood) minorities, considered that the deletion of the express inclusion of Métis would enable them to deny aboriginal status to the Métis's land and other legal claims.

It is arguable whether section 34 added anything not already included in section 25 (which was to remain in the charter) or anything that the courts could not reach by ordinary interpretation of the constitutional category of aboriginal peoples and aboriginal rights. Nevertheless, the four western premiers had expressly insisted upon excluding section 34 from the charter as the price of their accord. This raised quite understandable concerns on the part of Indian and native leaders and immediately brought them the support of other, non-Indian, public interest groups, who concluded that what the remnants of the gang of eight could unite upon to exclude from the charter must be worth the fight of restoring. Faced with the rallying of a general public support for the Indian and native peoples, the premiers gave way once more. They agreed to the restoration of section 34 (now renumbered as section 35) to the charter; but Premier Lougheed, their most powerful member, had the last word by successfully insisting that the 'aboriginal and treaty rights' to be 'recognized and affirmed' in section 35(1) should now carry the prefix 'existing.' Only 'existing aboriginal and treaty rights' would thus be constitutionally entrenched under section 35(1).

What was the purpose behind Lougheed's insistence on 'existing,' and what would be the legal consequences of so inserting it? The purpose was undoubtedly mischievous and was understood as such by Indian leaders and their legion of non-Indian supporters who immediately protested to the prime minister.[10] The legal effect was less clear: on one view, the prefix 'existing' might help persuade timid judges to give a purely static interpretation – nineteenth century or earlier time of origin – to aboriginal rights, thereby excluding that form of 'progressive,' 'generic' interpretation that imaginative judges had applied, for example, on the World Court in *Western Sahara* in 1975[11] in insisting on expanding and up-dating legal principles to meet the conditions of today, including the more enlightened conceptions of human and group rights. If that were so, it would surely represent a somewhat pessimistic view of the judicial process and of the capacity of judges to respond creatively and imaginatively to new problems. Federal Justice Minister Jean Chrétien justified the concession on the score that it was purely verbal and without substantive legal consequences; while the prime minister spoke of the need to press on with adoption of the resolution. A last-minute attempt in Parliament, by the NDP, to delete the prefix was defeated, as was an NDP attempt to give the Indian and native peoples a veto on any future constitutional amendments affecting them.

Prime Minister Trudeau cited the nine premiers as having gone on record, on 27 November 1981, through Premier Bennett, to the effect that the accord should be approved, as is, by Parliament; 'additional constitutional change should only be considered in Canada following the patriation of our constitution.' Further negotiation might 'put at risk the accord.'[12] There is no evidence that Trudeau had inspired this telexed request from the nine premiers[13]; but there is no doubt he breathed a sigh of relief, for the lunatic fringe had begun to emerge and demand the inclusion of special causes in the charter.

The premiers had begun to realize that their image was sullied by the evidence of their cynical horse-trading and seemed resolved to bring the whole affair to an end as quickly and quietly as possible and so escape with the least possible damage. The Conservatives among them were also reported to be concerned by Joe Clark's seeming desire to prolong the constitutional debate in Parliament by making demands for further changes in an apparent attempt to retrieve whatever he had lost by his campaign, only just abandoned, against patriation and the Charter of Rights in the name of 'provincial rights.'

Clark's stated concern was to bring the Quebec government into the final accord. He communicated directly with Premier Lévesque, suggesting, among other things, that he amend Bill 101. The constitutional propriety of his so communicating, as federal Opposition Leader, with a dissident premier, not of his own party, while delicate negotiations were proceeding, and this without the leave of the prime minister, was open to question. The political wisdom seemed even more faulty, for Clark ran the risk of being seen as trying to make an alliance with the premier of Quebec in an attempt to retrieve his own fortunes. Unholy alliances of this sort carried their own in-built sanctions, as the anglophone seven had found in the bitter recriminations that flowed from their desertion of Lévesque. Lévesque rescued Clark from the trap by rejecting his intervention in Quebec affairs.

Two other Conservative bids to stall or change the charter also failed. The Conservative opposition had made a surprise injection of the abortion issue into the constitutional debate, following days of intense lobbying by 'pro-life' groups who refused to accept the self-evident proposition that the charter was neutral on the issue of whether or not there was a constitutional right to abortion and that Parliament would retain its existing authority over abortion laws.[14] It is an axiom of constitutional science – amply confirmed by the unfortunate example of the Eighteenth (Prohibition) Amendment to the US Constitution that eventually had to be repealed, after enormous social cost, by the Twenty-first Amendment – that constitutional charters should not become havens for single-issue pressure groups determined to impose their own transient conceptions of social morality on other people.[15] This Conservative initiative seemed ill timed, ill advised, and a self-serving surrender on a controversial issue on which further public debate was needed.

A second Conservative amendment had more apparent merit. It was directed to an apparent oversight resulting from telex diplomacy. The revised constitutional amending machinery did not merely eliminate the provision for a referendum in case of deadlock in negotiations – a significant step backward in terms of participatory democracy and the chances of constitutional change. It also, seemingly by indirection, subjected, in section 40(e), the process of creation of new provinces in 41(f) – hitherto a matter for federal legislative power alone, under section 91(1) of the BNA Act – to amendment by Parliament with the concurrence of resolutions of at least seven provinces having at least 50 per cent of the population (section 37).

Some suggested that this had always been a design of the more expansionist provinces such as Alberta with ill-concealed ambitions of extending their frontiers into the northern territories. However, 'the extension of existing provinces into the territories' was made subject to the same process, in section 41(e). A better conclusion seems to be that it was arrived at unintentionally in the general rush preceding the accord. A sensible Conservative amendment stipulating that any Yukon or Northwest Territories accession to provincial status could be effected by federal action alone[16] was lost in the last-minute impatience with what were viewed as still further delaying tactics.

Premier Lévesque was still smarting after the humiliation of having been deserted by his former allies. He complained that it was Quebec that was isolated, but it began to look as if it were the premier who was isolated. After his first public indications of a new Quebec referendum on separation or a fresh provincial election, he retreated into statements that he would boycott further federal-provincial conferences, and finally that he would 'exercise Quebec's traditional right of veto' in regard to the patriation project and the Charter of Rights.

Just what Lévesque meant by the veto was not clear. Its authority rested upon the claimed examples of, first, Premier Lesage in 1965, and then Premier Bourassa in 1971, reneging on then unanimous accords on constitutional amending machinery and seeing the federal government and the other provinces drop the whole project. Can you convert a rule of prudence into a normative and binding constitutional principle? Prime Minister Trudeau suggested that, even if there were such a veto, Lévesque had effectively compromised it by his own voluntary abandonment of it in April 1981. Jean Chrétien treated Lévesque's assertion of a Quebec veto right with humour, with the simile of a Quebec government command to the Heavens not to let snow fall in Quebec in December.

There was, of course, a King Canute quality to Lévesque's gesture. The federal government dismissed the claim, and the other premiers either rejected it outright or simply ignored it. Quebec's agent-general in London wrote to all 635 members of the British Parliament invoking their help in rejecting the patriation package. This hardly seemed promising ground: even Sir Anthony Kershaw, after all the wounds he and his committee had suffered when they first presented their report, seemed now to have abandoned the provincial cause.[17] Other opposition seemed to have collapsed with the Supreme Court decision on legality and, even more, the 5 November accord. There was no further profit, in London, in trying to pull Canadian provincial chestnuts out of the fire.

A bid by Lévesque to the courts might seem to be worth the gamble, but it could not go directly to the Supreme Court without direct federal government help, and thus seemed confined to the Quebec Court of Appeal. There was no reason, in law or in equity, why the federal government should wait on any such action and delay presentation of the resolution to the British Parliament. Lévesque had had his day in court and had failed to canvass the existence or overwise of a Quebec veto.

Lévesque, facing a sea of economic troubles and an unpopular Budget, had seemed to become merely boring outside the province. He had lost significant support among English-speaking Canadians outside Quebec by the inconsistency of championing separatism and then both invoking the aid of British parliamentarians to block patriation and a Charter of Rights for English-Canadians and also making Quebec a leading force in organizing the gang of eight in opposition to the federal government. Recent Quebec premiers had always sensibly distinguished Quebec's long-range interests from any purely negative, destructive tactics aimed at blocking general reforms of the federal system desired by English-Canadians. Lévesque's constitutional strategy appeared cynical and amoral; it became only poetic justice to have him so abruptly and unceremoniously deserted by his seven colleagues.

Lévesque might still have salvaged a good deal through negotiations with Ottawa: if not constitutional recognition of a Quebec veto over constitutional amendments touching Quebec's special interests (which Lévesque had already bargained away), then at least a right to opt out of the minority-language guarantees (section 23) so far as they applied to Quebec, or a moratorium of three to five years in the application of those portions of the charter to Quebec. Instead of negotiating, Lévesque proposed these items, as well as recognition of the 'deux nations' concept, as demands to the federal government from the Quebec national assembly, and so himself closed the constitutional dossier.[18] Prime Minister Trudeau might well have chosen – profiting from the examples of East-West *détente* – to offer all or most of these things to Quebec, voluntarily and unilaterally, as part of the 'politic of mutual example,' but he chose not to do so.

Although the Indian and native peoples came out of the revisions of the accord better than expected, it was clear that they needed, in Trudeau's words, to 'get their act together' and develop some minimum common front. Moderate Indian and native leaders were negotiating with the federal government, in good faith, in Ottawa, for accommodations on the constitutional issues. At the same time 100 British Columbia Indian activists were travelling through Germany, France, Belgium, and Holland, at not inconsiderable expense, trying to get audiences with those countries' governments on Canadian issues. Fifty BC activists were lobbying in London in the crucial first week of November. The four European governments had no wish to become involved in Canadian internal affairs, and the Kershaw committee had changed its tune.[19] The BC Indian Chief who confronted Trudeau in Kamloops and accused him of lying on the constitutional issues announced to the television cameras that he had just returned from four weeks of lobbying in London. He had wasted his own and other people's time and money that might more profitably have been spent in the hard, often dull work of negotiating within Canada itself. He had simply been in the wrong place, at the wrong time, like the American Indians from Oregon who burnt the Canadian flag outside the hotel in Vancouver where Premier Bennett was addressing his party's annual convention.[20]

The public opinion aroused following the 5 November accord presaged significant changes in constitutional decision-making in Canada. The vigorous interest groups and pressure groups swept away the reluctant premiers in their path. Something has now changed. Constitutional law is being recognized as a continuing interaction of different, sometimes directly competing social interests; constitutional law-making is becoming the resolution or synthesis of those conflicts. It is all rather American, with the courts destined, as in the United States, to be at the heart of the process, whether they like it or not. The seven English-speaking premiers in the gang of eight, who fought such a desperate rearguard action to keep the constitution 'English' and to bar reception of all 'American' constitutional institutions and values, have, in losing so completely and so utterly in the end, simply speeded up the 'Americanization' (or modernization) of Canadian constitutional law.

On 2 December, the House of Commons adopted the final revised constitutional resolution, by a vote of 246 to 24.[21] The hold-outs – 17 Conservatives, 5 Liberals, and 2 New Democrats – voted against the resolution for quite diverse reasons. An anglophone Liberal from Quebec and former federal cabinet minister, Warren Allmand, felt the charter did not sufficiently protect the English minority in Quebec. The sole Conservative from Quebec and former federal cabinet minister, Roch LaSalle, objected to the lack of special constitutional status for Quebec. New Democrats strongly attacked the dilution of protection of Indian and native rights. A Conservative had wanted anti-abortion provisions included in the charter; a New Democrat (and Roman Catholic priest) abstained on the same point, as a 'silent protest.' A Conservative was angry because the charter did not include a formal right to private property.[22] Immediately the vote had been announced, members burst into 'O Canada.'

Premier Lévesque immediately ordered all flags on Quebec government buildings to be flown at half-mast. The national assembly had adopted a motion, the previous day, by 70 to 38, along strict party lines, laying down what Lévesque described as 'the bottom line' for Quebec participation in further constitutional talks. The four conditions were recognition that the two founding peoples of Canada are fundamentally equal and that Quebec forms a distinct society; acceptance of an amending formula that gives Quebec a veto, or else provides complete financial compensation for opting out; implementation of a watered-down rights charter that would permit Quebec to opt in to education guarantees for its English minority; and carrying out of promises regarding equalization payments and increased provincial control over natural resources.[23]

Prime Minister Trudeau, in a letter to Lévesque on 1 December, had already reminded him that the federal government had, historically, defended Quebec's right to a constitutional veto, and that successive Quebec governments had refused to support the federal constitutional packages containing such a veto for Quebec. Trudeau commented, pointedly, that Lévesque had himself abandoned 'any claim for a Quebec veto in any amending formula as early as September, 1980' as part of the deal with the seven other premiers. As he remarked on the Quebec claim to veto: 'We only abandoned this after your Government did.'[24]

Lévesque was rapidly running out of options and by now prudently disinclined to pursue his earlier hints of a new referendum or a snap election (which, in view of Quebec's draconian budget and a sharply declining provincial economy, might well turn on economic and not constitutional issues). He announced that he would seek an advisory opinion from the Quebec Court of Appeal on the claimed Quebec veto. Once again, he was hoist with his own petard. Quebec ought sensibly to have posed that question to the Quebec Court of Appeal twelve months earlier. Now it was simply too late! The federal government had never been legally obligated to wait on the earlier rulings on constitutionality of the patriation project, but for good and sufficient reasons (the impact in London, for example) had decided to do so. It had resolved, this time, to brook no further delay but to proceed immediately to London, once the resolution had been adopted by Parliament. Lévesque's last legal gesture was reduced thereby to a command by Canute.

The government leader in the Senate, Ray Perrault, insisted that the upper house should not try to stall or delay unnecessarily passage of the resolution approved by the popularly elected House of Commons. Final adoption occurred on 8 December[25] and the measure was rushed to London immediately afterwards.

Did Prime Minister Trudeau have any second thoughts about the patriation project and, in particular, the revised Charter of Rights? By now, he appeared more detached,[26] having by now clearly routed the constitutional enemy and put it to flight. While the concessions meant that the charter might not be as attractive a document as the one originally released, he had not had to bargain away any federal powers to the provinces, as he had been prepared to do in the summer of 1980 as the price of provincial acquiescence. The premiers had gained nothing substantive from seventeen and a half months of stalling tactics other than the dubious distinction of a right of opting out of fundamental freedoms, legal rights, and equality rights plus some modifications in the amending machinery (principally the elimination of direct popular participation, through referendum, in the constituent process). When Joe Clark prided himself on the 'improvements' his party's prolonged war of attrition in the House of Commons had effected to the charter, a similar comment seemed apt. How much better might the Charter have been if premiers and federal opposition had resolved, instead, on an affirmative public debate on its constitutional merits and bent their best energies to improving it?

A hint of the constitutional future, however, was provided by a decision of the Supreme Court, on 1 December 1981.[27] Former Manitoba cabinet minister Joseph Borowski, a militant campaigner against the 1969 federal Criminal Code amendments establishing ground rules for therapeutic abortions, was given legal standing-to-sue to challenge the constitutionality of permitting or facilitating abortions. The Supreme Court ruled by a surprisingly decisive, seven-to-two majority. Chief Justice Laskin pointed out in his dissenting opinion that while allowing legal standing-to-sue is a matter of judicial discretion, Mr Borowski had no direct interest in the application of the abortion laws: 'Mere distaste has never been a ground upon which to seek the assistance of a court.' The majority opinion was, however, written by Mr Justice Martland, the most senior member of the Court. Perhaps he was emboldened by the public plaudits for the six-man majority opinion on conventionality, which he clearly had authored. He had been a judicial conservative committed to a strict and complete legalism and to the deliberate eschewing of 'policy' in law, but he now left the Court a Pandora's box of policy issues. A court appointed by the executive was granting permission to a wide range of interest groups to raise before it high political issues which, it might be argued, might more properly be decided by the elected branches of government.

12

The constitution
and the future

Our basic conclusion has been, and must remain, that constitution-making 1979–1982 was a flawed exercise, yielding only limited and imperfect results. We saw one of those rare moments in a nation's history when the time and circumstances were ripe for a successful exercise in constituent power. The failure – albeit partial – to profit from that opportunity was due to a number of errors, some perhaps necessary but others for the most part foreseeable and avoidable.

The locking-in of the constituent process to the first ministers' forum and federal-provincial diplomacy no doubt falls into the first category. There were ill omens, based on the past half-century and more of failure by that route. Yet it would have been viewed as a form of constitutional *violence* if a prime minister, too often accused of being arrogant, had by-passed it from the beginning in favour of other, more direct methods. The (predictable) failure of that approach required bolder methods, lest the opportunity should disappear. The device of the parliamentary joint committee was chosen as a more 'democratic' method after the not very clear or persuasive Supreme Court ruling, in December 1979, on Senate reform.

It is perhaps too harsh to dismiss the decision to make a last approach to London as essentially timid and conservative. All the political advantages of public involvement and legitimation were certainly foresworn. One can criticize the joint committee: too large to function efficiently and yet too small and inexpert to operate through subcommittee. Above all, there was confusion in the committee members' minds between a parliamentary committee and a public commission of enquiry. In opting for the latter role, the committee lost further valuable time. It did imperfectly what had already been done, systematically and scientifically, by the Pépin-Robarts commission and several other recent special commissions. The consultation of the general public is a pre-condition for constitution-making in a liberal democratic society. As operated by the committee, however, participatory democracy involved a false dialectical operation. A highly selective approach was used in choosing witnesses. Too many of the groups represented seemed ad hoc; they were never examined as to their representativeness, and their members played musical chairs, by sometimes appearing more than once. Some individuals were involved at the same time as salaried governmental adviser and as independent expert witness and critic of the constitutional draft. There was no genuine clash of ideas, no real probing and testing through accepted legal processes, and no constitutional dialectic in any real sense of the word.

The patriation package that emerged in April 1981 lacked the crispness and sparkle and that characterized comparable exercises in the United States, France, West Germany, and other societies with comparable traditions.[1] The patriation package is prolix, loosely constructed, and rambling; pedestrian in literary style and drafting; and conservative, traditional, and unimaginative in content and elaborations. It is a grey document and certainly nothing to light bonfires about. And yet as a result of the whole exercise, flawed as it might have been, a number of quite positive points emerged.

1 It had become apparent, by the end of the summer of 1980, that the constitution-making game had been too artificial and limited in scope and outlook, with too small and restricted a group of players. Whatever else happens, it should no longer be possible to limit fundamental decisions as to Canada's future to the prime minister and the premiers. New players, such as the mayors of the great cities, and the Indian and native communities, must challenge the legitimacy of the first ministers' claims to speak on their behalf, and they are hardly likely to tolerate such claims indefinitely.

2 The premiers, by and large, demonstrated themselves as out of touch with the times and with their own constituencies. Provincial electoral laws are too heavily weighted to sparse rural constituencies, and the new, post-war immigrant communities have failed to penetrate into the provincial political processes. The social base of provincial government is too limited, restrictive, and non-representative, and it will have to change dramatically if premiers' demands to be able to veto fundamental constitutional change are to be accorded credibility.

3 The patriation exercise has certainly speeded up the historical process of cutting the last imperial ties with Britain. It was inelegant, even indecent, for premiers who had lost out by the ordinary constitutional and political processes in Canada to lobby British parliamentarians to do for them what they were evidently incapable of doing, at home. There was also something absurd in British MPs trying to set up shop as 'champions' of the Canadian

provinces. Prime Minister Thatcher and her cabinet maintained at all times a constitutionally correct position in regard to Canada. Yet back-benchers' committees claimed that they were still today, somehow or other, the legal 'guardians' of the Canadian constitution or 'trustees' of premiers' special interests. Such claims were not merely anachronistic and unacceptable, but legal nonsense in the light of Canada's full juridical sovereignty. Canada today is the product of immigration from all parts of the globe, and seeing such latter-day claims asserted by members of a foreign legislature – even at the behest of provincial premiers – should, for better or worse, speed up the dissolution of the last constitutional links binding Canada to Britain.

4 Even though the patriation package may be dull and grey and unimaginative, it does not differ substantially, thereby, from the BNA Act of 1867; for it also is a homely document. These negative elements have not prevented the original act from developing an independent life and being of its own. Its very open-endedness and neutrality has facilitated its creative evolution and pragmatic adaptation to a rapidly evolving society. Canada has avoided the tensions between a too precisely formulated charter and a society in the throes of rapid change that have marked many other countries. There is every reason to believe that a similar adaptation could now take place with the new Charter of Rights in the patriation package.

5 It is likely that the Supreme Court of Canada, *faute de mieux* and in the absence of corresponding, political initiatives from the other arms of government, will play a major role in implementing the new Charter of Rights and translating its abstract norms into concrete reality. Such a role does not differ generically from that exercised by the Imperial Privy Council from 1867 until 1949 and by the Supreme Court of Canada ever since. But the sheer volume of case law from the new civil rights jurisdiction is likely to produce a quantitative, and ultimately a qualitative, change in the Court's work and function. It will pose certain problems of constitutional 'legitimacy' for the Court. Some changes in the Court's constitution and jurisdiction seem implied by this new situation; but there are adequate precedents and models available from other countries' experience, and the correctives involved would seem capable of being achieved incrementally.

6 The limited and traditional character of the patriation package, and the fact that it is not holistic and does not address major problems of Canadian society, mean that adjustments and compromises can continue to occur, as in the past, outside the formal constitutional structure and machinery. These basic political compromises are the starting-point of any constitutional society and are difficult to legislate, perhaps best not legislated. They are pre-legal, meta-legal facts.

One such fundamental compromise in Canada has involved the relations between the two founding nations, French and English. The original compromise was embodied in the Quebec Act of 1774, but new content has been given to it in the give-and-take between Quebec and English Canada. It probably involves now de facto acceptance by English Canada of a Quebec that is as French as, say, Ontario is English, and of the substance and philosophy (if not necessarily all the details) of Bill 22 and Bill 101. It involves, further, acceptance by Quebec, as expressed in the referendum vote, that French-Canadian self-determination is to occur *within* Canadian federalism, in line with these general principles. A federal bilingualism policy, applied to federal governmental institutions, but applied benignly and pragmatically, seems also to have emerged as part of the fundamental language compromise in Canada. There is every reason to expect that this compromise, and similar ones in other areas, will continue to be made and to evolve, outside the strict letter of the constitutional charter but in accord with its main philosophy.

7 While the patriation package is autonomous and self-contained, and capable of operating in conjunction with the BNA Act of 1867, as amended, there is absolutely no reason to regard its adoption as completing the constituent process. The constitution-making game can and should continue; but it should involve many things besides those issues of federal-provincial powers that preoccupied us in yesteryear. It should address the issue of modernization of the whole constitutional and governmental system, to meet the demands of post-industrial society. The patriation exercise can be viewed as an essentially limited, *first* phase in constitution-making.

The patriation exercise will have long-range consequences. It will help reshape Canadian-British relations and Canada's general position in the Commonwealth. It will affect the careers of various political leaders and parties who were identified with one or more of the alternative constitutional options. It seems to have been less a clash of contending, clearly defined, historical forces or of rival ideologies – a genuine dialectical operation – than an exercise in political theatre in which personalities were often more important than the ideas they claimed to represent. If it was not, at times, a dress rehearsal in the theatre of the absurd, some of the players seemed casual characters wandering on and off the stage in search of an author and a script, without always being certain about their lines or why they were there in the first place.

The British connection is perhaps the best demonstration of this truth, in the context of a single act with several different scenes. The British government, which had – in the end elegantly, if not always happily or easily –

accepted the loss of its empire, seemed to have forgotten some of its earlier lessons. The question of provincial consent obscured the fact that Britain could have responded to a request for patriation by treating the issue as a request from one sovereign government to another. It could have declared that, with the evolution of inter-Commonwealth conventional law, the British Parliament today no longer had any constitutional competence to legislate as to Canada, even at the express request of the Canadian government and the Canadian Parliament. Such a declaration would have thrown the ball right back into the Canadian court. It would have left the Canadian government obliged to do what so many other governments have done in similar circumstances, of devising constituent power of its own accord, and presumably, because of the desire to obtain legitimation, of going to the people in a referendum.

Once this, the most obvious and contemporary solution, had been overlooked, the British government fulfilled its role correctly and in accordance with the letter of international law. It would deal only with the Canadian government. Provincial premiers and their minions would be treated with civility and ordinary courtesy, but would not be heard.

Bodies such as the Kershaw committee had a certain nuisance value in sponsoring or promoting Provincial interests not receivable by the government; but the Kershaw committee quickly impaired its own claims to credibility by rushing to judgment on Canadian constitutional law questions not within its competence and even before the joint resolution had been voted on in the Canadian Parliament. Whatever authority its report might have had seemed vitiated by sloppy research methods; it relied solely on British specialists not expert in Canadian law and in any case under professional retainer to the Quebec or other provincial governments.

Those provincial governments that carried their case to the Kershaw committee and otherwise lobbied British parliamentarians, ministers, and officials raised questions as to their faith in the democratic processes and their willingness to fight their battles inside Canada. Further, Britain was a foreign power as far as Canada, legally, was concerned. The Quebec premier never attempted to explain away the irony in his seeking to maximize imperial links to frustrate the Canadian government.

The dissident provinces had quite disparate, often directly conflicting interests and entered too easily into a common front. The coalition could only yield gains if it could be maintained to the end and cause the federal government to compromise. Anything less than that would be a Pyrrhic victory, at best. Individual provinces might have done better to emulate Premier Davis of Ontario and try to negotiate bilaterally with the federal government for special constitutional arrangements to accommodate their invariably single issue of concern. Such an approach could hardly have been less barren than the obstinate 'no-deal' strategy actually developed.

Premier Lougheed, the most astute of the premiers and the one with the strongest base, borrowed from Davis's example, but even more effectively, in negotiating, on a direct, bilateral basis with Prime Minister Trudeau, a new energy price agreement governing oil prices and the sharing of oil revenues and taxation between Ottawa and Alberta. The agreement, signed on 1 September 1981, went far to meeting Lougheed's original contention that oil prices in Canada should move towards world prices and also involved Ottawa's withdrawing its export tax on natural gas produced in Alberta – another major grievance. Quiet diplomacy, exercised with finesse and a minimum of name-calling achieved such positive results that one wondered why other provinces did not reach similar agreements, and at a much earlier time.

An agreement exempting British Columbia from federal export tax on its natural gas should have been achieved quickly and easily. The government of British Columbia sought a confrontation, deliberately withholding payment of the federal export tax and defying the federal government to take it to court to enforce payment. Such an approach set a bad example to private citizens as to defaulting on their tax obligations and contravened the principles of federal good manners. As punishment for its tax delinquency, British Columbia was not included in the Ottawa-Alberta agreement but would have to wait its turn to try to negotiate its own special agreement with Ottawa. Quiet diplomacy and low-key methods carry their own bonus.

At the federal level, the negotiating postures assumed by the different players raise interesting questions. The Conservative party, perhaps because of the internal challenges to its leadership, opted for an aggressive role that involved challenging the federal government at every point. This role was developed with a considerable tactical skill that masked the strategic question of where it would all lead. The party could claim Diefenbaker's Bill of Rights and the whole tory radical tradition. It could have fought for an entrenched bill of rights incorporating individualistic values in the social and property fields and seeking to limit big government. Such an approach would have reflected some major trends in North America and no doubt been popular.

There were risks involved in being associated with a last-ditch opposition to 'Canadianizing' the constitution, with a campaign abroad to achieve that objective against the Canadian government, and with opposition to the principle of an entrenched bill of rights of whatever character and content. The Conservative approach, in retrospect, appears to have been overly clever and preoccupied with securing short-term debating points, without any overall strategy.

By the same token, the New Democratic Party chose very early and at considerable cost (in terms of party unity) to support the patriation package. It obtained a little less than it might, in return, by way of giving the new charter a more genuinely social democratic orientation.

The federal Liberal party held a clear majority in both houses of Parliament, but strived to produce a consensus – even an artificial one – in support of its charter; a consensus could presumably influence the British government to ratify automatically any request for a formal amendment of the BNA Act. But the party perhaps gave away too much to the objective of unity, thereby producing a bland charter that makes, it might be argued, no breakthrough sufficient to warrant all the investment in the patriation project.

What challenges would be opened up once repatriation should have been successfully achieved? Extrapolation of the main historical trends in democratic constitutionalism throughout the world would suggest the following main implications for constitutional process and substance.

1 There is a clear trend, observable throughout the world and almost without exception, to 'bring the people in' to any process for drafting and adoption of a new constitutional charter, or even for substantial renewal of an old one. The trend is clearly away from closed assemblies in favour of popularly elected constituent assemblies, followed by referenda for adoption. The trend is from an élitist to a democratic approach – participatory democracy in the best sense of the word. The limitations of Canada's old-style approach are too patent to need further demonstration. It rests upon a legal fiction that the historian knows to be untrue – that the constitution is a contract between provincial princes. It has meant, in practice, a more or less permanent veto for the provinces on all other than purely inconsequential changes.

2 The BNA Act of 1867 responded to the needs of mid-nineteenth-century Canada, not those of the essentially urban nation of today. The development of commerce and industry and the resulting movements of population, plus large-scale immigration, have produced an urban, post-industrial society characterized by large new metropolitan concentrations and marked imbalances in terms of wealth, population, and social and economic opportunity. Other federal systems have moved to correct such imbalances by readjusting provincial boundaries, or amalgamating or abolishing some existing provinces, or creating new ones, and by up-grading the cities and municipalities, where the major social problems exist, to the status of provinces.[2]

A new Canadian constitution must start with the premise that nothing is sacred. Save for Quebec which should be preserved as an entity, existing provincial frontiers and the notion of a federal system of ten provinces need to be re-examined. The larger cities might become provinces. Or the federal system could be conceived and restructured in terms of three levels of government – federal, provincial, and municipal – each with its own law-making and taxation powers (or at least full participation in existing tax-sharing agreements).[3] The city is where all the action is. It has organized crime, the drug traffic, juvenile delinquency, urban decay, and grossly inadequate housing and public transportation facilities and neither the powers nor the finances to resolve those problems. It is the mere creature of the province and must go cap-in-hand each year to usually unsympathetic (and often unrepresentative) provincial legislatures. Its new role is reflected in the high quality of the candidates now presenting themselves for municipal elections in comparison to those running in provincial elections. A new constitution should correct the imbalance by allocating power where the problems exist, and this means a constitutional status for Canadian municipalities.

3 The recognition of the legal rights of the native and Indian peoples based on international and treaty law requires implementation of the principle of full political, social, and economic self-determination within Canadian federalism. This could mean either the creation of new, Indian-majority provinces out of the territories of existing provinces and the federal territories; or a system of personality-based special rights and privileges for the Indian nations, existing side-by-side with and in addition to general Canadian and provincial law; or a combination of the two. The express constitutional entrenchment of the new constitutional role of the native and Indian peoples remains the necessary conclusion.[4]

4 The existing language situation – the compromise of the 1970s – involves affirmative federal bilingualism and federal tolerance of a Quebec that is establishing French as official language, language of work, and language of education. This accommodation should be recognized in a new constitution.

5 The trend in democratic constitutionalism away from purely appointive or indirectly elected offices towards direct popular election should be accepted and applied to all federal institutions. Purported 'reforms,' such as the proposal to replace the existing Senate by a new body appointed by the provinces, are a step backward and should be rejected.

6 The democratic constitutional trend towards legislative assemblies that more nearly reflect actual voting patterns point to consideration of proportional representation. That system tends to produce minority governments and coalitions. Such a result is often healthy since it compels compromise. Too sudden a switch could be avoided by combining it with the single-member constituency approach (as is done in some federal systems on a fifty-fifty basis) or by applying it to a popularly elected Senate alone.

7 The marked attrition of the legislative processes, observable in all liberal democratic societies, and the corresponding burgeoning of executive power, have seriously disturbed the classical system of constitutional checks and balances.[5] The solution lies in developing new sources of countervailing power. For some countries, the approach is by way of entrenched bills of rights, aided by specialized constitutional tribunals. For other countries, the approach is through administrative procedure codes, special laws on the responsibility of public officials, and specialized administrative review and control tribunals – *conseils d'état*. Still others create administrative watch-dog agencies (less than tribunals) – Soviet-style *procurators* or Scandinavian-style *ombudsmen*.

In the new Canadian constitution, all of these approaches should be used, with emphasis on judicially based constitutional and administrative review. Specialized tribunals would go beyond the controls now exercised by the Supreme Court. The Charter of Rights and Freedoms should be expanded to include, also, the new social and economic rights.

8 The likelihood is that the challenge of continually redefining relations between man and the state will remain the main constitutional challenge for Canada. The problem is too important to be left to provincial premiers, and too heavy a burden to be solved through informal modes – creative judicial interpretation, and governmental glosses on an original charter. Referenda on proposed amendments, and perhaps also a right of popular initiative in constitutional change, are the unmistakeable trend in liberal democratic systems. In Canada, we could see constitutional amendments adopted when ratified by a nation-wide majority which included a majority in more than half the provinces or regions. This would see participatory democracy applied to continuing constituent power. It would seem a logical conclusion to patriation of the BNA Act to Canada, and it would help to render that whole protracted exercise worthwhile.

The quest for a new constitution has sometimes been presented as a panacea for all our assorted national ills, as if all our problems would be resolved once and for all, and the need for imagination, courage, and the normal skills of political compromise would somehow disappear.

Such an approach displays a profound misunderstanding of constitutional law and those principles and processes which we designate as constitutionalism. A charter that is genuinely normative, and not simply nominal, will proceed from and reflect a reasonable consensus among the main societal forces and interest groups; it will set out the institutions and processes through which the society makes its decisions; and it will offer guidance as to the values to be applied in arriving at those decisions and the standards to be applied in administering or enforcing them. But the constitutional charter cannot resolve every problem, and it cannot be a substitute for what Judge Learned Hand called the 'spirit of moderation,' which is vital to the survival and functioning of a federal state.

While the impasse of the 1960s and 1970s as to changes in the BNA Act continued, nothing in the existing constitutional system inhibited compromises in language and culture and in the distribution of taxation revenues. These adjustments are the life-blood of a federal system and operate as informal glosses on the constitutional charter. Such a process can go on as it has in the past, whether or not we see substantive changes in institutions, processes, and values.

The great virtue of our constitutional system has been its relative lack of legal barriers to new ideas or to social and economic change. This has been, of course, a principal reason for its survival, where so many other, more artfully conceived documents have fallen by the wayside. We could say much the same about the patriation package, whatever our regrets that it was not more boldly conceived and executed. The future of Canadian federalism is therefore likely to be optimistic, so long as community decision-makers (executive, legislative, and judicial) continue to display the skills of compromise and the ability to make adjustments in old institutions that they have shown since 1867.

A new and more truly 'modern' constitutional charter would certainly help greatly to lighten the burden of that 'trust for salvation' cast upon executive, legislature, and judiciary today. But it should not be at the expense of, or a substitute for, the building of fundamental consensus in other areas – the difficult issues of social and economic choice and of redefinition of values in every post-industrial society today. This is the case, in the end, for participatory democracy and bringing the people in to the constituent process itself.

13

Constitutional postscript

Once adopted by both houses of the federal Parliament in December 1981, the patriation resolution was rushed to London for formal enactment by the British Parliament. A concerted effort began, in British officialdom, to overcome any diplomatic bad blood still remaining from the feeling, in Canada, that certain British parliamentarians – the Kershaw group, in particular – had been almost indecently anxious to espouse the political cause of the recalcitrant premiers, and that they had rushed ill-advisedly into constitutional issues that might prudently have been left to Prime Minister Thatcher or to resolution within Canada itself.

It was immediately announced that the Queen would come to Canada to participate in official ceremonies marking patriation of the constitution, the exact date to be determined after formal enactment by the British Parliament. The British Secretary of State for Foreign and Commonwealth Affairs, Lord Carrington, at the same time released a six-page policy paper – evidently held up, pending adoption of the patriation resolution by the Canadian Parliament – in which he indicated that the British government would, indeed, sponsor legislation formally enacting the resolution:

The statements by Ministers of successive Governments that it would be in accordance with precedent for the Government to introduce, and for Parliament to enact, legislation on the basis of a Canadian request have been statements of fact: in every case where there has been a request from the Federal Parliament for amendment, the Government have introduced, and Parliament has enacted, legislation in accordance with it. While the Government accept that there is never an exact precedent for a particular constitutional amendment, the consistent practice has been to act in accordance with the request and consent of the Federal Parliament. The force of this consistent practice cannot be ignored. This does not mean the United Kingdom Parliament is under some legal obligation automatically to enact whatever Canadian proposals are put before it; but it does point overwhelmingly in the direction of acceding to an agreed request for patriation.[1]

Lord Carrington and Mrs Thatcher could feel amply vindicated by events. The British government's graceful closing of the Canadian constitutional books represented a vindication, also, of the traditional techniques of quiet diplomacy, patiently, politely, and effectively practised by Lord Carrington and Canadian external affairs secretary Mark MacGuigan and their staffs and advisers.

The Kershaw committee, on 18 January 1982, issued still another report indicating that it would endorse parliamentary enactment of the patriation resolution. By this stage, however, the committee seemed no more than an irrelevant footnote to a problem that had been resolved by other players. Having by now resolved, to its own satisfaction at least, the Gibraltar and the Canadian problems, it could turn its intellectual energies to solving the Northern Ireland problem.

Mrs Thatcher courteously but firmly rejected[2] a request by Premier Lévesque that the British Parliament delay formal enactment of the patriation resolution until the Quebec government had a ruling on a Quebec right of veto on amendments to the BNA Act.[3] Was he serious in this approach or was he simply seeking to make political points, to use in Quebec? The comments of his vice-premier, Jacques-Yvan Morin, on the English sense of 'fair play'[4] would seem to imply the latter. For Mrs Thatcher to await completion of a second round of litigation would have meant a further delay – twelve months, perhaps more. In a twenty-line reply to Lévesque's nine-page missive, she reminded him that further legal proceedings in Canada were 'entirely a Canadian matter'; she added that she was sorry Quebec had been unable to reach agreement with Ottawa and the other nine provinces.[5]

In Quebec, the reaction to and disillusionment with the collapse of the gang of eight brought angry recriminations at the Parti québécois policy convention in December 1981, and soul-searching on the part of key participants in that strategy. In early January 1982, the minister of intergovernmental affairs and principal architect of the step-by-step approach to separation (*étapisme*), Claude Morin, resigned his cabinet post.[6] Morin had begun his career as a young provincial civil servant with Premier Jean Lesage and had been the trusted constitutional adviser of the Union nationale governments of Daniel Johnson and Jean-Jacques Bertrand and of the Liberal government of

Robert Bourassa. He left the civil service to run as a Parti québécois candidate and became a minister in the Lévesque government.

Morin evolved from a federalist seeking accommodations in favour of Quebec special interests to an outright separatist committed to the deliberately veiled (perhaps overly clever) sovereignty-association formula submitted in the 1980 referendum. His evolution owes something, perhaps, to that special Quebec mood described by scholar Léon Dion in his telling phrase: 'I am a tired federalist.'[7] Nothing perhaps became Morin quite so much as his manner of leaving office: voluntarily, without any blame or reproach to others, and with grace. He presumably recognized the failure of his strategy. Yet étapisme had secured a wide degree of public support, in the 1976 election, in the high tally of separatist votes in the referendum, and in the triumphant re-election in 1981. It had been much more popular than other approaches, such as the decision to abandon Quebec's insistence on 'special' status in favour of a common front against Ottawa.

Morin expressed keen disappointment at the final collapse of the gang of eight, and well he might, for his anglophone colleagues behaved, to say the least, churlishly. They abandoned him without the courtesy of any prior notification or personal apology. But what can you expect if you are willing to equate national self-determination (inside or outside Confederation) with someone else's demands for more taxation points on oil or natural gas? Morin, in making an unholy alliance against Ottawa, assimilated Quebec's special case to the assorted causes of the seven anglophone premiers. An essentially noble, poetic cause (whatever one might think of its merits) became part of a low-level commercial barter operation. Morin's departure was the honourable way of atoning for that error and allowing his successors to try to retrieve Quebec's original position.

It was perhaps fitting that Jacques-Yvan Morin, the vice-premier, became the new constitutional strong-man. As a young professor at the Université de Montréal in the early years of the Quiet Revolution, he had been the principal progenitor of Quebec's case for 'special' status,[8] the case so eloquently argued by Jean Lesage and his original équipe de tonnerre, including René Lévesque.

Would special constitutional arrangements have a political future in Canada in the post-patriation era? While Prime Minister Trudeau and the federal forces had fairly consistently opposed what was characterized as a 'checkerboard quilt' pattern of rules, this policy seemed directed more at the absurdity of any such notion for English Canada than at a denial of the theory of deux nations. Trudeau had to a large extent accepted the coexistence of federal bilingual and Quebec unilingual policies. He noted that the federal government

did consider a number of options with respect to section 23 of the Charter and its application to Quebec; including opting-in and opting-out as well as the delay provision ...

It was decided that the mix found in the resolution approved by Parliament was the most suitable. The 'Canada clause' provides a minimum of reciprocity between Quebec and the other provinces. The Quebec government had previously acknowledged that reciprocity was desirable and had made provision for this in Bill 101. In fact, the resolution does little more than give effect to section 86 of that law.

Section 23(1)(a) was not imposed on Quebec because of the province's concern that the majority of new citizens would assimilate with the minority language group when the desire is to have them identify with the majority language population. Section 59 will allow Quebec to opt-in to the 'mother tongue' provision once the National Assembly signifies its approval of this section in respect of Quebec.

Regarding the notwithstanding clause ... I did not like to see it added to the Charter, but I am not too concerned as it will be politically very difficult for a government to introduce a measure which applies notwithstanding the Charter of Rights without a very good reason.[9]

Lévesque was not the only player in the constitution-making game to try a British ploy. Various Indian groups not only revived their attempts to lobby back-benchers but also sought to defeat patriation by various forms of legal process before the British courts. Prime Minister Thatcher's government maintained, from the beginning, that any legal obligations existing between Britain and the Indian and native peoples of Canada had passed to the Canadian government with Canada's attainment of independence. This legal position had been advanced by the Foreign Office in Parliament[10] and was repeated in Lord Carrington's policy paper of December 1981, with the addition that

all relevant treaty obligations with the Indian peoples in so far as they still subsisted became the responsibility of the Government of Canada with the attainment of independence, at the latest with the Statute of Westminster 1931 ... The Government believe that any amendment of the provisions [in the patriation resolution] relating to aboriginal rights unless requested and consented to by the Canadian Government – as with any other amendments – would constitute an act of interference in the internal affairs of Canada.[11]

Even the Kershaw committee, in a curious self-contradiction, had ruled that while Canada must be considered, in effect, as less than 'sovereign,' with Britain as 'guardian' and 'trustee' of the Canadian federal system, Britain nevertheless had legally washed her hands of her original legal obligations to the Indian nations. Since British courts must accept the ruling of the Foreign Office as binding in respect to the existence and extent of treaty and other international law-based obligations, Lord Carrington's statements meant that there would be no way for Canadian Indian groups to bar parliamentary enactment of the patriation resolution through legal actions in the British courts.

What might have seemed a sensible tactical move by Canadian Indian leaders in the spring and summer of 1981 had, by December, become a lost cause. The timing of raising and then compromising a constitutional claim was always crucial. The legal actions in the British courts in December 1981 and January and February 1982[12] were too late. That these actions were persisted in, and at enormous expense, may say something as to the legal advice the Indian leaders were receiving in Britain.

Governor-General Edward Schreyer, in an interview on 21 January 1982 marking the completion of the third year of his term of office, threw some additional light on the background to the patriation conflict.[13] But he also, and much more importantly, indirectly reminded Canadians that constitutional custom and convention are never dead but in constant movement; and that the office of governor-general continues to evolve in its interactions with the other institutions of government. Schreyer (in remarks that he subsequently stated had been taken out of context, 'dealing in the abstract, or in a hypothetical sense, and not in a factual sense')[14] indicated that if the final constitutional conference had broken down and there had been 'an absolute absence of willingness to discuss anything any further ... the only way out ... would have been to cause an election to be held and the Canadian people asked to decide.'[15] His remarks were strongly criticized, on a number of grounds, by a number of people. Premier Lévesque angrily accused him of applying a double standard: 'now that English Canada's provinces are satisfied, Mr. Schreyer apparently feels nothing more is indicated so he could go back to sleep, which is his normal occupation.'[16]

Eugene Forsey focused on the propriety of the governor-general's discussing such matters in public, the governor-general's comments, in his view, being 'indiscreet beyond belief,' for even if Schreyer had been contemplating calling an election, 'he shouldn't go blathering about it now.'[17]

Forsey suggested that Schreyer was 'completely out of line' in saying he could have ordered an election: 'The classic phrase is that the Crown has the right to advise, to encourage and to warn,' with any stronger interpretations of the crown's authority as 'obsolete.'[18] James Mallory was prepared to concede a power of the governor-general to dismiss the prime minister and, in effect, force general elections, if he should feel that the prime minister was 'behaving totally unreasonably or going against the Constitution.'[19]

Yet most of the arguments for the alleged disappearance, through developing constitutional custom and convention, of the reserve, discretionary, prerogative powers of the governor-general stem from examples that no longer seem applicable to Canadian conditions. In 1926 the governor-general, Lord Byng, refused the request for a dissolution of Parliament made by Prime Minister Mackenzie King and transferred power to the Conservative leader, Arthur Meighen. A little later, after Meighen's defeat in the House, Byng granted the dissolution he had refused to King. Byng's recall to England – in embarrassment, if not in disgrace, after King's triumph in the election – has been widely considered (though never, it must be said, by Forsey) as establishing the convention that the governor-general must defer absolutely to the wishes of the prime minister.

The affair should perhaps be viewed, more correctly, as confirming the emergence of another and different convention. An 'alien' (British, and imperially appointed) governor-general could, by 1926, no longer resist the advice of the Canadian government. Why should not a Canadian governor-general who is both a Canadian citizen and also effectively appointed by the government of Canada, exercise the reserve, discretionary, prerogative powers conferred upon him by the BNA Act (sections 50 and 54–7).

The argument the other way is that such express powers have been cut down by developing custom and convention. That convention can break positive law is, technically speaking, difficult to demonstrate: even the Supreme Court, in its ruling of 28 September 1981, found it impossible to go as far as that. But the claimed conventions that would override the positive law powers of the governor-general rest on two conditions no longer applicable; in Canada the powers are no longer exercised (as in the past) by an 'alien' or (as in Britain) by a hereditary monarch. The governor-general is a truly Canadian office-holder, and, unlike the British monarch, he has his position for a limited term only. He may well conclude that he has a constitutional legitimacy in his own right, and that he has his own role to play as part of the system of checks and balances if the need for exercise of his legal powers should arise in his own proper, constitutional judgment.

The mild impatience which Schreyer's remarks reveal should be taken not only as reflecting an intellectually vigorous and still young incumbent who was only forty-three at the time of his appointment, and would be only forty-eight on retirement; but also as an indication of the potential revival, conventionally, of the office itself. Perhaps the 'Canadianization' of the constitution signals the revival of a once moribund institution. Would some of the currently fashionable proposals for election, at least indirect election, of the governor-general as head of state change and magnify that office by conferring upon it its own constitutional mandate? Such proposals should be approached soberly and not simply because they are 'trendy,' and they should be weighed and evaluated with due regard to their potential effects upon the office itself and upon its delicate interrelations with other institutions. The arguments for silent exercise of the office's discretionary powers need evaluation in the light of any changes in the positive law and conventional base of the office itself.[20]

On 28 January 1982, the British Court of Appeal unanimously rejected arguments advanced by the Alberta Indian Association, the Union of Nova Scotia Indians, and the Union of New Brunswick Indians that the British government still retained legal responsibility for treaty obligations concluded between the Crown and the Indian peoples of Canada.[21] The three-man court, led by Lord Denning, dismissed the Indian arguments on every legal point, saying that the treaty obligations (such as they might be), between the Crown and the Canadian Indian peoples had long since passed to the Canadian government. All Indian legal claims arising under those treaties must, henceforward, properly be addressed to Ottawa. The traditional concept of the Crown as legally one and indivisible had disappeared with the emergence of full Canadian sovereignty and independence. Instead of the one Crown Imperial, there was a separate and autonomous Crown in Canada, legally distinct from the Crown in Britain.

Lord Denning, echoing Chief Justice Bora Laskin in earlier litigation on other issues, concluded that the proclamation of 1763 and the treaties between the British Crown and the Indian peoples were akin to an Indian bill of rights, a sort of Magna Carta: 'No parliament should do anything to lessen ... these guarantees ... so long as the sun rises and the river flows.'[22] Such a statement, coming from the heart and with all Lord Denning's enormous prestige behind it, might help make up, in moral force, all that it lacked in strict legal authority in Canada. It was likely to go ringing through the years of continuing dialogue, still ahead, between the Canadian government and the Indian and native peoples as to a just and equitable constitutional settlement of their historic legal claims.

On 29 January 1982, the British Court of Appeal refused permission to the three Indian groups concerned to appeal the court's ruling to the House of Lords, the highest British court.[23] The three Indian groups might still choose to go directly to the House of Lords to apply for leave to appeal. Saskatchewan Indian leaders promptly announced that they would pursue the same legal arguments through another route – the Chancery Division of the High Court. Quebec Indian leaders announced yet another delegation to London to lobby British parliamentarians.[24] But the 'British strategy' of attempting to use British parliamentary lobbies and British court processes to frustrate patriation of the BNA Act had, by now, demonstrably failed.

The time was clearly ripe for Indian and native leaders to attempt a cool and sober cost-benefit analysis of the whole London operation. Why had it failed? Why had it been continued so long after its main *raison d'être* – its nuisance value as an inducement to the federal government to make generous concessions at a time when it desperately needed allies – had ended?

A National Indian Brotherhood report prepared in December 1981 estimated that Indian groups had already spent three to four million dollars on the London lobby, and this did not include the main legal costs for the court arguments which took place in January 1982.[25] The Indian Association of Alberta reported, officially, that it had spent $190,000 on its London efforts. The Saskatchewan Indians had spent $400,000. The Union of BC Indian Chiefs had sold Indian artifacts as part of a fund-raising campaign and claimed that the lobby had 'financially decimated' its organization; but Reeves Haggan of the staff of the Canadian high commission in London was reported as suggesting that, in the end, it would all come out of the Canadian taxpayers' pocket.[26]

Where did the money all go? Apart from the costs of air fares and hotel expenses for the very large Indian delegations (sometimes as large as fifty in number) involved in public demonstrations, and the Indians' own lawyers' expenses (one of them was reported to have made six visits to London in 1981), there were the professional fees for the British lawyers and for the British public relations firms that had encouraged and stage-managed the last-ditch battle. One of these, a British firm called External Development Services Consultants, in London, admitted that its fee was $88 per hour, and the Alberta Indians acknowledged that this firm alone had been paid, on average, $11,000 per month since the spring of 1981. The British firm had used a Conservative back-bencher, Sir Bernard Braine, as its main parliamentary spokesman, and he had been one of the main members of the back-benchers' informal committee opposing Prime Minister Thatcher's endorsement of the patriation project.[27]

Yet, by now, the British establishment had finally come to rally around Mrs Thatcher. The door in the wall, in Downing Street as in Buckingham Palace, had been closed, all along, to provincial premiers and their agents-general bearing gifts; and all the other doors in London now slammed shut to the still-intransigent Quebec government, to Indian and native leaders, and other anti-federal government special interest groups. *The Times* of London – under Canadian ownership a year and more before – had frowned on Prime Minister Trudeau and actively espoused the premiers' cause; now, under Australian ownership, it opined editorially, after the Court of Appeal's rejection of the Indian claims, that 'the United Kingdom Parliament has now no legal or constitutional or political option but to pass the Canada Bill and send the Constitution where it belongs.'[28]

This had been Mrs Thatcher's public position from the beginning. What had now developed in Britain was one of those more or less spontaneous acts of collective consensus in which the British establishment decided that the 'Canadian caper' had gone on long enough. It did not make sense for Britain, with its balance-of-payments problems at home and its 'running ulcer' of Northern Ireland next door, to be involved any longer in a political adventure in Canada in which there was no discernible gain for Britain itself. Sir Anthony Kershaw jovially entered into the new spirit of the game, formally asking in the House of Commons on 4 February why the British government was taking so long to present its Canada Bill, formally enacting the patriation project, for second reading.

For Canadian Indian and native leaders it would be back to Canada and the negotiation table for phase two of constitution-making. A constitutional conference, in terms of the patriation package, must take place within twelve months of proclamation of the new Canada Act, must include 'aboriginal rights' in its agenda, and must have representatives of the Indian and native peoples 'participating' in the debate on such an item. The inter-governmental negotiating arena within Canada and also the Canadian courts would, henceforth, have to be the principal outlets for Indian and native activism in support of their constitutional rights.

By way of comparison, no official information is available as to the costs of the dissident premiers' lobbying in London in 1980 and throughout most of 1981. Such provincial lobbying certainly included costs of retainers and general legal fees for British lawyers, fees for British public relations firms and professional lobbyists, and the cost of lavish entertainment, luncheons, and dinners for British MPs from all parties. From their very scale, particularly on the part of the Quebec government and the western provinces, one can reasonably conclude that the expenses vastly exceeded those of the Indian and native groups. The result, of course, was the same, and predictably the same. The real difference perhaps is that the dissident premiers (apart from Quebec) knew when to break off their London strategy – after the 5 November compromise agreement with the federal government.

In mid-March 1982, a panel of five judges of the House of Lords, the highest English court, turned down an application by the Alberta Indians for special leave to appeal to the House of Lords a decision of the British Court of Appeal of January 1982. The Court of Appeal had categorically rejected, on the merits, all of the Indians' legal arguments against the patriation project. In a second, procedural ruling of 29 January 1982, it had refused permission to appeal to the House of Lords. With the March ruling, all legal doors in Britain finally closed to the Indians.

In early March 1982, the federal government, after some weeks' delay, appointed Justice Bertha Wilson of the Ontario Court of Appeal to the Supreme Court of Canada, to the seat left vacant by Justice Martland's retirement. Justice Wilson was the first woman to be appointed to the Supreme Court. Her appointment came on the very eve of the adoption of the Charter of Rights and Freedoms, with the radical transformation in the traditional role of the Court that that presaged. It would have been an ideal occasion to undertake some public discussion of the candidate's philosophy of law and legal development (as with President Reagan's nomination of the first woman justice to the US Supreme Court the previous year) and to debate the new role of the Canadian Supreme Court. Structural changes in the Court and in the judicial appointing process might have been discussed; they may be necessary so as more fully to integrate the Court into the new system of constitutional checks and balances and also the better to legitimate its new and expanded law-making responsibilities.

On 9 March 1982, the British House of Commons, by a vote of 177 to 33, gave final approval to the Canadian constitutional bill, and it was then sent on to the House of Lords. Less than a third of all MPs bothered to turn up for the third reading and to vote at the conclusion of the debate, in spite of the modest pressures exercised by the party whips. This is a commentary both on what British parliamentarians thought of the quality of the debate and also on the ultimate political irrelevance of the enormously expensive 'battle of the dining tables' mounted in London by the eight provincial premiers opposed to the project. Independent Labour MP George Cunningham referred to Prime Minister Trudeau's quip that British MPs should, if need be, 'hold their noses and pass the [Patriation] bill' and commented: 'I think Mr. Trudeau was imprudent in the extreme. But we have paid him back in spades. Our impudence has greatly exceeded his.' He added: 'Only boundless presumption, a characteristic which has marked the English through the centuries,' had persuaded certain British MPs that they could constitutionally refuse a legitimate request from Canada.[29]

In the House of Lords, the debate was mercifully brief. There was a rallying of senior cabinet ministers, former ministers, Law Lords, and others to prevent any repetition of the studied irrelevancies and talking to the galleries that had marked the Commons proceedings. On 25 March 1982, the House of Lords voted to adopt the Canadian bill, thus formally ending the last vestigial legal links tying Canada to Britain. On 17 April 1982, the measure was officially proclaimed in Ottawa by the Queen and entered into the Canadian constitution.

In Canada, constitutional attention had already shifted to matters of significance, really, to phase two of constitution-making. The first two weeks of March 1982 were occupied, in Ottawa, by the 'battle of the parliamentary division bells.' The Conservative opposition decided to boycott the sittings of the House of Commons – in stated protest against the government's package bill on energy, though the Conservative strategy seemed related also to intra-party feuds over leadership and the desire of the Clark forces to mount a political show of strength. The government, surprisingly, seemed to acquiesce in this immobilizing of Parliament – perhaps waiting for public opinion to turn in its favour and wishing to avoid being seen as reacting 'prematurely' – though it had all the votes necessary to proceed with the ordinary business of Parliament, in the absence of the Conservatives.

Perhaps sensing an unfavourable public reaction to MPs continuing to draw their full salaries while deliberately absenting themselves from their parliamentary duties, the Conservatives called the parliamentary boycott off, after two weeks. All the public opinion soundings, at the time, showed a significant rise in NDP support at the expense of the two other parties.

But the incident raised interesting questions as to the relevance of the parliamentary system. Many back-benchers feel helpless when faced with the rise of executive power. The British parliamentary executive is not working today, and has not worked for many years (in Britain or in the Commonwealth) according to classical models. Should not phase two of constitution-making examine new patterns of executive-legislative relations, new constitutional checks and balances, as a means of giving Parliament a more meaningful role and establishing it, once again, as an effective countervailing power to the executive? Patriation could liberate Canada from a hitherto too exclusive concern for British precedents and open the door to study of other models – the fifth French Republic, the Bonn system of 1949, the post-war Japanese system – where all these crucial problems have had to be faced and resolved in quite contemporary constitutional terms.

On 26 March 1982, an anglophone businessman from Montreal, Allan Singer, lost out in the Quebec Cour supérieure in his attempt to have Quebec's Bill 101 of 1977 declared unconstitutional.

In London, sixty-nine Saskatchewan Indians, joining with seventy-eight British Columbia, Manitoba, and Ontario Indian chiefs, found still more British lawyers prepared to accept their briefs, to argue before British courts that the treaties signed by the British Crown with Canadian Indians were still binding on the British government, notwithstanding the passage by both British houses of Parliament of the Canadian constitutional bill. Those Canadian Indian leaders even found a judge of the Chancery Division of the British High Court of Justice prepared, only one day after passage of the Canada bill through the British Parliament, to grant them at least a tentative June hearing for their cases, despite the contention by the lawyers representing the British government that the Canadian Indian leaders were 'suing the wrong defendant in the wrong court in the wrong country.'

Meanwhile, Joe Clark was arguing for a 'low-key' patriation ceremony in Ottawa, expressing the hope that plans for the Queen's visit to Canada would take into account possible negative reaction in Quebec or other parts of the country so as to avoid 'provid[ing] an opportunity for people who might become angered by what is going on to have that anger deepened.'[30] The objection seemed to come strangely from a leader who had hardly been noticeable for his efforts to dissuade his provincial cohorts from using the 'British connection' in their vain attempt to block patriation. It did at least direct attention to one final, crowning irony in the whole exercise: that a project designed to complete Canada's 'decolonization' should have the prime living representative of the imperial past as the key actor in the final official ceremony to that effect.

The federal government sought to maximize the public relations aspects of this ceremony in order to reap the greatest possible political advantages from it. There was lavish entertainment, at the government's expense, for 2,300 specially invited guests. Premier Lévesque threatened to stage 'counter-events' in Montreal on the same days as the Ottawa celebrations; he was politely but firmly reproved by Claude Ryan for wanting to waste Quebec public monies at a time of drastic restraint in Quebec health, education, and social services expenditures. Lévesque then scaled down the Quebec counter-ceremony to a mass street march in Montreal. He also sent a letter to Quebec Lieutenant-Governor Pierre Côté (a federal appointee, of course), asking him not to attend the Ottawa ceremony. Claude Ryan announced that he himself had not been invited to attend the Ottawa ceremonies, but that, even if he had, he would not have gone anyway: 'The absence of a person like myself will serve as a reminder that there are still important issues to resolve: this agreement [on the constitution] was arrived at without Quebec's consent.'

For those premiers who did choose to attend the Ottawa ceremony, Prime Minister Trudeau had his own honorific award to confer: the ten current premiers, plus recently defeated Manitoba Premier Sterling Lyon and federal NDP leader Ed Broadbent, would all be sworn in as members of the Queen's (Canadian) Privy Council. There was a certain conscious irony in Trudeau's gesture: most of the premiers had fought the patriation project tooth and nail, had bitterly opposed its Charter of Rights, and must bear a principal responsibility for the charter's obvious gaps and its frequent weaknesses in facing up to the pressing new issues of Canadian society. Newly elected Manitoba Premier Howard Pawley, who, as a late entry on the political scene, was free from any blame for the shortcomings of the patriation project, remarked tartly that naming the premiers to the Privy Council would not improve federal-provincial relations: 'The responsibility of a premier or any political leader is not to be influenced by the handing out of honours or perks such as this. I don't think it is a solution to anything.'

Premier Lévesque lost out in Quebec's highest court, the Cour d'Appel; a five-man bench unanimously rejected on 7 April the Lévesque argument that the 5 November 1981 constitutional accord was illegal since obtained without Quebec's consent. Applying the Supreme Court's ruling on the constitutionality of the patriation package, the court ruled that there was, indeed, a sufficiency of provincial consent, even without Quebec; and thus it delivered the legal quietus to Quebec's traditional claim to a legal right of veto over constitutional change in Canada. The court, in passing, also indicated that Quebec's character as a distinct society within Canadian federalism did not carry with it any corresponding special constitutional-legal status different from that of the other provinces: 'Articles 91 and 92 of the BNA Act give the smallest Provinces the same rights as the largest.' Having lost absolutely before the Quebec court, there was nothing left for Premier Lévesque but to swallow his pride and announce he would appeal the ruling to the Supreme Court.

With the long-range goals in public life that he had originally set for himself largely attained, speculation arose once more that Prime Minister Trudeau might consider retiring again, as he had prematurely announced in late 1979 after his general election defeat earlier in the same year. However, musing aloud, the prime minister indicated that he might indeed stay around a little longer to tackle, this time, economic problems. As for the constitution and phase two of constitution-making, going to basic institutions and processes of government, he proclaimed himself 'a little bit hesitant.'[31] The patriation project did, in terms (section 37), commit the federal government to holding a further constitutional conference, within a year after patriation, on Indian and native rights. Anything beyond that would depend on public opinion and direct pressures upon political leaders. The public mood on the constitution appeared now to be one of profound ennui, and no one in the cabinet, not even the prime minister, and no one in the opposition parties seemed disposed to take the political risks of trying to change that, at least for the moment.

Behind the surface illusion that patriation meant an entirely new constitutional order for Canada lay the modest reality that patriation itself was an essentially symbolic act that would change nothing in and of itself. The new constitutional amending machinery probably wouldn't work, so that this might have been the last clear chance for a constitutional breakthrough for a number of years. The new Charter of Rights reached only quite limited, albeit important, sectors of Canadian constitutionalism. Institutional changes in the Supreme Court would have been needed to give the expected new wave of judicial legislation technical sophistication (in community policy-making terms) and constitutional legitimacy (in liberal-democratic terms). For resolution of all the other pressing new constitutional problems, involving redefinition of the relation of man and state in post-industrial society, Canadians would have to get along, as before, with the old BNA Act of 1867, trendily retitled now the Constitution Acts 1867 to 1982. We had, of course, done reasonably well over the past 115 years with the old constitutional charter, with its ideological neutrality or at least open-endedness, and its quieter, homelier virtues. Eugene Forsey had reminded us, before, that the original founding fathers of 1867 – Canadian and British – had not served us so badly; and newer generations of constitutional founding fathers would now have to find the imagination, wit, and civil courage to do even better, with the patriation project finally achieved.

Introduction

The resolution on the constitution adopted by the two houses of Parliament and formally enacted by the British Parliament is presented hereunder in its four successive versions. The first draft (Appendix A), by the prime minister's civil service staff, was released by Prime Minister Trudeau in a nation-wide television address on 2 October 1980. The second version (Appendix B), the result of the joint committee and its impact upon the first draft, was tentatively accepted by all parties, pending ruling by the Supreme Court on its constitutionality, on 24 April 1981. The Supreme Court ruled on 28 September 1981. The prime minister and the nine anglophone premiers arrived at a constitutional accord (Appendix C) on 5 November 1981. This accord gave rise to the third version (Appendix D), released on 18 November 1981, with the federal government incorporating and translating into precise legal terms the modifications that had been agreed upon in that accord. The public criticisms of the third version, particularly by women's groups and Indian and native peoples, led to further modifications, some of which were cleared with the nine anglophone premiers, but others of which seem to have been made on the federal government's own initiative. It is this fourth version, of 8 December 1981 (Appendix E), that was adopted by joint resolution of the two federal houses and formally enacted by the British Parliament.

Why publish (even in abridged form) all four versions (and the accord of 5 November), since only the fourth version has binding legal authority? First, the successive drafts are part of the general legislative history of the resolution as finally adopted. They may, as *travaux préparatoires*, be cited, in the courts and elsewhere, as official guides to its interpretation and application in cases of legal ambiguity or doubt. Second, the patriation project has been an exercise in constitution-making; the successive draft versions expose, better than anything else, the motives and strategy of the main constitutional players, the tactical development of their plans, and the compromises and bargains that they were compelled to make. The constitution-making game stands thus revealed – at its best as a model of the skills of compromise, and at its worst as, all too frequently, an example of naked cynicism in the pursuit of low-level political gains.

To avoid unnecessary repetition, only those parts of the first three versions of the resolution are published that change significantly from one draft to another. The final version is published in full. The first was current when the Manitoba, Newfoundland, and Quebec courts of appeal (see Appendix G) were giving their rulings in early 1981; the second was current for purposes of the appeal to the Supreme Court (see Appendix H). The 5 November accord is reproduced in full, or at least in the complete text released by all the parties at that time. It is clear, however, that that text is somewhat elliptic, and it certainly fails to mention at least several key elements of the accord that all parties, subsequently, had no difficulty in acknowledging as part of their consensus. The explanation would appear to be not that the official text is accompanied by any secret protocols but that in the hurry of reducing to writing a political compromise the parties employed a sort of diplomatic shorthand and failed to include some agreed items, through simple oversight or negligence.

We have also included in the appendixes extracts from all main court judgments bearing upon the patriation project as a whole or, more specifically, the constitutional resolution. Publication of the Supreme Court's advisory opinion of 21 December 1979 on Senate reform (Appendix F) may seem strange; but that brief, unsigned opinion appears to have been a factor persuading the federal government to amend the constitution by way of formal statute of the British Parliament. As for the various court decisions on the constitutionality of the patriation project, the rulings of the provincial courts of appeal (Appendix G) are more coherent, tidier, and better organized, and in consequence easier to comprehend in their legal reasoning, than the Supreme Court ruling on appeal (Appendix H). Indeed, the opinion of Chief Justice Samuel Freedman of Manitoba is intellectually innovatory and persuasive and impressive in its own right. I have therefore taken key passages from the provincial court rulings, particularly those of Manitoba and Quebec, and much lengthier selections from all of the opinions filed to the Supreme Court's final judgment – the 'group-of-seven' opinion on legality, the parallel 'group-of-six' opinion on conventionality, the two-man 'conservative' dissent to the first of these, and the three-man 'liberal' dissent to the second.

Proposed resolution first draft (extracts)

Proposed Resolution for a Joint Address to Her Majesty the Queen respecting the Constitution of Canada [2 October 1980]

WHEREAS in the past certain amendments to the Constitution of Canada have been made by the Parliament of the United Kingdom at the request and with the consent of Canada;

AND WHEREAS it is in accord with the status of Canada as an independent state that Canadians be able to amend their Constitution in Canada in all respects;

AND WHEREAS it is also desirable to provide in the Constitution of Canada for the recognition of certain fundamental rights and freedoms and to make other amendments to that Constitution.

NOW THEREFORE the Senate and the House of Commons, in Parliament assembled, resolve that a respectful address be presented to Her Majesty the Queen in the following words:

To the Queen's Most Excellent Majesty:
Most Gracious Sovereign:

We, Your Majesty's loyal subjects, the Senate and the House of Commons of Canada in Parliament assembled, respectfully approach Your Majesty, requesting that you may graciously be pleased to cause to be laid before the Parliament of the United Kingdom a measure containing the recitals and clauses hereinafter set forth:

An Act to amend the Constitution of Canada

Whereas Canada has requested and consented to the enactment of an Act of the Parliament of the United Kingdom to give effect to the provisions hereinafter set forth and the Senate and the House of Commons of Canada in Parliament assembled have submitted an address to Her Majesty requesting that Her Majesty may graciously be pleased to cause a Bill to be laid before the Parliament of the United Kingdom for that purpose.

Be it therefore enacted by the Queen's Most Excellent Majesty, by and with the advice and consent of the Lords Spiritual and Temporal, and Commons, in this present Parliament assembled, and by the authority of the same, as follows:

[THE CANADA ACT]

1 The *Constitution Act, 1980* set out in Schedule B to this Act is hereby enacted for and shall have the force of law in Canada and shall come into force as provided in that Act.

Constitution Act, 1980 enacted

2 No Act of the Parliament of the United Kingdom passed after the *Constitution Act, 1980* comes into force shall extend to Canada as part of its law.

Parliament of United Kingdom not to legislate for Canada

3 So far as it is not contained in Schedule B, the French version of this Act is set out in Schedule A to this Act and has the same authority in Canada as the English version thereof.

French version

4 This Act may be cited as the *Canada Act*.

Short title

SCHEDULE B
CONSTITUTION ACT, 1980

PART I CANADIAN CHARTER OF RIGHTS AND FREEDOMS

Guarantee of Rights and Freedoms
1 *The Canadian Charter of Rights and Freedoms* guarantees the rights and freedoms set out in it subject only to such reasonable limits as are generally accepted in a free and democratic society with a parliamentary system of government.

Rights and Freedoms in Canada

Fundamental Freedoms
2 Everyone has the following fundamental freedoms:
(*a*) freedom of conscience and religion;
(*b*) freedom of thought, belief, opinion and expression, including freedom of the press and other media of information; and
(*c*) freedom of peaceful assembly and of association.

Fundamental freedoms

Democratic Rights
3 Every citizen of Canada has, without unreasonable distinction or limitation, the right to vote in an election of members of the House of Commons or of a legislative assembly and to be qualified for membership therein.

Democratic rights of citizens

4(1) No House of Commons and no legislative assembly shall continue for longer than five years from the date fixed for the return of the writs at a general election of its members.

Duration of elected legislative bodies

(2) In time of real or apprehended war, invasion or insurrection, a House of Commons may be continued by Parliament and a legislative

Continuation in special circumstances

143 Proposed resolution, first draft

assembly may be continued by the legislature beyond five years if such continuation is not opposed by the votes of more than one-third of the members of the House of Commons or the legislative assembly, as the case may be.

5 There shall be a sitting of Parliament and of each legislature at least once every twelve months.

Mobility Rights
6(1) Every citizen of Canada has the right to enter, remain in and leave Canada.

(2) Every citizen of Canada and every person who has the status of a permanent resident of Canada has the right
(*a*) to move to and take up residence in any province; and
(*b*) to pursue the gaining of a livelihood in any province.

(3) The rights specified in subsection (2) are subject to
(*a*) any laws or practices of general application in force in a province other than those that discriminate among persons primarily on the basis of province of present or previous residence; and
(*b*) any laws providing for reasonable residency requirements as a qualification for the receipt of publicly provided social services.

Legal Rights
7 Everyone has the right to life, liberty and security of the person and the right not to be deprived thereof except in accordance with the principles of fundamental justice.

8 Everyone has the right not to be subjected to search or seizure except on grounds, and in accordance with procedures, established by law.

9 Everyone has the right not to be detained or imprisoned except on grounds, and in accordance with procedures, established by law.

10 Everyone has the right on arrest or detention
(*a*) to be informed promptly of the reasons therefor;
(*b*) to retain and instruct counsel without delay; and
(*c*) to have the validity of the detention determined by way of *habeas corpus* and to be released if the detention is not lawful.

11 Anyone charged with an offence has the right
(*a*) to be informed promptly of the specific offence;
(*b*) to be tried within a reasonable time;
(*c*) to be presumed innocent until proven guilty according to law in a fair and public hearing by an independent and impartial tribunal;
(*d*) not to be denied reasonable bail except on grounds, and in accordance with procedures, established by law;
(*e*) not to be found guilty on account of any act or omission that at the time of the act or omission did not constitute an offence;
(*f*) not to be tried or punished more than once for an offence of which he or she has been finally convicted or acquitted; and
(*g*) to the benefit of the lesser punishment where the punishment for an offence of which he or she has been convicted has been varied between the time of commission and the time of sentencing.

12 Everyone has the right not to be subjected to any cruel and unusual treatment or punishment. *Treatment or punishment*

13 A witness has the right when compelled to testify not to have any incriminating evidence so given used to incriminate him or her in any other proceedings, except a prosecution for perjury or for the giving of contradictory evidence. *Self-crimination*

14 A party or witness in any proceedings who does not understand or speak the language in which the proceedings are conducted has the right to the assistance of an interpreter. *Interpreter*

Non-discrimination Rights

15(1) Everyone has the right to equality before the law and to the equal protection of the law without discrimination because of race, national or ethnic origin, colour, religion, age or sex. *Equality before the law and equal protection of the law*

(2) This section does not preclude any law, program or activity that has as its object the amelioration of conditions of disadvantaged persons or groups. *Affirmative action programs*

Official Languages of Canada

16(1) English and French are the official languages of Canada and have equality of status and equal rights and privileges as to their use in all institutions of the Parliament and government of Canada. *Official languages of Canada*

(2) Nothing in this Charter limits the authority of Parliament or a legislature to extend the status or use of English and French or either of those languages. *Extension of status and use*

17 Everyone has the right to use English or French in any debates and other proceedings of Parliament. *Proceedings of Parliament*

18 The statutes, records and journals of Parliament shall be printed and published in English and French and both language versions are equally authoritative. *Parliamentary statutes and records*

19 Either English or French may be used by any person in, or in any pleading in or process issuing from, any court established by Parliament. *Proceedings in courts established by Parliament*

20 Any member of the public in Canada has the right to communicate with, and to receive available services from, any head or central office of an institution of the Parliament or government of Canada in English or French, as he or she may choose, and has the same right with respect to any other office of any such institution where that office is located within an area of Canada in which it is determined, in such manner as may be prescribed or authorized by Parliament, that a substantial number of persons within the population use that language. *Communications by public with federal institutions*

21 Nothing in sections 16 to 20 abrogates or derogates from any right, privilege or obligation with respect to the English and French languages, or either of them, that exists or is continued by virtue of any other provision of the Constitution of Canada. *Continuation of existing constitutional provisions*

22 Nothing in sections 16 to 20 abrogates or derogates from any legal or customary right or privilege acquired or enjoyed either before *Rights and privileges preserved*

or after the coming into force of this Charter with respect to any language that is not English or French.

Minority Language Educational Rights
23(1) Citizens of Canada whose first language learned and still understood is that of the English or French linguistic minority population of the province in which they reside have the right to have their children receive their primary and secondary school instruction in that minority language if they reside in an area of the province in which the number of children of such citizens is sufficient to warrant the provision out of public funds of minority language educational facilities in that area.

Language of instruction

(2) Where a citizen of Canada changes residence from one province to another and, prior to the change, any child of that citizen has been receiving his or her primary or secondary school instruction in either English or French, that citizen has the right to have any or all of his or her children receive their primary and secondary school instruction in that same language if the number of children of citizens resident in the area of the province to which the citizen has moved, who have a right recognized by this section, is sufficient to warrant the provision out of public funds of minority language educational facilities in that area.

Continuity of language of instruction

Undeclared Rights and Freedoms
24 The guarantee in this Charter of certain rights and freedoms shall not be construed as denying the existence of any other rights or freedoms that exist in Canada, including any rights or freedoms that pertain to the native peoples of Canada.

Undeclared rights and freedoms

General
25 Any law that is inconsistent with the provisions of this Charter is, to the extent of such inconsistency, inoperative and of no force or effect.

Primacy of Charter

26 No provision of this Charter, other than section 13, affects the laws respecting the admissibility of evidence in any proceedings or the authority of Parliament or a legislature to make laws in relation thereto.

Laws respecting evidence

27 A reference in this Charter to a province or to the legislative assembly of a province shall be deemed to include a reference to the Yukon Territory and the Northwest Territories, or to the appropriate legislative authority thereof, as the case may be.

Application to territories and territorial authorities

28 Nothing in this Charter extends the legislative powers of any body or authority.

Legislative powers not extended

Application of Charter
29(1) This Charter applies
(*a*) to the Parliament and government of Canada and to all matters within the authority of Parliament including all matters relating to the Yukon Territory and Northwest Territories; and
(*b*) to the legislature and government of each province and to all matters within the authority of the legislature of each province.

Application of Charter

(2) Notwithstanding subsection (1), section 15 shall not have appli-   Exception
cation until three years after this Act, except Part V, comes into force.

Citation
30 This Part may be cited as the *Canadian Charter of Rights and Free-*   Citation
doms.

PART II EQUALIZATION AND REGIONAL DISPARITIES

31 (1) Without altering the legislative authority of Parliament or of the   Commitment to
provincial legislatures, or the rights of any of them with respect to the   promote equal
exercise of their legislative authority, Parliament and the legislatures,   opportunities
together with the government of Canada and the provincial govern-
ments, are committed to
(*a*) promoting equal opportunities for the well-being of Canadians;
(*b*) furthering economic development to reduce disparity in opportunities; and
(*c*) providing essential public services of reasonable quality to all Canadians.
    (2) Parliament and the government of Canada are committed to   Commitment
taking such measures as are appropriate to ensure that provinces are   respecting
able to provide the essential public services referred to in paragraph   essential public
(1)(*c*) without imposing an undue burden of provincial taxation.   services

PART III CONSTITUTIONAL CONFERENCES

32 Until Part V comes into force, a constitutional conference com-   Constitutional
posed of the Prime Minister of Canada and the first ministers of the   conferences
provinces shall be convened by the Prime Minister of Canada at least
once in every year unless, in any year, a majority of those composing
the conference decide that it shall not be held.

...

PART V PROCEDURE FOR AMENDING CONSTITUTION OF CANADA

41 (1) An amendment to the Constitution of Canada may be made by   General
proclamation issued by the Governor General under the Great Seal of   procedure for
Canada where so authorized by   amending
(*a*) resolutions of the Senate and House of Commons; and   Constitution of
(*b*) resolutions of the legislative assemblies of at least a majority of the   Canada
provinces that includes
    (i) every province that at any time before the issue of the proclama-
tion had, according to any previous general census, a population of
at least twenty-five per cent of the population of Canada,
    (ii) at least two of the Atlantic provinces that have, according to the
then latest general census, combined populations of at least fifty per
cent of the population of all the Atlantic provinces, and

(iii) at least two of the Western provinces that have, according to the then latest general census, combined populations of at least fifty per cent of the population of all the Western provinces.

(2) In this section,

'Atlantic provinces' means the provinces of Nova Scotia, New Brunswick, Prince Edward Island and Newfoundland;

'Western provinces' means the provinces of Manitoba, British Columbia, Saskatchewan and Alberta.

Definitions
'Atlantic provinces'

'Western provinces'

...

48 Subject to section 50, Parliament may exclusively make laws amending the Constitution of Canada in relation to the executive government of Canada or the Senate or House of Commons.

Amendments by Parliament

49 Subject to section 50, the legislature of each province may exclusively make laws amending the constitution of the province.

Amendments by provincial legislatures

50 An amendment to the Constitution of Canada in relation to the following matters may be made only in accordance with a procedure prescribed by section 41 or 42:

(a) the office of the Queen, the Governor General and the Lieutenant Governor of a province;

(b) the Canadian Charter of Rights and Freedoms;

(c) the commitments relating to equalization and regional disparities set out in section 31;

(d) the powers of the Senate;

(e) the number of members by which a province is entitled to be represented in the Senate and the residence qualifications of Senators;

(f) the right of a province to a number of members in the House of Commons not less than the number of Senators representing the province; and

(g) the principles of proportionate representation of the provinces in the House of Commons prescribed by the Constitution of Canada.

Matters requiring amendment under general formula

51 Class 1 of section 91 and class 1 of section 92 of the Constitution Act, 1867 (formerly named the British North America Act, 1867), the British North America (No. 2) Act, 1949, referred to in item 21 of Schedule I to this Act and Parts III and IV of this Act are repealed.

Consequential amendments

PART VI GENERAL

52(1) The Constitution of Canada includes

(a) the Canada Act;

(b) the Acts and orders referred to in Schedule I; and

(c) any amendment to any Act or order referred to in paragraph (a) or (b).

Constitution of Canada

(2) Amendments to the Constitution of Canada shall be made only in accordance with the authority contained in the Constitution of Canada.

Amendments to Constitution of Canada

53(1) The enactments referred to in Column I of Schedule I are   Repeals and
hereby repealed, or amended to the extent indicated in Column II   new names
thereof, and, unless repealed, shall continue as law in Canada under
the names set out in Column III thereof.

...

59 This Schedule may be cited as the *Constitution Act, 1980* and the   Citations
Constitution Acts, 1867 to 1975 (No. 2) and this Act may be cited
together as the *Constitution Acts, 1867 to 1980.*

[Schedule I to the Constitution Act, 1980 is omitted.]

Consolidated resolution (extracts)

Consolidation of proposed constitutional resolution tabled by the Minister of Justice in the House of Commons on February 13, 1981 with the amendments approved by the House of Commons on April 23, 1981 and by the Senate on April 24, 1981

THAT, WHEREAS in the past certain amendments to the Constitution of Canada have been made by the Parliament of the United Kingdom at the request and with the consent of Canada;

AND WHEREAS it is in accord with the status of Canada as an independent state that Canadians be able to amend their Constitution in Canada in all respects;

AND WHEREAS it is also desirable to provide in the Constitution of Canada for the recognition of certain fundamental rights and freedoms and to make other amendments to that Constitution;

A respectful address be presented to Her Majesty the Queen in the following words:

To the Queen's Most Excellent Majesty:
    Most Gracious Sovereign:

We, Your Majesty's loyal subjects, the House of Commons of Canada in Parliament assembled, respectfully approach Your Majesty, requesting that you may graciously be pleased to cause to be laid before the Parliament of the United Kingdom a measure containing the recitals and clauses hereinafter set forth:

An Act to give effect to a request by the Senate and House of Commons of Canada

Whereas Canada has requested and consented to the enactment of an Act of the Parliament of the United Kingdom to give effect to the provisions hereinafter set forth and the Senate and the House of Commons of Canada in Parliament assembled have submitted an address to

Her Majesty requesting that Her Majesty may graciously be pleased to cause a Bill to be laid before the Parliament of the United Kingdom for that purpose.

Be it therefore enacted by the Queen's Most Excellent Majesty, by and with the advice and consent of the Lords Spiritual and Temporal, and Commons, in this present Parliament assembled, and by the authority of the same, as follows:

[THE CANADA ACT]

1 The *Constitution Act, 1981* set out in Schedule B to this Act is hereby enacted for and shall have the force of law in Canada and shall come into force as provided in that Act. — *Constitution Act, 1981* enacted

2 No Act of the Parliament of the United Kingdom passed after the *Constitution Act, 1981* comes into force shall extend to Canada as part of its law. — Termination of power to legislate for Canada

3 So far as it is not contained in Schedule B, the French version of this Act is set out in Schedule A to this Act and has the same authority in Canada as the English version thereof. — French version

4 This Act may be cited as the *Canada Act*. — Short title

SCHEDULE B
CONSTITUTION ACT, 1981

PART I CANADIAN CHARTER OF RIGHTS AND FREEDOMS

Whereas Canada is founded upon principles that recognize the supremacy of God and the rule of law:

Guarantee of Rights and Freedoms
1 The *Canadian Charter of Rights and Freedoms* guarantees the rights and freedoms set out in it subject only to such reasonable limits prescribed by law as can be demonstrably justified in a free and democratic society. — Rights and freedoms in Canada

Fundamental Freedoms
2 Everyone has the following fundamental freedoms: — Fundamental freedoms
(a) freedom of conscience and religion;
(b) freedom of thought, belief, opinion and expression, including freedom of the press and other media of communication;
(c) freedom of peaceful assembly; and
(d) freedom of association.

Democratic Rights
3 Every citizen of Canada has the right to vote in an election of members of the House of Commons or of a legislative assembly and to be qualified for membership therein. — Democratic rights of citizens

151 Consolidated resolution

4(1) No House of Commons and no legislative assembly shall continue for longer than five years from the date fixed for the return of the writs at a general election of its members.

(2) In time of real or apprehended war, invasion or insurrection, a House of Commons may be continued by Parliament and a legislative assembly may be continued by the legislature beyond five years if such continuation is not opposed by the votes of more than one-third of the members of the House of Commons or the legislative assembly, as the case may be.

5 There shall be a sitting of Parliament and of each legislature at least once every twelve months.

Mobility Rights

6(1) Every citizen of Canada has the right to enter, remain in and leave Canada.

(2) Every citizen of Canada and every person who has the status of a permanent resident of Canada has the right

(*a*) to move to and take up residence in any province; and

(*b*) to pursue the gaining of a livelihood in any province.

(3) The rights specified in subsection (2) are subject to

(*a*) any laws or practices of general application in force in a province other than those that discriminate among persons primarily on the basis of province of present or previous residence; and

(*b*) any laws providing for reasonable residency requirements as a qualification for the receipt of publicly provided social services.

Legal Rights

7 Everyone has the right to life, liberty and security of the person and the right not to be deprived thereof except in accordance with the principles of fundamental justice.

8 Everyone has the right to be secure against unreasonable search or seizure.

9 Everyone has the right not to be arbitrarily detained or imprisoned.

10 Everyone has the right on arrest or detention

(*a*) to be informed promptly of the reasons therefor;

(*b*) to retain and instruct counsel without delay and to be informed of that right; and

(*c*) to have the validity of the detention determined by way of *habeas corpus* and to be released if the detention is not lawful.

11 Any person charged with an offence has the right

(*a*) to be informed without unreasonable delay of the specific offence;

(*b*) to be tried within a reasonable time;

(*c*) not to be compelled to be a witness in proceedings against that person in respect of the offence;

(*d*) to be presumed innocent until proven guilty according to law in a fair and public hearing by an independent and impartial tribunal;

(*e*) not to be denied reasonable bail without just cause;

(*f*) except in the case of an offence under military law tried before a military tribunal, to the benefit of trial by jury where the maximum punishment for the offence is imprisonment for five years or a more severe punishment;

(*g*) not to be found guilty on account of any act or omission unless, at the time of the act or omission, it constituted an offence under Canadian or international law or was criminal according to the general principles of law recognized by the community of nations;

(*h*) if finally acquitted of the offence, not to be tried for it again and, if finally found guilty and punished for the offence, not to be tried or punished for it again; and

(*i*) if found guilty of the offence and if the punishment for the offence has been varied between the time of commission and the time of sentencing, to the benefit of the lesser punishment.

12 Everyone has the right not to be subjected to any cruel and unusual treatment or punishment. Treatment or punishment

13 A witness who testifies in any proceedings has the right not to have any incriminating evidence so given used to incriminate that witness in any other proceedings, except in a prosecution for perjury or for the giving of contradictory evidence. Self-crimination

14 A party or witness in any proceedings who does not understand or speak the language in which the proceedings are conducted or who is deaf has the right to the assistance of an interpreter. Interpreter

Equality Rights

15(1) Every individual is equal before and under the law and has the right to the equal protection and equal benefit of the law without discrimination and, in particular, without discrimination based on race, national or ethnic origin, colour, religion, sex, age or mental or physical disability. Equality before and under law and equal protection and benefit of law

(2) Subsection (1) does not preclude any law, program or activity that has as its object the amelioration of conditions of disadvantaged individuals or groups including those that are disadvantaged because of race, national or ethnic origin, colour, religion, sex, age or mental or physical disability. Affirmative action programs

Official Languages of Canada

16(1) English and French are the official languages of Canada and have equality of status and equal rights and privileges as to their use in all institutions of the Parliament and government of Canada. Official languages of Canada

(2) English and French are the official languages of New Brunswick and have equality of status and equal rights and privileges as to their use in all institutions of the legislature and government of New Brunswick. Official languages of New Brunswick

(3) Nothing in this Charter limits the authority of Parliament or a legislature to advance the equality of status or use of English and French. Advancement of status and use

17(1) Everyone has the right to use English or French in any debates and other proceedings of Parliament. Proceedings of Parliament

153 Consolidated resolution

(2) Everyone has the right to use English or French in any debates and other proceedings of the legislature of New Brunswick.

Proceedings of New Brunswick legislature

18(1) The statutes, records and journals of Parliament shall be printed and published in English and French and both language versions are equally authoritative.

Parliamentary statutes and records

(2) The statutes, records and journals of the legislature of New Brunswick shall be printed and published in English and French and both language versions are equally authoritative.

New Brunswick statutes and records

19(1) Either English or French may be used by any person in, or in any pleading in or process issuing from, any court established by Parliament.

Proceedings in courts established by Parliament

(2) Either English or French may be used by any person in, or in any pleading in or process issuing from, any court of New Brunswick.

Proceedings in New Brunswick courts

20(1) Any member of the public in Canada has the right to communicate with, and to receive available services from, any head or central office of an institution of the Parliament or government of Canada in English or French, and has the same right with respect to any other office of any such institution where

Communications by public with federal institutions

(a) there is a significant demand for communications with and services from that office in such language; or

(b) due to the nature of the office, it is reasonable that communications with and services from that office be available in both English and French.

(2) Any member of the public in New Brunswick has the right to communicate with, and to receive available services from, any office of an institution of the legislature or government of New Brunswick in English or French.

Communications by public with New Brunswick institutions

21 Nothing in sections 16 to 20 abrogates or derogates from any right, privilege or obligation with respect to the English and French languages, or either of them, that exists or is continued by virtue of any other provision of the Constitution of Canada.

Continuation of existing constitutional provisions

22 Nothing in sections 16 to 20 abrogates or derogates from any legal or customary right or privilege acquired or enjoyed either before or after the coming into force of this Charter with respect to any language that is not English or French.

Rights and privileges preserved

Minority Language Educational Rights
23(1) Citizens of Canada

(a) whose first language learned and still understood is that of the English or French linguistic minority population of the province in which they reside, or

Language of instruction

(b) who have received their primary school instruction in Canada in English or French and reside in a province where the language in which they received that instruction is the language of the English or French linguistic minority population of the province,

have the right to have their children receive primary and secondary school instruction in that language in that province.

(2) Citizens of Canada of whom any child has received or is receiving primary or secondary school instruction in English or French in Canada, have the right to have all their children receive primary and secondary school instruction in the same language. *Continuity of language instruction*

(3) The right of citizens of Canada under subsections (1) and (2) to have their children receive primary and secondary school instruction in the language of the English or French linguistic minority population of a province *Application where numbers warrant*

(a) applies wherever in the province the number of children of citizens who have such a right is sufficient to warrant the provision to them out of public funds of minority language instruction; and

(b) includes, where the number of those children so warrants, the right to have them receive that instruction in minority language educational facilities provided out of public funds.

Enforcement

24(1) Anyone whose rights or freedoms, as guaranteed by this Charter, have been infringed or denied may apply to a court of competent jurisdiction to obtain such remedy as the court considers appropriate and just in the circumstances. *Enforcement of guaranteed rights and freedoms*

(2) Where, in proceedings under subsection (1), a court concludes that evidence was obtained in a manner that infringed or denied any rights or freedoms guaranteed by this Charter, the evidence shall be excluded if it is established that, having regard to all the circumstances, the admission of it in the proceedings would bring the administration of justice into disrepute. *Exclusion of evidence bringing administration of justice into disrepute*

General

25 The guarantee in this Charter of certain rights and freedoms shall not be construed so as to abrogate or derogate from any aboriginal, treaty or other rights or freedoms that pertain to the aboriginal peoples of Canada including *Aboriginal rights and freedoms not affected by Charter*

(a) any rights or freedoms that have been recognized by the Royal Proclamation of October 7, 1763; and

(b) any rights or freedoms that may be acquired by the aboriginal peoples of Canada by way of land claims settlement.

26 The guarantee in this Charter of certain rights and freedoms shall not be construed as denying the existence of any other rights or freedoms that exist in Canada. *Other rights and freedoms not affected by Charter*

27 This Charter shall be interpreted in a manner consistent with the preservation and enhancement of the multicultural heritage of Canadians. *Multicultural heritage*

28 Notwithstanding anything in this Charter, the rights and freedoms referred to in it are guaranteed equally to male and female persons. *Rights guaranteed equally to both sexes*

29 Nothing in this Charter abrogates or derogates from any rights or privileges guaranteed by or under the Constitution of Canada in respect of denominational, separate or dissentient schools. *Rights respecting certain schools preserved*

155 Consolidated resolution

30 A reference in this Charter to a province or to the legislative assembly or legislature of a province shall be deemed to include a reference to the Yukon Territory and the Northwest Territories, or to the appropriate legislative authority thereof, as the case may be.

Application to territories and territorial authorities

31 Nothing in this Charter extends the legislative powers of any body or authority.

Legislative powers not extended

Application of Charter
32(1) This Charter applies
(*a*) to the Parliament and government of Canada and to all matters within the authority of Parliament including all matters relating to the Yukon Territory and Northwest Territories; and
(*b*) to the legislature and government of each province and to all matters within the authority of the legislature of each province.

Application of Charter

(2) Notwithstanding subsection (1), section 15 shall not have effect until three years after this Act, except Part VI, comes into force.

Exception

Citation
33 This Part may be cited as the *Canadian Charter of Rights and Freedoms*.

Citation

PART II RIGHTS OF THE ABORIGINAL PEOPLES OF CANADA

34(1) The aboriginal and treaty rights of the aboriginal peoples of Canada are hereby recognized and affirmed.

Recognition of aboriginal and treaty rights

(2) In this Act, 'aboriginal peoples of Canada' includes the Indian, Inuit and Métis peoples of Canada.

Definition of 'aboriginal peoples of Canada'

PART III EQUALIZATION AND REGIONAL DISPARITIES

35(1) Without altering the legislative authority of Parliament or of the provincial legislatures, or the rights of any of them with respect to the exercise of their legislative authority, Parliament and the legislatures, together with the government of Canada and the provincial governments, are committed to
(*a*) promoting equal opportunities for the well-being of Canadians;
(*b*) furthering economic development to reduce disparity in opportunities; and
(*c*) providing essential public services of reasonable quality to all Canadians.

Commitment to promote equal opportunities

(2) Parliament and the government of Canada are committed to the principle of making equalization payments to ensure that provincial governments have sufficient revenues to provide reasonably comparable levels of public services at reasonably comparable levels of taxation.

Commitment respecting public services

PART IV CONSTITUTIONAL CONFERENCES

36(1) Until Part VI comes into force, a constitutional conference composed of the Prime Minister of Canada and the first ministers of the

Constitutional conferences

provینces shall be convened by the Prime Minister of Canada at least once in every year.

(2) A conference convened under subsection (1) shall have included in its agenda an item respecting constitutional matters that directly affect the aboriginal peoples of Canada, including the identification and definition of the rights of those peoples to be included in the Constitution of Canada, and the Prime Minister of Canada shall invite representatives of those peoples to participate in the discussions on that item. *Participation of aboriginal peoples*

(3) The Prime Minister of Canada shall invite elected representatives of the governments of the Yukon Territory and the Northwest Territories to participate in the discussions on any item on the agenda of a conference convened under subsection (1) that, in the opinion of the Prime Minister, directly affects the Yukon Territory and the Northwest Territories. *Participation of territories*

PART V INTERIM AMENDMENT PROCEDURE AND
RULES FOR ITS REPLACEMENT

37 Until Part VI comes into force, an amendment to the Constitution of Canada may be made by proclamation issued by the Governor General under the Great Seal of Canada where so authorized by resolutions of the Senate and House of Commons and by the legislative assembly or government of each province. *Interim procedure for amending Constitution of Canada*

38 Until Part VI comes into force, an amendment to the Constitution of Canada in relation to any provision that applies to one or more, but not all, provinces may be made by proclamation issued by the Governor General under the Great Seal of Canada where so authorized by resolutions of the Senate and House of Commons and by the legislative assembly or government of each province to which the amendment applies. *Amendment of provisions relating to some but not all provinces*

39(1) Notwithstanding section 41, an amendment to the Constitution of Canada *Amendments respecting certain language rights*

(a) adding a province as a province named in subsection 16(2), 17(2), 18(2), 19(2) or 20(2), or

(b) otherwise providing for any or all of the rights guaranteed or obligations imposed by any of those subsections to have application in a province to the extent and under the conditions stated in the amendment, may be made by proclamation issued by the Governor General under the Great Seal of Canada where so authorized by resolutions of the Senate and House of Commons and the legislative assembly of the province to which the amendment applies.

(2) The procedure for amendment prescribed by subsection (1) may be initiated only by the legislative assembly of the province to which the amendment applies. *Initiation of amendment procedure*

40(1) The procedures for amendment prescribed by sections 37 and 38 may be initiated either by the Senate or House of Commons or by the legislative assembly or government of a province. *Initiation of amendment procedures*

(2) A resolution made or other authorization given for the purposes *Revocation of authorization*

of this Part may be revoked at any time before the issue of a proclamation authorized by it.

41 Sections 37 and 38 do not apply to an amendment to the Constitution of Canada where there is another provision in the Constitution for making the amendment, but the procedure prescribed by section 37 shall be used to amend the *Canadian Charter of Rights and Freedoms* and any provision for amending the Constitution, including this section.

Limitation on use of interim amendment procedure

42 Part VI shall come into force

Coming into force of Part VI

(*a*) with or without amendment, on such day as may be fixed by proclamation issued pursuant to the procedure prescribed by section 37, or

(*b*) on the day that is two years after the day this Act, except Part VI, comes into force,

whichever is the earlier day but, if a referendum is required to be held under subsection 43(3), Part VI shall come into force as provided in section 44.

43(1) The legislative assemblies of seven or more provinces that have, according to the then latest general census, combined populations of at least eighty per cent of the population of all the provinces may make a single proposal to substitute for paragraph 46(1)(*b*) such alternative as they consider appropriate.

Provincial alternative procedure

(2) One copy of an alternative proposed under subsection (1) may be deposited with the Chief Electoral Officer of Canada by each proposing province within two years after this Act, except Part VI, comes into force but, prior to the expiration of that period, any province that has deposited a copy may withdraw that copy.

Procedure for perfecting alternative

(3) Where copies of an alternative have been deposited as provided by subsection (2) and, on the day that is two years after this Act, except Part VI, comes into force, at least seven copies remain deposited by provinces that have, according to the then latest general census, combined populations of at least eighty per cent of the population of all the provinces, the government of Canada shall cause a referendum to be held within two years after that day to determine whether

Referendum

(*a*) paragraph 46(1)(*b*) or any alternative thereto approved by resolutions of the Senate and House of Commons and deposited with the Chief Electoral Officer at least ninety days prior to the day on which the referendum is held, or

(*b*) the alternative proposed by the provinces,

shall be adopted.

44 Where a referendum is held under subsection 43(3), a proclamation under the Great Seal of Canada shall be issued within six months after the date of the referendum bringing Part VI into force with such modifications, if any, as are necessary to incorporate the proposal approved by a majority of the persons voting at the referendum and with such other changes as are reasonably consequential on the incorporation of that proposal.

Coming into force of Part VI where referendum held

45(1) Every citizen of Canada has, subject only to such reasonable limits prescribed by law as can be demonstrably justified in a free and democratic society, the right to vote in a referendum held under subsection 43(3).

Right to vote

(2) If a referendum is required to be held under subsection 43(3), a Referendum Rules Commission shall forthwith be established by commission issued under the Great Seal of Canada consisting of

(a) the Chief Electoral Officer of Canada, who shall be chairman of the Commission;

(b) a person appointed by the Governor General in Council; and

(c) a person appointed by the Governor General in Council

(i) on the recommendation of the governments of a majority of the provinces, or

(ii) if the governments of a majority of the provinces do not recommend a candidate within thirty days after the Chief Electoral Officer of Canada requests such a recommendation, on the recommendation of the Chief Justice of Canada from among persons recommended by the governments of the provinces within thirty days after the expiration of the first mentioned thirty day period or, if none are so recommended, from among such persons as the Chief Justice considers qualified.

Establishment of Referendum Rules Commission

(3) A Referendum Rules Commission shall cause rules for the holding of a referendum under subsection 43(3) approved by a majority of the Commission to be laid before Parliament within sixty days after the Commission is established or, if Parliament is not then sitting, on any of the first ten days next thereafter that Parliament is sitting.

Duty of Commission

(4) Subject to subsection (1) and taking into consideration any rules approved by a Referendum Rules Commission in accordance with subsection (3), Parliament may enact laws respecting the rules applicable to the holding of a referendum under subsection 43(3).

Rules for referendum

(5) If Parliament does not enact laws under subsection (4) respecting the rules applicable to the holding of a referendum within sixty days after receipt of a recommendation from a Referendum Rules Commission, the rules recommended by the Commission shall forthwith be brought into force by proclamation issued by the Governor General under the Great Seal of Canada.

Proclamation

(6) Any period when Parliament is prorogued or dissolved shall not be counted in computing the sixty day period referred to in subsection (5).

Computation of period

(7) Subject to subsection (1), rules made under this section have the force of law and prevail over other laws made under the Constitution of Canada to the extent of any inconsistency.

Rules to have force of law

PART VI PROCEDURE FOR AMENDING CONSTITUTION OF CANADA

46(1) An amendment to the Constitution of Canada may be made by proclamation issued by the Governor General under the Great Seal of Canada where so authorized by

(a) resolutions of the Senate and House of Commons; and

(b) resolutions of the legislative assemblies of at least a majority of the provinces that includes

General procedure for amending Constitution of Canada

(i) every province that at any time before the issue of the proclamation had, according to any previous general census, a population of at least twenty-five per cent of the population of Canada,

(ii) two or more of the Atlantic provinces, and

(iii) two or more of the Western provinces.

(2) In this section,

'Atlantic provinces' means the provinces of Nova Scotia, New Brunswick, Prince Edward Island and Newfoundland;

'Western provinces' means the provinces of Manitoba, British Columbia, Saskatchewan and Alberta.

Definitions
'Atlantic provinces'

'Western provinces'

47(1) An amendment to the Constitution of Canada may be made by proclamation issued by the Governor General under the Great Seal of Canada where so authorized by a referendum held throughout Canada under subsection (2) at which

(a) a majority of persons voting thereat, and

(b) a majority of persons voting thereat in each of the provinces, resolutions of the legislative assemblies of which would be sufficient, together with resolutions of the Senate and House of Commons, to authorize the issue of a proclamation under subsection 46(1),

have approved the making of the amendment.

Amendment authorized by referendum

(2) A referendum referred to in subsection (1) shall be held where directed by proclamation issued by the Governor General under the Great Seal of Canada, which proclamation may be issued where

(a) an amendment to the Constitution of Canada has been authorized under paragraph 46(1)(a) by resolutions of the Senate and House of Commons;

(b) the requirements of paragraph 46(1)(b) in respect of the proposed amendment have not been satisfied within twelve months after the passage of the resolutions of the Senate and House of Commons; and

(c) the issue of the proclamation has been authorized by the Governor General in Council.

Authorization of referendum

(3) A proclamation issued under subsection (2) in respect of a referendum shall provide for the referendum to be held within two years after the expiration of the twelve month period referred to in paragraph (b) of that subsection.

Time limit for referendum

48 An amendment to the Constitution of Canada in relation to any provision that applies to one or more, but not all, provinces may be made by proclamation issued by the Governor General under the Great Seal of Canada where so authorized by resolutions of the Senate and House of Commons and of the legislative assembly of each province to which the amendment applies.

Amendment of provisions relating to some but not all provinces

49(1) Notwithstanding section 55, an amendment to the Constitution of Canada

(a) adding a province as a province named in subsection 16(2), 17(2), 18(2), 19(2) or 20(2), or

(b) otherwise providing for any or all of the rights guaranteed or obligations imposed by any of those subsections to have application in a province to the extent and under the conditions stated in the amendment,

Amendments respecting certain language rights

may be made by proclamation issued by the Governor General under the Great Seal of Canada where so authorized by resolutions of the Senate and House of Commons and the legislative assembly of the province to which the amendment applies.

(2) The procedure for amendment prescribed by subsection (1) may be initiated only by the legislative asembly of the province to which the amendment applies. *Initiation of amendment procedure*

50(1) The procedures for amendment prescribed by subsection 46(1) and section 48 may be initiated either by the Senate or House of Commons or by the legislative assembly of a province. *Initiation of amendment procedures*

(2) A resolution made for the purposes of this Part may be revoked at any time before the issue of a proclamation authorized by it. *Revocation of authorization*

51(1) Every citizen of Canada has, subject only to such reasonable limits prescribed by law as can be demonstrably justified in a free and democratic society, the right to vote in a referendum held under section 47. *Right to vote*

(2) Where a referendum is to be held under section 47, a Referendum Rules Commission shall forthwith be established by commission issued under the Great Seal of Canada consisting of *Establishment of Referendum Rules Commission*

(a) the Chief Electoral Officer of Canada, who shall be chairman of the Commission;

(b) a person appointed by the Governor General in Council; and

(c) a person appointed by the Governor General in Council

(i) on the recommendation of the governments of a majority of the provinces, or

(ii) if the governments of a majority of the provinces do not recommend a candidate within thirty days after the Chief Electoral Officer of Canada requests such a recommendation, on the recommendation of the Chief Justice of Canada from among persons recommended by the governments of the provinces within thirty days after the expiration of the first mentioned thirty day period or, if none are so recommended, from among such persons as the Chief Justice considers qualified.

(3) A Referendum Rules Commission shall cause rules for the holding of a referendum under section 47 approved by a majority of the Commission to be laid before Parliament within sixty days after the Commission is established or, if Parliament is not then sitting, on any of the first ten days next thereafter that Parliament is sitting. *Duty of Commission*

(4) Subject to subsection (1) and taking into consideration any rules approved by a Referendum Rules Commission in accordance with subsection (3), Parliament may enact laws respecting the rules applicable to the holding of a referendum under section 47. *Rules for referendum*

(5) If Parliament does not enact laws under subsection (4) respecting the rules applicable to the holding of a referendum within sixty days after receipt of a recommendation from a Referendum Rules Commission, the rules recommended by the Commission shall forthwith be brought into force by proclamation issued by the Governor General under the Great Seal of Canada. *Proclamation*

161 Consolidated resolution

(6) Any period when Parliament is prorogued or dissolved shall not be counted in computing the sixty day period referred to in subsection (5). Computation of period

(7) Subject to subsection (1), rules made under this section have the force of law and prevail over other laws made under the Constitution of Canada to the extent of any inconsistency. Rules to have force of law

52(1) The procedures prescribed by section 46, 47 or 48 do not apply to an amendment to the Constitution of Canada where there is another provision in the Constitution for making the amendment, but the procedures prescribed by section 46 or 47 shall, nevertheless, be used to amend any provision for amending the Constitution, including this section. Limitation on use of general amendment procedure

(2) The procedures prescribed by section 46 or 47 do not apply in respect of an amendment referred to in section 48. Idem

53 Subject to section 55, Parliament may exclusively make laws amending the Constitution of Canada in relation to the executive government of Canada or the Senate or House of Commons. Amendments by Parliament

54 Subject to section 55, the legislature of each province may exclusively make laws amending the constitution of the province. Amendments by provincial legislatures

55 An amendment to the Constitution of Canada in relation to the following matters may be made only in accordance with a procedure prescribed by section 46 or 47: Matters requiring amendment under general amendment procedure

(*a*) the office of the Queen, the Governor General and the Lieutenant Governor of a province;

(*b*) the *Canadian Charter of Rights and Freedoms*;

(*c*) the rights of the aboriginal peoples of Canada set out in Part II;

(*d*) the commitments relating to equalization and regional disparities set out in section 35;

(*e*) the powers of the Senate;

(*f*) the number of members by which a province is entitled to be represented in the Senate;

(*g*) the method of selecting Senators and the residence qualifications of Senators;

(*h*) the right of a province to a number of members in the House of Commons not less than the number of Senators representing the province; and

(*i*) the principles of proportionate representation of the provinces in the House of Commons prescribed by the Constitution of Canada.

56(1) Class 1 of section 91 and class 1 of section 92 of the *Constitution Act, 1867* (formerly named the *British North America Act, 1867*), the *British North America (No. 2) Act, 1949*, referred to in item 22 of Schedule I to this Act and Parts IV and V of this Act are repealed. Consequential amendments

(2) When Parts IV and V of this Act are repealed, this section may be repealed and this Act may be renumbered, consequential upon the repeal of those Parts and this section, by proclamation issued by the Governor General under the Great Seal of Canada. Idem

PART VII AMENDMENT TO THE CONSTITUTION ACT, 1867

57 The *Constitution Act, 1867* (formerly named the *British North America Act, 1867*) is amended by adding thereto, immediately after section 92 thereof, the following heading and section:

Amendment to *Constitution Act, 1867*

'Non-Renewable Natural Resources, Forestry Resources and Electrical Energy
92A(1) In each province, the legislature may exclusively make laws in relation to
(*a*) exploration for non-renewable natural resources in the province;
(*b*) development, conservation and management of non-renewable natural resources and forestry resources in the province, including laws in relation to the rate of primary production therefrom; and
(*c*) development, conservation and management of sites and facilities in the province for the generation and production of electrical energy.

Laws respecting non-renewable natural resources, forestry resources and electrical energy

(2) In each province, the legislature may make laws in relation to the export from the province to another part of Canada of the primary production from non-renewable natural resources and forestry resources in the province and the production from facilities in the province for the generation of electrical energy, but such laws may not authorize or provide for discrimination in prices or in supplies exported to another part of Canada.

Export from provinces of resources

(3) Nothing in subsection (2) derogates from the authority of Parliament to enact laws in relation to the matters referred to in that subsection and, where such a law of Parliament and a law of a province conflict, the law of Parliament prevails to the extent of the conflict.

Authority of Parliament

(4) In each province, the legislature may make laws in relation to the raising of money by any mode or system of taxation in respect of
(*a*) non-renewable natural resources and forestry resources in the province and the primary production therefrom, and
(*b*) sites and facilities in the province for the generation of electrical energy and the production therefrom,
whether or not such production is exported in whole or in part from the province, but such laws may not authorize or provide for taxation that differentiates between production exported to another part of Canada and production not exported from the province.

Taxation of resources

(5) The expression "primary production" has the meaning assigned by the Sixth Schedule.

'Primary production'

(6) Nothing in subsections (1) to (5) derogates from any powers or rights that a legislature or government of a province had immediately before the coming into force of this section.'

Existing powers or rights

58 The said Act is further amended by adding thereto the following Schedule:

Idem

'THE SIXTH SCHEDULE

Primary Production from Non-Renewable Natural Resources and Forestry Resources

163 Consolidated resolution

1 For the purposes of section 92A of this Act,
(*a*) production from a non-renewable natural resource is primary production therefrom if
    (i) it is in the form in which it exists upon its recovery or severance
    from its natural state, or
    (ii) it is a product resulting from processing or refining the resource,
    and is not a manufactured product or a product resulting from
    refining crude oil, refining upgraded heavy crude oil, refining gases
    or liquids derived from coal or refining a synthetic equivalent of
    crude oil; and
(*b*) production from a forestry resource is primary production therefrom if it consists of sawlogs, poles, lumber, wood chips, sawdust or
any other primary wood product, or wood pulp, and is not a product
manufactured from wood.'

PART VIII GENERAL

59(1) The Constitution of Canada is the supreme law of Canada, and any law that is inconsistent with the provisions of the Constitution is, to the extent of the inconsistency, of no force or effect. *[Primacy of Constitution of Canada]*

(2) The Constitution of Canada includes *[Constitution of Canada]*
(*a*) the *Canada Act*;
(*b*) the Acts and orders referred to in Schedule I; and
(*c*) any amendment to any Act or order referred to in paragraph (*a*) or (*b*).

(3) Amendments to the Constitution of Canada shall be made only in accordance with the authority contained in the Constitution of Canada. *[Amendments to Constitution of Canada]*

60(1) The enactments referred to in Column I of Schedule I are hereby repealed or amended to the extent indicated in Column II thereof and, unless repealed, shall continue as law in Canada under the names set out in Column III thereof. *[Repeals and new names]*

(2) Every enactment, except the *Canada Act*, that refers to an enactment referred to in Schedule I by the name of Column I thereof is hereby amended by substituting for that name the corresponding name in Column III thereof, and any British North America Act not referred to in Schedule I may be cited as the *Constitution Act* followed by the year and number, if any, of its enactment. *[Consequential amendments]*

61 A French version of the portions of the Constitution of Canada referred to in Schedule I shall be prepared by the Minister of Justice of Canada as expeditiously as possible and, when any portion thereof sufficient to warrant action being taken has been so prepared, it shall be put forward for enactment by proclamation issued by the Governor General under the Great Seal of Canada pursuant to the procedure then applicable to an amendment of the same provisions of the Constitution of Canada. *[French version of Constitution of Canada]*

62 Where any portion of the Constitution of Canada has been or is enacted in English and French or where a French version of any portion of the Constitution is enacted pursuant to section 61, the English *[English and French versions of certain constitutional texts]*

and French versions of that portion of the Constitution are equally authoritative.

63 The English and French versions of this Act are equally authoritative.

English and French versions of this Act

64 Subject to section 65, this Act shall come into force on a day to be fixed by proclamation issued by the Governor General under the Great Seal of Canada.

Commencement

65 Part VI shall come into force as provided in Part V.

Exception

66 This Schedule may be cited as the *Constitution Act, 1981*, and the Constitution Acts 1867 to 1975 (No. 2) and this Act may be cited together as the *Constitution Acts, 1867 to 1981*.

Short title and citations

[Schedule I to the Constitution Act, 1981, Modernisation of the Constitution, is omitted.]

Accord of
5 November 1981

Text of constitutional agreement between Prime Minister Trudeau and the nine (anglophone) premiers (Ottawa), 5 November 1981:

In an effort to reach an acceptable consensus on the constitutional issue which meets the concerns of the federal government and a substantial number of provincial governments, the undersigned governments have agreed to the following:

(1) Patriation

(2) Amending Formula:
- Acceptance of the April Accord Amending Formula with the deletion of Section 3 which provides for fiscal compensation to a province which opts out of a constitutional amendment.
- The Delegation of Legislative Authority from the April Accord is deleted.

(3) Charter of Rights and Freedoms:
- The entrenchment of the full Charter of Rights and Freedoms now before Parliament with the following changes:
    (a) With respect to Mobility Rights the inclusion of the right of a province to undertake affirmative action programs for socially and economically disadvantaged individuals as long as a province's employment rate was below the National average.
    (b) A 'notwithstanding' clause covering sections dealing with Fundamental Freedoms, Legal Rights and Equality Rights. Each 'notwithstanding' provision would require reenactment not less frequently than once every five years.
    (c) We have agreed that the provisions of Section 23 in respect of Minority Language Education Rights will apply to our provinces.

(4) The provisions of the Act now before Parliament relating to Equalization and Regional Disparities, and Non Renewable Natural Resources, Forestry Resources and Electrical Energy would be included.

(5) A constitutional conference as provided for in clause 36 of the Resolution, including in its agenda an item respecting constitutional matters that directly affect

the Aboriginal peoples of Canada, including the identification and definition of the rights of those peoples to be included in the Constitution of Canada, shall be provided for in the Resolution. The Prime Minister of Canada shall invite representatives of the Aboriginal peoples of Canada to participate in the discussion of that item.

FACT SHEET THE NOTWITHSTANDING OR OVERRIDE CLAUSE
AS APPLIED TO THE CHARTER OF RIGHTS & FREEDOMS

A notwithstanding clause is one which enables a legislative body (federal and provincial) to enact expressly that a particular provision of an Act will be valid, notwithstanding the fact that it conflicts with a specific provision of the Charter of Rights and Freedoms. The notwithstanding principle has been recognized and is contained in a number of bills of rights, including the Canadian Bill of Rights (1960), the Alberta Bill of Rights (1972), The Quebec Charter of Rights and Freedoms (1975), the Saskatchewan Human Rights Code (1979), and Ontario's Bill 7 to Amend its Human Rights Code (1981).

How it would be applied
Any enactment overriding any specific provisions of the Charter would contain a clause expressly declaring that a specific provision of the proposed enactment shall operate, notwithstanding a specific provision of the Charter of Rights and Freedoms.

Any notwithstanding enactment would have to be reviewed and renewed every five years by the enacting legislature if it were to remain in force.

Amended resolution (extracts)

Patriation resolution, amended version (18 November 1981): new or amended sections only

Mobility Rights
6(1) Every citizen of Canada has the right to enter, remain in and leave Canada.

(2) Every citizen of Canada and every person who has the status of a permanent resident of Canada has the right;
(*a*) to move to and take up residence in any province; and
(*b*) to pursue the gaining of a livelihood in any province.

(3) The rights specified in subsection (2) are subject to
(*a*) any laws or practices of general application in force in a province other than those that discriminate among persons primarily on the basis of province of present of previous residence; and
(*b*) any laws providing for reasonable residency requirements as a qualification for the receipt of publicly provided social services.

(4) Subsections (2) and (3) do not preclude any law, program or activity that has as its object the amelioration in a province of conditions of individuals in that province who are socially or economically disadvantaged if the rate of employment in that province is below the rate of employment in Canada.

General
25 The guarantee in this charter of certain rights and freedoms shall not be construed so as to abrogate or derogate from any aboriginal rights or freedoms that pertain to the aboriginal peoples of Canada, including
(*a*) any rights or freedoms that have been recognized by the Royal Proclamation of October 7, 1763; and
(*b*) any rights or freedoms that may be acquired by the aboriginal peoples of Canada by way of land claims settlement.

...

28 Notwithstanding anything in this charter, except Section 33, the rights and freedoms referred to in it are guaranteed equally to male and female persons.

Application of Charter
32(1) This charter applies
(*a*) to the Parliament and Government of Canada in respect of all matters within the authority of Parliament including all matters relating to the Yukon Territory and the Northwest Territories; and
(*b*) to the Legislature and Government of each province in respect of all matters within the authority of the Legislature of each province.
(2) Notwithstanding subsection (1), Section 15 shall not come into effect until three years after this section comes into force.
33(1) Parliament or the Legislature of a province may expressly declare in an Act of Parliament or of the Legislature, as the case may be, that the act or a provision thereof shall operate notwithstanding a provision included in Section 2 or Sections 7 to 15 of this charter, or Section 28 of this charter in its application to discrimination based on sex referred to in Section 15.
(2) An act or a provision of an act in respect of which a declaration made under this section is in effect shall have such operation as it would have but for the provision of this charter referred to in the declaration.
(3) A declaration made under sub-section (1) shall cease to have effect five years after it comes into force or on such earlier date as may be specified in the declaration.
(4) Parliament or the Legislature of a province may re-enact a declaration made under subsection (1).
(5) Subsection (3) applies in respect of a re-enactment made under subsection (4).

Citation
34 This part may be cited as the Canadian Charter of Rights and Freedoms.

PART III CONSTITUTIONAL CONFERENCE

36(1) A constitutional conference composed of the Prime Minister of Canada and the first ministers of the provinces shall be convened by the Prime Minister of Canada within one year after this Part comes into force.
(2) The conference convened under subsection (1) shall have included in its agenda an item respecting constitutional matters that directly affect the aboriginal peoples of Canada, including the identification and definition of the rights of those peoples to be included in the Constitution of Canada, and the Prime Minister of Canada shall invite representatives of those peoples to participate in the discussions on that item.
(3) The Prime Minister of Canada shall invite elected representatives of the Governments of the Yukon Territory and the Northwest Territories to participate in the discussions on any item on the agenda of the conference convened under subsection (1) that, in the opinion of the Prime Minister, directly affects the Yukon Territory and the Northwest Territories.

PART IV PROCEDURE FOR AMENDING CONSTITUTION

37(1) An amendment to the Constitution of Canada may be made by proclamation issued by the Governor-General under the Great Seal of Canada where so authorized by

169 Amended resolution

(*a*) resolutions of the Senate and House of Commons; and
(*b* resolutions of the legislative assemblies of at least two-thirds of the provinces that have, in the aggregate, according to the then latest general census, at least fifty per cent of the population of all the provinces.

(2) An amendment made under subsection (1) that derogates from the legislative powers, the proprietary rights or any other rights or privileges of the Legislature or Government of a province shall require a resolution supported by a majority of the members of each of the Senate, the House of Commons and the legislative assemblies required under subsection (1).

(3) An amendment referred to in subsection (2) shall not have effect in a province the legislative assembly of which has expressed its dissent thereto by resolution supported by a majority of its members prior to the issue of the proclamation to which the amendment relates unless that legislative assembly, subsequently, by resolution supported by a majority of its members, revokes its dissent and authorizes the amendment.

(4) A resolution of dissent made for the purposes of subsection (3) may be revoked at any time before or after the issue of the proclamation to which it relates.

38(1) A proclamation shall not be issued under subsection 37(1) before the expiration of one year from the adoption of the resolution initiating the amendment procedure thereunder, unless the legislative assembly of each province has previously adopted a resolution of assent or dissent.

(2) A proclamation shall not be issued under subsection 37(1) after the expiration of three years from the adoption of the resolution initiating the amendment procedure thereunder.

39 Where an amendment is made under subsection 37(1) that transfers provincial legislative powers relating to education or other cultural matters from provincial Legislatures to Parliament, Canada shall provide reasonable compensation to any province to which the amendment does not apply.

40 An amendment to the Constitution of Canada in relation to the following matters may be made by proclamation issued by the Governor-General under the Great Seal of Canada only where authorized by resolutions of the Senate and House of Commons and of the legislative assembly of each province:
(*a*) the office of the Queen, the Governor-General and the Lieutenant-Governor of a province;
(*b*) the right of a province to a number of members in the House of Commons not less than the number of Senators by which the province is entitled to be represented at the time this part comes into force;
(*c*) subject to Section 42, the use of the English or the French language;
(*d*) the composition of the Supreme Court of Canada; and
(*e*) an amendment to this Part.

41(1) An amendment to the Constitution of Canada in relation to the following matters may be made only in accordance with subsection 37(1):
(*a*) the principle of proportionate representation of the provinces in the House of Commons prescribed by the Constitution of Canada;
(*b*) the powers of the Senate and the method of selecting Senators;
(*c*) the number of members by which a province is entitled to be represented in the Senate and the residence qualifications of Senators;
(*d*) subject to paragraph 40(*d*), the Supreme Court of Canada;
(*e*) the extension of existing provinces into the territories; and

(*f*) notwithstanding any other law of practice, the establishment of new provinces.

(2) Subsections 37(2) to (4) do not apply in respect of amendments in relation to matters referred to in subsection (1).

42 An amendment to the Constitution of Canada in relation to any provision that applies to one, or more, but not all, provinces, including

(*a*) any alteration to boundaries between provinces and,

(*b*) any amendment to any provision that relates to the use of the English or the French language within a province,

may be made by proclamation issued by the Governor-General under the Great Seal of Canada only where so authorized by resolutions of the Senate and House of Commons and of the legislative assembly of each province to which the amendment applies.

43 Subject to Sections 40 and 41, Parliament may exclusively make laws amending the Constitution of Canada in relation to the executive Government of Canada or the Senate and House of Commons.

44 Subject to Section 40, the Legislature of each province may exclusively make laws amending the constitution of the province.

45(1) The procedures for amendment under Sections 37, 40, 41 and 42 may be initiated either by the Senate or the House of Commons or by the legislative assembly of a province.

(2) A resolution of assent made for the purposes of this part may be revoked at any time before the issue of a proclamation authorized by it.

46(1) An amendment to the Constitution of Canada made by proclamation under Sections 37, 40, 41 or 42 may be made without a resolution of the Senate authorizing the issue of the proclamation if, within 180 days after the adoption by the House of Commons of a resolution authorizing its issue, the Senate has not adopted such a resolution and if, at any time after the expiration of that period, the House of Commons again adopts the resolution.

(2) Any period when Parliament is prorogued or dissolved shall not be counted in computing the 180-day period referred to in subsection (1).

47 The Queen's Privy Council for Canada shall advise the Governor-General to issue a proclamation under this part forthwith on the adoption of the resolutions required for an amendment made by proclamation under this part.

48 A constitutional conference composed of the Prime Minister of Canada and the first ministers of the provinces shall be convened by the Prime Minister of Canada within 15 years after this part comes into force to review the provisions of this part.

PART V AMENDMENT TO THE CONSTITUTION ACT, 1867

[Sections 49 and 50 involve renumbering of Part VII, setions 57 and 58, of the consolidated resolution]

PART VI GENERAL

[Sections 51 to 59 involve renumbering of Part VIII, sections 59 to 66, of the consolidated resolution: however, section 53 is entirely new, and section 58 replaces the previously bland section 65.]

53 Part III is repealed on the day that is one year after this part comes into force and this section may be repealed and this act renumbered, consequential upon the

repeal of Part III and this section, by proclamation issued by the Governor-General under the Great Seal of Canada.

58(1) Paragraph 23(1)(a) shall come into force in respect of Quebec on a day to be fixed by proclamation issued by the Queen or the Governor-General under the Great Seal of Canada.

(2) A proclamation under subsection (1) shall be issued only where authorized by the Legislative Assembly or Government of Quebec.

(3) This section may be repealed on the day paragraph 23(1)(a) comes into force in respect of Quebec and this act amended and renumbered, consequential upon the repeal of this section, by proclamation issued by the Queen or the Governor-General under the Great Seal of Canada.

Final resolution

Patriation resolution, final version (8 December 1981), [as adopted by Parliament]

THAT, WHEREAS in the past certain amendments to the Constitution of Canada have been made by the Parliament of the United Kingdom at the request and with the consent of Canada;

AND WHEREAS it is in accord with the status of Canada as an independent state that Canadians be able to amend their Constitution in Canada in all respects;

AND WHEREAS it is also desirable to provide in the Constitution of Canada for the recognition of certain fundamental rights and freedoms and to make other amendments to that Constitution;

A respectful address be presented to Her Majesty the Queen in the following words:

To the Queen's Most Excellent Majesty:
Most Gracious Sovereign:

We, Your Majesty's loyal subjects, the House of Commons of Canada in Parliament assembled, respectfully approach Your Majesty, requesting that you may graciously be pleased to cause to be laid before the Parliament of the United Kingdom a measure containing the recitals and clauses hereinafter set forth:

SCHEDULE A [THE CANADA ACT]

An act to give effect to a request by the Senate and House of Commons of Canada
Whereas Canada has requested and consented to the enactment of an act of the Parliament of the United Kingdom to give effect to the provisions hereinafter set forth and the Senate and the House of Commons of Canada in Parliament assembled have submitted an address to Her Majesty requesting that Her Majesty may graciously be pleased to cause a bill to be laid before the Parliament of the United Kingdom for that purpose.

Be it therefore enacted by the Queen's Most Excellent Majesty, by and with the advice and consent of the Lords Spiritual and Temporal, and Commons, in this present Parliament assembled, and by the authority of the same, as follows:

1 The *Constitution Act, 1981*, set out in Schedule B to this act is hereby enacted for and shall have the force of law in Canada and shall come into force as provided in that act.

2 No act of the Parliament of the United Kingdom passed after the *Constitution Act, 1981*, comes into force shall extend to Canada as part of its law.

3 So far as it is not contained in Schedule B, the French version of this act is set out in Schedule A to this act and has the same authority in Canada as the English version thereof.

4 This act may be cited as the Canada Act.

SCHEDULE B
CONSTITUTION ACT, 1981

PART I CANADIAN CHARTER OF RIGHTS AND FREEDOMS

Whereas Canada is founded upon principles that recognize the supremacy of God and the rule of law:

Guarantee of Rights and Freedoms
1 The Canadian Charter of Rights and Freedoms guarantees the rights and freedoms set out in it subject only to such reasonable limits prescribed by law as can be demonstrably justified in a free and democratic society.

Fundamental Freedoms
2 Everyone has the following fundamental freedoms:
(*a*) freedom of conscience and religion;
(*b*) freedom of thought, belief, opinion and expression, including freedom of the press and other media of communication;
(*c*) freedom of peaceful assembly; and
(*d*) freedom of association.

Democratic Rights
3 Every citizen of Canada has the right to vote in an election of members of the House of Commons or of a legislative assembly and to be qualified for membership therein.

4(1) No House of Commons and no legislative assembly shall continue for longer than five years from the date fixed for the return of the writs at a general election of its members.

(2) In time of real or apprehended war, invasion or insurrection, a House of Commons may be continued by Parliament and a legislative assembly may be continued by the Legislature beyond five years if such continuation is not opposed by the votes of more than one-third of the members of the House of Commons or the legislative assembly, as the case may be.

5 There shall be a sitting of Parliament and of each Legislature at least once every 12 months.

Mobility Rights
6(1) Every citizen of Canada has the right to enter, remain in and leave Canada.

(2) Every citizen of Canada and every person who has the status of a permanent resident of Canada has the right
(a) to move to and take up residence in any province; and
(b) to pursue the gaining of a livelihood in any province.

(3) The rights specified in subsection (2) are subject to
(a) any laws or practices of general application in force in a province other than those that discriminate among persons primarily on the basis of province of present or previous residence; and
(b) any laws providing for reasonable residency requirements as a qualification for the receipt of publicly provided social services.

(4) Subsections (2) and (3) do not preclude any law, program or activity that has as its object the amelioration in a province of conditions of individuals in that province who are socially or economically disadvantaged if the rate of employment in that province is below the rate of employment in Canada.

Legal Rights
7 Everyone has the right to life, liberty and security of the person and the right not to be deprived thereof except in accordance with the principles of fundamental justice.

8 Everyone has the right to be secure against unreasonable search or seizure.

9 Everyone has the right not to be arbitrarily detained or imprisoned.

10 Everyone has the right on arrest or detention;
(a) to be informed promptly of the reasons therefor;
(b) to retain and instruct counsel without delay and to be informed of that right; and
(c) to have the validity of the detention determined by way of *habeas corpus* and to be released if the detention is not lawful.

11 Any person charged with an offence has the right:
(a) to be informed without unreasonable delay of the specific offence;
(b) to be tried within a reasonable time;
(c) not to be compelled to be a witness in proceedings against that person in respect of the offence;
(d) to be presumed innocent until proven guilty according to law in a fair and public hearing by an independent and impartial tribunal;
(e) not to be denied reasonable bail without just cause;
(f) except in the case of an offence under military law tried before a military tribunal, to the benefit of trial by jury where the maximum punishment for the offence is imprisonment for five years or a more severe punishment;
(g) not to be found guilty on account of any act or omission unless, at the time of the act or omission, it constituted an offence under Canadian or international law or was criminal acording to the general principles of law recognized by the community of nations;
(h) if finally acquitted of the offence, not to be tried for it again and, if finally found guilty and punished for the offence, not to be tried or punished for it again; and
(i) if found guilty of the offence and if the punishment for the offence has been varied between the time of commission and the time of sentencing, to the benefit of the lesser punishment.

12 Everyone has the right not to be subjected to any cruel and unusual treatment or punishment.

13 A witness who testifies in any proceedings has the right not to have any incriminating evidence so given used to incriminate that witness in any other proceedings, except in a prosecution for perjury or for the giving of contradictory evidence.

14 A party or witness in any proceedings who does not understand or speak the language in which the proceedings are conducted or who is deaf has the right to the assistance of an interpreter.

Equality Rights

15(1) Every individual is equal before and under the law and has the right to the equal protection and equal benefit of the law without discrimination and, in particular, without discrimination based on race, national or ethnic origin, color, religion, sex, age or mental or physical disability.

(2) Subsection (1) does not preclude any law, program or activity that has as its object the amelioration of conditions of disadvantaged individuals or groups including those that are disadvantaged because of race, national or ethnic origin, color, religion, sex, age or mental or physical disability.

Official Languages

16(1) English and French are the official languages of Canada and have equality of status and equal rights and privileges as to their use in all institutions of the Parliament and government of Canada.

(2) English and French are the official languages of New Brunswick and have equality of status and equal rights and privileges as to their use in all institutions of the Legislature and government of New Brunswick.

(3) Nothing in this charter limits the authority of Parliament or a Legislature to advance the equality of status or use of English and French.

17(1) Everyone has the right to use English or French in any debates and other proceedings of Parliament.

(2) Everyone has the right to use English or French in any debates and other proceedings of the Legislature of New Brunswick.

18(1) The statutes, records and journals of Parliament shall be printed and published in English and French and both language versions are equally authoritative.

(2) The statutes, records and journals of the Legislature of New Brunswick shall be printed and published in English and French and both language versions are equally authoritative.

19(1) Either English or French may be used by any person in, or in any pleading in or process issuing from, any court established by Parliament.

(2) Either English or French may be used by any person in, or in any pleading in or process issuing from, any court of New Brunswick.

20(1) Any member of the public in Canada has the right to communicate with, and to receive available services from, any head or central office of an institution of the Parliament or government of Canada in English or French, and has the same right with respect to any other office of any such institution where
(*a*) there is a significant demand for communications with and services from that office in such language; or
(*b*) due to the nature of the office, it is reasonable that communications with and services from that office be available in both English and French.

(2) Any member of the public in New Brunswick has the right to communicate with, and to receive available services from, any office of an institution of the Legislature or government of New Brunswick in English or French.

21 Nothing in sections 16 to 20 abrogates or derogates from any right, privilege or obligation with respect to the English and French languages, or either of them, that exists or is continued by virtue of any other provision of the Constitution of Canada.

22 Nothing in sections 16 to 20 abrogates or derogates from any legal or customary right or privilege acquired or enjoyed either before or after the coming into force of this charter with respect to any language that is not English or French.

Minority Language Educational Rights
23(1) Citizens of Canada
(*a*) whose first language learned and still understood is that of the English or French linguistic minority population of the province in which they reside, or
(*b*) who have received their primary school instruction in Canada in English or French and reside in a province where the language in which they received that instruction is the language of the English or French linguistic minority population of the province,
have the right to have their children receive primary and secondary school instruction in that language in that province.

(2) Citizens of Canada of whom any child has received or is receiving primary or secondary school instruction in English or French in Canada, have the right to have all their children receive primary and secondary school instruction in the same language.

(3) The right of citizens of Canada under subsections (1) and (2) to have their children receive primary and secondary school instruction in the language of the English or French linguistic minority population of a province
(*a*) applies wherever in the province the number of children of citizens who have such a right is sufficient to warrant the provision to them out of public funds of minority language instruction; and
(*b*) includes, where the number of those children so warrants, the right to have them receive that instruction in minority language educational facilities provided out of public funds.

Enforcement
24(1) Anyone whose rights or freedoms, as guaranteed by this Charter, have been infringed or denied may apply to a court of competent jurisdiction to obtain such remedy as the court considers appropriate and just in the circumstances.

(2) Where, in proceedings under subsection (1), a court concludes that evidence was obtained in a manner that infringed or denied any rights or freedoms guaranteed by this Charter, the evidence shall be excluded if it is established that, having regard to all the circumstances, the admission of it in the proceedings would bring the administration of justice into disrepute.

General
25 The guarantee in this Charter of certain rights and freedoms shall not be construed so as to abrogate or derogate from any aboriginal, treaty or other rights or freedoms that pertain to the aboriginal peoples of Canada including

(a) any rights or freedoms that have been recognized by the Royal Proclamation of October 7, 1763; and

(b) any rights or freedoms that may be acquired by the aboriginal peoples of Canada by way of land claims settlement.

26 The guarantee in this Charter of certain rights and freedoms shall not be construed as denying the existence of any other rights or freedoms that exist in Canada.

27 This Charter shall be interpreted in a manner consistent with the preservation and enhancement of the multicultural heritage of Canadians.

28 Notwithstanding anything in this Charter, the rights and freedoms referred to in it are guaranteed equally to male and female persons.

29 Nothing in this Charter abrogates or derogates from any rights or privileges guaranteed by or under the Constitution of Canada in respect of denominational, separate or dissentient schools.

30 A reference in this Charter to a province or to the legislative assembly or Legislature of a province shall be deemed to include a reference to the Yukon Territory and the Northwest Territories, or to the appropriate legislative authority thereof, as the case may be.

31 Nothing in this Charter extends the legislative powers of any body or authority.

Application of Charter

32(1) This Charter applies

(a) to the Parliament and government of Canada in respect of all matters within the authority of Parliament including all matters relating to the Yukon Territory and Northwest Territories; and

(b) to the Legislature and government of each province in respect of all matters within the authority of the Legislature of each province.

(2) Notwithstanding subsection (1), section 15 shall not have effect until three years after this section comes into force.

33(1) Parliament or the Legislature of a province may expressly declare in an Act of Parliament or of the Legislature, as the case may be, that the act or a provision thereof shall operate notwithstanding a provision included in section 2 or sections 7 to 15 of this Charter.

(2) An act or a provision of an act in respect of which a declaration made under this section is in effect shall have such operation as it would have but for the provision of this Charter referred to in the declaration.

(3) A declaration made under subsection (1) shall cease to have effect five years after it comes into force or on such earlier date as may be specified in the declaration.

(4) Parliament or a Legislature of a province may re-enact a declaration made under subsection (1).

(5) Subsection (3) applies in respect of a re-enactment made under subsection (4).

Citation

34 This Part may be cited as the Canadian Charter of Rights and Freedoms.

PART II RIGHTS OF THE ABORIGINAL PEOPLES OF CANADA

35(1) The existing aboriginal and treaty rights of the aboriginal peoples of Canada are hereby recognized and affirmed.

(2) In this act, 'aboriginal peoples of Canada' includes the Indian, Inuit and Métis peoples of Canada.

PART III EQUALIZATION AND REGIONAL DISPARITIES

36(1) Without altering the legislative authority of Parliament or of the provincial Legislatures, or the rights of any of them with respect to the exercise of their legislative authority, Parliament and the Legislatures, together with the government of Canada and the provincial governments, are committed to
(a) promoting equal opportunities for the well-being of Canadians;
(b) furthering economic development to reduce disparity in opportunities; and
(c) providing essential public services of reasonable quality to all Canadians.

(2) Parliament and the government of Canada are committed to the principle of making equalization payments to ensure that provincial governments have sufficient revenues to provide reasonably comparable levels of public services at reasonably comparable levels of taxation.

PART IV CONSTITUTIONAL CONFERENCE

37(1) A constitutional conference composed of the Prime Minister of Canada and the first ministers of the provinces shall be convened by the Prime Minister of Canada within one year after this part comes into force.

(2) The conference convened under subsection (1) shall have included in its agenda an item respecting constitutional matters that directly affect the aboriginal peoples of Canada, including the identification and definition of the rights of those peoples to be included in the Constitution of Canada, and the Prime Minister of Canada shall invite representatives of those peoples to participate in the discussions on that item.

(3) The Prime Minister of Canada shall invite elected representatives of the Governments of the Yukon Territory and the Northwest Territories to participate in the discussions on any item on the agenda of the conference convened under subsection (1) that, in the opinion of the Prime Minister, directly affects the Yukon Territory and the Northwest Territories.

PART V PROCEDURE FOR AMENDING CONSTITUTION OF CANADA

38(1) An amendment to the Constitution of Canada may be made by proclamation issued by the Governor General under the Great Seal of Canada where so authorized by
(a) resolutions of the Senate and House of Commons; and
(b) resolutions of the legislative assemblies of at least two-thirds of the province that have, in the aggregate, according to the then latest general census, at least fifty per cent of the population of all the provinces.

(2) An amendment made under subsection (1) that derogates from the legislative powers, the proprietary rights or any other rights or privileges of the Legislature or government of a province shall require a resolution supported by a majority of the members of each of the Senate, the House of Commons and the legislative assemblies required under subsection (1).

179 Final resolution

(3) An amendment referred to in subsection (2) shall not have effect in a province the legislative assembly of which has expressed its dissent thereto by resolution supported by a majority of its members prior to the issue of the proclamation to which the amendment relates unless that legislative assembly, subsequently, by resolution supported by a majority of its members, revokes its dissent and authorizes the amendment.

(4) A resolution of dissent made for the purposes of subsection (3) may be revoked at any time before or after the issue of the proclamation to which it relates.

39(1) A proclamation shall not be issued under subsection 38(1) before the expiration of one year from the adoption of the resolution initiating the amendment procedure thereunder, unless the legislative assembly of each province has previously adopted a resolution of assent or dissent.

(2) A proclamation shall not be issued under subsection 38(1) after the expiration of three years from the adoption of the resolution initiating the amendment procedure thereunder.

40 Where an amendment is made under subsection 38(1) that transfers provincial legislative powers relating to education or other cultural matters from provincial Legislatures to Parliament, Canada shall provide reasonable compensation to any province to which the amendment does not apply.

41 An amendment to the Constitution of Canada in relation to the following matters may be made by proclamation issued by the Governor-General under the Great Seal of Canada only where authorized by resolutions of the Senate and House of Commons and of the legislative assembly of each province:

(a) the office of the Queen, the Governor-General and the Lieutenant-Governor of a province;

(b) the right of a province to a number of members in the House of Commons not less than the number of Senators by which the province is entitled to be represented at the time this part comes into force;

(c) subject to section 43, the use of the English or the French language;

(d) the composition of the Supreme Court of Canada; and

(e) an amendment to this part.

42(1) An amendment to the Constitution of Canada in relation to the following matters may be made only in accordance with subsection 38(1):

(a) the principle of proportionate representation of the provinces in the House of Commons prescribed by the Constitution of Canada;

(b) the powers of the Senate and the method of selecting Senators;

(c) the number of members by which a province is entitled to be represented in the Senate and the residence qualifications of Senators;

(d) subject to paragraph 41(d), the Supreme Court of Canada;

(e) the extension of existing provinces into the territories; and

(f) notwithstanding any other law or practice, the establishment of new provinces.

(2) Subsections 38(2) to (4) do not apply in respect of amendments in relation to matters referred to in subsection (1).

43 An amendment to the Constitution of Canada in relation to any provision that applies to one or more, but not all, provinces, including

(a) any alteration to boundaries between provinces, and

(b) any amendment to any provision that relates to the use of the English or the French language within a province, may be made by proclamation issued by the Governor-General under the Great Seal of Canada only where so authorized by resolutions of the Senate and House of Commons and of the legislative assembly of each province to which the amendment applies.

44 Subject to sections 41 and 42, Parliament may exclusively make laws amending the Constitution of Canada in relation to the executive government of Canada or the Senate and House of Commons.

45 Subject to section 41, the Legislature of each province may exclusively make laws amending the constitution of the province.

46(1) The procedures for amendment under sections 38, 41, 42 and 43 may be initiated either by the Senate or the House of Commons or by the legislative assembly of a province.

(2) A resolution of assent made for the purposes of this part may be revoked at any time before the issue of a proclamation authorized by it.

47(1) An amendment to the Constitution of Canada made by proclamation under sections 38, 41, 42 or 43 may be made without a resolution of the Senate authorizing the issue of the proclamation if, within one hundred and eighty days after the adoption by the House of Commons of a resolution authorizing its issue, the Senate has not adopted such a resolution and if, at any time after the expiration of that period, the House of Commons again adopts the resolution.

(2) Any period when Parliament is prorogued or dissolved shall not be counted in computing the one hundred and eighty day period referred to in subsection (1).

48 The Queen's Privy Council for Canada shall advise the Governor-General to issue a proclamation under this part forthwith on the adoption of the resolutions required for an amendment made by proclamation under this part.

49 A constitutional conference composed of the Prime Minister of Canada and the first ministers of the provinces shall be convened by the Prime Minister of Canada within 15 years after this part comes into force to review the provisions of this part.

PART VI AMENDMENT TO THE CONSTITUTION ACT, 1867

50 The *Constitution Act, 1867* (formerly named the *British North America Act, 1867*) is amended by adding thereto, immediately after section 92 thereof, the following heading and section:

'*Non-Renewable Natural Resources, Forestry Resources and Electrical Energy*
92A(1) In each province, the Legislature may exclusively make laws in relation to
(a) exploration for non-renewable natural resources in the province;
(b) development, conservation and management of non-renewable natural resources and forestry resources in the province, including laws in relation to the rate of primary production therefrom; and
(c) development, conservation and management of sites and facilities in the province for the generation and production of electrical energy.

(2) In each province, the Legislature may make laws in relation to the export from the province to another part of Canada of the primary production from non-renewable natural resources and forestry resources in the province and the production from facilities in the province for the generation of electrical energy, but such laws may not authorize or provide for discrimination in prices or in supplies exported to another part of Canada.

(3) Nothing in subsection (2) derogates from the authority of Parliament to enact laws in relation to the matters referred to in that subsection and, where such a law of Parliament and a law of a province conflict, the law of Parliament prevails to the extent of the conflict.

(4) In each province, the Legislature may make laws in relation to the raising of money by any mode or system of taxation in respect of

(a) non-renewable natural resources and forestry resources in the province and the primary production therefrom, and

(b) sites and facilities in the province for the generation of electrical energy and the production therefrom,

whether or not such production is exported in whole or in part from the province, but such laws may not authorize or provide for taxation that differentiates between production exported to another part of Canada and production not exported from the province.

(5) The expression "primary production" has the meaning assigned by the Sixth Schedule.

(6) Nothing in subsections (1) to (5) derogates from any powers or rights that a Legislature or government of a province had immediately before the coming into force of this section.'

51 The said act is further amended by adding thereto the following schedule:

'THE SIXTH SCHEDULE

Primary Production from Non-Renewable Natural Resources and Forestry Resources.

1 For the purposes of section 92A of this act,

(a) production from a non-renewable natural resource is primary production therefrom if

(i) it is in the form in which it exists upon its recovery or severance from its natural state, or

(ii) it is a product resulting from processing or refining the resource, and is not a manufactured product or a product resulting from refining crude oil, refining upgraded heavy crude oil, refining gases or liquids derived from coal or refining a synthetic equivalent of crude oil; and

(b) production from a forestry resource is primary production therefrom if it consists of sawlogs, poles, lumber, wood chips, sawdust or any other primary wood product, or wood pulp, and is not a product manufactured from wood.'

PART VII GENERAL

52(1) The Constitution of Canada is the supreme law of Canada, and any law that is inconsistent with the provisions of the Constitution is, to the extent of the inconsistency, of no force or effect.

(2) The Constitution of Canada includes

(a) the *Canada Act*, including this act;

(b) the acts and orders referred to in Schedule I; and

(c) any amendment to any act or order referred to in paragraph (a) or (b).

(3) Amendments to the Constitution of Canada shall be made only in accordance with the authority contained in the Constitution of Canada.

53(1) The enactments referred to in Column I of Schedule I are hereby repealed or amended to the extent indicated in Column II thereof and, unless repealed, shall continue as law in Canada under the names set out in Column III thereof.

(2) Every enactment, except the *Canada Act*, that refers to an enactment referred to in Schedule I by the name in Column I thereof is hereby amended by substituting for that name the corresponding name in Column III thereof, and any British North America Act not referred to in Schedule I may be cited as the *Constitution Act* followed by the year and number, if any, of its enactment.

54 Part IV is repealed on the day that is one year after this Part comes into force and this section may be repealed and this Act renumbered, consequential upon the repeal of Part IV and this section, by proclamation issued by the Governor-General under the Great Seal of Canada.

55 A French version of the portions of the Constitution of Canada referred to in Schedule I shall be prepared by the Minister of Justice of Canada as expeditiously as possible and, when any portion thereof sufficient to warrant action being taken has been so prepared, it shall be put forward for enactment by proclamation issued by the Governor-General under the Great Seal of Canada pursuant to the procedure then applicable to an amendment of the same provisions of the Constitution of Canada.

56 Where any portion of the Constitution of Canada has been or is enacted in English and French or where a French version of any portion of the Constitution is enacted pursuant to section 55, the English and French versions of that portion of the Constitution are equally authoritative.

57 The English and French versions of this Act are equally authoritative.

58 Subject to section 59, this Act shall come into force on a day to be fixed by proclamation issued by the Queen or the Governor-General under the Great Seal of Canada.

59(1) Paragraph 23(1)(*a*) shall come into force in respect of Quebec on a day to be fixed by proclamation issued by the Queen or the Governor-General under the Great Seal of Canada.

(2) A proclamation under subsection (1) shall be issued only where authorized by the legislative assembly or government of Quebec.

(3) This section may be repealed on the day paragraph 23(1)(*a*) comes into force in respect of Quebec and this Act amended and renumbered, consequential upon the repeal of this section, by proclamation issued by the Queen or the Governor-General under the Great Seal of Canada.

60 This Act may be cited as the *Constitution Act, 1981*, and the *Constitution Acts 1867 to 1975 (No. 2)* and this Act may be cited together as the *Constitution Acts, 1867 to 1981*.

Supreme Court advisory opinion on Senate reform (extracts)

Reference re Legislative Authority of Parliament to Alter or Replace the Senate

102 DLR (3d) 1 (1979).

Supreme Court of Canada, Laskin, C.J.C., Martland, Ritchie, Pigeon, Dickson, Estey, Pratte and McIntyre, JJ. December 21, 1979.

THE COURT:—By Order in Council PC 1978-3581, dated November 23, 1978, the Governor-General in Council, pursuant to s. 55 of the *Supreme Court Act*, RSC 1970, c. S-19, referred to this Court for hearing and consideration the following two questions:

1 Is it within the legislative authority of the Parliament of Canada to repeal sections 21 to 36 of the *British North America Act, 1867*, as amended, and to amend other sections thereof so as to delete any reference to an Upper House or the Senate? If not, in what particular or particulars and to what extent?

2 Is it within the legislative authority of the Parliament of Canada to enact legislation altering, or providing a replacement for, the Upper House of Parliament, so as to effect any or all of the following:
(a) to change the name of the Upper House;
(b) to change the numbers and proportions of members by whom provinces and territories are represented in that House;
(c) to change the qualifications of members of that House;
(d) to change the tenure of members of that House;
(e) to change the method by which members of that House are chosen by
(i) conferring authority on provincial legislative assemblies to select, on the nomination of the respective Lieutenant Governors in Council, some members of the Upper House, and, if a legislative assembly has not selected such members within the time permitted, authority on the House of Commons to select those members on the nomination of the Governor General in Council, and
(ii) conferring authority on the House of Commons to select, on the nomination of the Governor General in Council, some members of the Upper House from each province, and, if the House of Commons has not selected such members

from a province within the time permitted, authority on the legislative assembly of the province to select those members on the nomination of the Lieutenant Governor in Council.

(iii) conferring authority on the Lieutenant Governors in Council of the provinces or on some other body or bodies to select some or all of the members of the Upper House, or

(iv) providing for the direct election of all or some of the members of the Upper House by the public; or

(f) to provide that Bills approved by the House of Commons could be given assent and the force of law after the passage of a certain period of time notwithstanding that the Upper House has not approved them?

If not, in what particular or particulars and to what extent?

...

It is clear that Question I in essence, although not in terms, asks whether the Parliament of Canada has legislative authority to abolish the Senate. The Attorney-General of Canada contends that the question should be answered in the affirmative. All of the Attorneys-General of the Provinces, represented on the hearing, contended that the question should be answered in the negative.

The Attorney-General of Canada bases his submission upon the provisions of Class 1 of the subject-matters enumerated in s. 91 of the Act. Section 91, which appears in Part VI of the Act, under the heading 'Powers of the Parliament', defines the legislative authority of the Parliament of Canada. The opening words of this section are as follows:

91 It shall be lawful for the Queen, by and with the Advice and Consent of the Senate and House of Commons, to make Laws for the Peace, Order and good Government of Canada, in relation to all Matters not coming within the Classes of Subjects by this Act assigned exclusively to the Legislatures of the Provinces; and for greater Certainty, but not so as to restrict the Generality of the foregoing Terms of this Section, it is hereby declared that (notwithstanding anything in this Act) the exclusive Legislative Authority of the Parliament of Canada extends to all Matters coming within the Classes of Subjects next herein-after enumerated ...

Class 1 of s. 91 was added to it by an amendment to the Act enacted by the British Parliament on December 16, 1949 ...

Prior to 1949, in most respects, the Act did not provide for its amendment by any legislative authority in Canada. Accordingly, as it was a statute enacted by the British Parliament, any changes in its content had to be made by way of an amending Act enacted by that Parliament. Many amendments have been made in that way ...

The apparent intention of the 1949 amendment to the Act which enacted s. 91(1) was to obviate the necessity for the enactment of a statute of the British Parliament to effect amendments to the Act which theretofore had been obtained through a joint resolution of both Houses of Parliament and without provincial consent. Legislation enacted since 1949 pursuant to s. 91(1) has not, to quote the White Paper, 'affected federal-provincial relationships.' The following statutes have been enacted by the Parliament of Canada:

(1) *The British North America Act, 1952*, effected a readjustment of representation in the House of Commons. The principle of representation by population was not affected by this legislation.

(2) *The British North America Act, 1965*, provided for the compulsory retirement of senators, henceforth appointed, at age seventy-five.

(3) *The British North America Act (No. 2), 1974*, repealed the provisions of the Act of 1952 and substituted a new readjustment of representation in the House of Commons. The principle of representation by population was maintained.

(4) *The British North America Act, 1975*, increased the representation of the Northwest Territories in the House of Commons from one to two members.

(5) *The British North America Act (No. 2), 1975*, increased the total number of senators from 102 to 104, and provided for representation in the Senate for the Yukon Territory and the Northwest Territories by one member each.

All of these measures dealt with what might be described as federal 'housekeeping' matters which, according to the practice existing before 1949, would have been referred to the British Parliament by way of a joint resolution of both Houses of Parliament, and without the consent of the Provinces. The last two of these statutes were within the power of the Parliament of Canada to enact by virtue of s. 1 of the *British North America Act, 1886*. Like the others they did not in any substantial way affect federal-provincial relationships.

The legislation contemplated in the first question is of an entirely different character. While it does not directly affect federal-provincial relationships in the sense of changing federal and provincial legislative powers, it does envision the elimination of one of the two Houses of Parliament, and so would alter the structure of the federal Parliament to which the federal power to legislate is entrusted under s. 91 of the Act.

The Senate has a vital role as an institution forming part of the federal system created by the Act. The recitals in the Act have some significance:

Whereas the Provinces of Canada, Nova Scotia, and New Brunswick have expressed their Desire to be federally united into One Dominion under the Crown of the United Kingdom of Great Britain and Ireland, with a Constitution similar in Principle to that of the United Kingdom:

And whereas such a Union would conduce to the Welfare of the Provinces and promote the Interests of the British Empire:

And whereas on the Establishment of the Union by Authority of Parliament it is expedient, not only that the Constitution of the Legislative Authority in the Dominion be provided for, but also that the Nature of the Executive Government therein be declared.

Under the Constitution of the United Kingdom, to which reference is made in the first recital, legislative power was and is exercised by the Queen, by and with the advice and consent of the House of Lords and the House of Commons. The Upper House was not and is not an elected body, the Lower House was and is ...

A primary purpose of the creation of the Senate, as a part of the federal legislative process, was, therefore, to afford protection to the various sectional interests in Canada in relation to the enactment of federal legislation ...

The power to enact federal legislation was given to the Queen by and with the advice and consent of the Senate and the House of Commons. Thus, the body which had been created as a means of protecting sectional and provincial interests was made a participant in this legislative process.

The amendment to the Act made in 1949 added an additional class of subject-matters to those which already existed. By that time the classes had been increased to thirty. The amendment was made on a joint resolution of both Houses of Parliament, but without the consent of the Provinces. It gave power to the Queen, by and with the advice and consent of the Senate and the House of Commons to amend 'the Constitution of Canada.' This power was made subject to certain specific exceptions, as follows: 'except as regards matters coming within the classes of subjects by this Act assigned exclusively to the Legislatures of the provinces, or as regards rights or privileges by this or any other Constitutional Act granted or secured to the Legislature or the Government of a province.'

...

In our opinion, the power of amendment given by s. 91(1) relates to the constitution of the federal Government in matters of interest only to that Government. The statutes enacted by the federal Parliament since 1949, to which we have previously referred, are illustrations of the exercise of that power.

The next question is whether, in that limited sense, s. 91(1) would permit the federal Parliament to abolish the Senate.

Bearing in mind the historical background in which the creation of the Senate as a part of the federal legislative process was conceived, the words of Lord Sankey, LC in *Re Aerial Navigation; A.-G. Can. v. A.-G. Ont. et al.*, [1932] 1 DLR 58 at p 65, [1932] AC 54 at p. 70. [1931] 3 WWR 625, although they were written in relation to the Act as originally enacted, are apt:

Inasmuch as the Act embodies a compromise under which the original Provinces agreed to federate, it is important to keep in mind that the preservation of the rights of minorities was a condition on which such minorities entered into the federation, and the foundation upon which the whole structure was subsequently erected. The process of interpretation as the years go on ought not to be allowed to dim or to whittle down the provisions of the original contract upon which the federation was founded, nor is it legitimate that any judicial construction of the provisions of ss. 91 and 92 should impose a new and different contract upon the federating bodies.

In our opinion, the power given to the federal Parliament by s. 91(1) was not intended to enable it to alter in any way the provisions of ss. 91 and 92 governing the exercise of legislative authority by the Parliament of Canada and the Legislatures of the Provinces. Section 91(1) is a particularization of the general legislative power of the Parliament of Canada. That general power can be exercised only by the Queen by and with the advice and consent of the Senate and the House of Commons. Section 91(1) cannot be construed to confer power to supplant the whole of the rest of the section. It cannot be construed as permitting the transfer of the legislative powers enumerated in s. 91 to some body or bodies other than those specifically designated in it.

This Court, in *A.-G. N.S. et al. v. A.-G. Can. et al.*, [1950] 4 DLR 369, [1951] SCR 31, determined that neither the Parliament of Canada nor a provincial Legislature could delegate to the other the legislative powers with which it has been vested nor receive from the other the powers with which the other has been vested. The elimination of the Senate would go much further in that it would involve a transfer by Parliament of all its legislative powers to a new legislative body of which the Senate would not be a member ...

The continued existence of the Senate as a part of the federal legislative process is implied in the exceptions provided in s. 91(1) ...

For the foregoing reasons, we would answer the first question in the negative.

Question 2
The Attorney-General of Canada submits that this question, in all its aspects, should be answered in the affirmative. Differing views were expressed by the Attorneys-General of the Provinces.

All of the provincial Attorneys-General, other than the Attorney-General of Prince Edward Island, submitted that para. (f) of Question 2 should be answered in the negative. This paragraph raises the question of the power of Parliament, under s. 91(1), to provide that all bills be given assent and the force of law after a certain time period notwithstanding that they had not been approved by the Upper House. The only provision presently existing, which limits the power of the Senate as compared with the power of the House of Commons, is s. 53 which provides that bills for appropriating any part of the public revenue or for imposing any tax or impost shall originate in the House of Commons.

A provision of the kind contemplated would seriously impair the position of the Senate in the legislative process because it would permit legislation to be enacted under s. 91 without the consent of the Senate. For the reasons already given in respect of Question 1, it is our view that Parliament cannot under s. 91(1) impair the role of the Senate in that process. We would answer this question in the negative.

With respect to the other portions of Question 2, the Attorney-General of Ontario and the Attorney-General of Nova Scotia submit that these subquestions cannot be answered categorically in the form in which they are asked. As the Attorney-General of Nova Scotia puts it, they cannot be answered 'in the absence of a factual context or actual draft legislation.' In our opinion there is merit in this contention. We will deal with the subquestions seriatim.

Subquestion (a) asks whether Parliament could change the name of the Upper House. We would assume that a change of name would be proposed only as a part of some scheme for the alteration of the Senate itself. If that scheme were to be held *ultra vires* of Parliament, then the change of name would probably go with it. We do not think the question can properly be answered in the absence of such a context.

Subquestion (b) involves changing the numbers and proportions of members by whom Provinces and Territories are represented in the Senate. None of the Provinces supported the federal submission on this point.

As previously noted, the system of regional representation in the Senate was one of the essential features of that body when it was created. Without it, the fundamental character of the Senate as part of the Canadian federal scheme would be eliminated. In the absence of a factual context, it is not possible to say whether a change contemplated by this question would be in keeping with that fundamental character.

Subquestion (c) deals with a change in the qualifications of senators. The difficulty here is that we have not been told what changes are contemplated. Some of the qualifications for senators prescribed in s. 23, such as the property qualifications, may not today have the importance which they did when the Act was enacted. On the other hand, the requirement that a senator should be resident in the Province for which he is appointed has relevance in relation to the sectional characteristic of the make-up of the Senate. In our opinion, the question cannot be answered categorically.

Subquestion (d) relates to the tenure of senators. At present, a senator, when appointed, has tenure until he attains the age of 75. At some point, a reduction of the term of office might impair the functioning of the Senate in providing what Sir John A. Macdonald described as 'the sober second thought in legislation.' The Act contemplated a constitution similar in principle to that of the United Kingdom, where members of the House of Lords hold office for life. The imposition of compulsory retirement at age 75 did not change the essential character of the Senate. However, to answer this question we need to know what change of tenure is proposed.

Subquestion (e), paras. (i), (ii) and (iii), contemplates changing the method of appointment of senators, presently the function of the Governor-General, by having 'some' members selected by provincial Legislatures, 'some' members by the House of Commons, 'some' members selected by the Lieutenant-Governor in Council or 'some other body or bodies.' The selection of senators by a provincial Legislature or by the Lieutenant-Governor of a Province would involve an indirect participation by the Provinces in the enactment of federal legislation and is contrary to the reasoning of this Court in the *A.-G. N.S. v. A.-G. Can.* case previously cited.

Again, we do not feel that we have a factual context in which to formulate a satisfactory answer.

Subquestion (e) (iv) deals with the possible selection of all or some members of the Senate by direct election by the public. The substitution of a system of election for a system of appintment would involve a radical change in the nature of one of the component parts of Parliament. As already noted, the preamble to the Act referred to 'a constitution similar in principle to that of the United Kingdom,' where the Upper House is not elected. In creating the Senate in the manner provided in the Act, it is clear that the intention was to make the Senate a thoroughly independent body which could canvass dispassionately the measures of the House of Commons. This was accomplished by providing for the appointment of members of the Senate with tenure for life. To make the Senate a wholly or partially elected body would affect a fundamental feature of that body. We would answer this subquestion in the negative.

Dealing generally with Question 2, it is our opinion that while s. 91(1) would permit some changes to be made by Parliament in respect of the Senate as now constituted, it is not open to Parliament to make alterations which would affect the fundamental features, or essential characteristics, given to the Senate as a means of ensuring regional and provincial representation in the federal legislative process. The character of the Senate was determined by the British Parliament in response to the proposals submitted by the three Provinces in order to meet the requirement of the proposed federal system. It was that Senate, created by the Act, to which a legislative role was given by s. 91. In our opinion, its fundamental character cannot be altered by unilateral action by the Parliament of Canada and s. 91(1) does not give that power.

We answer Question 1 in the negative. We answer subquestions 2(b), 2(e)(iv) and 2(f) in the negative. In our opinion, the other subquestions in Question 2, in the absence of a factual background, cannot be answered categorically.

References
to courts of appeal
re resolution (extracts)

1 Manitoba

IN THE MATTER OF An Act for Expediting the Decision of Constitutional and Other Provincial Questions, being Chapter c180, CCSM.
AND IN THE MATTER OF a Reference pursuant thereto by the Lieutenant Governor in Council to the Court of Appeal for Manitoba, for hearing and consideration, the questions concerning the amendment of the Constitution of Canada as set out in Order in Council No. 1020/80

COURT: Freedman, CJM; Hall, JA; Matas, JA; O'Sullivan, JA; Huband, JA.

February 3, 1981.

The Questions referred to the Court were as follows:
1 If the amendments to the Constitution of Canada sought in the 'Proposed Resolution for a Joint Address to Her Majesty the Queen respecting the Constitution of Canada,' or any of them, were enacted, would federal-provincial relationships or the powers, rights or privileges granted or secured by the Constitution of Canada to the provinces, their legislatures or governments be affected, and if so, in what respect or respects?
2 Is it a constitutional convention that the House of Commons and Senate of Canada will not request Her Majesty the Queen to lay before the Parliament of the United Kingdom of Great Britain and Northern Ireland a measure to amend the Constitution of Canada affecting federal-provincial relationships or the powers, rights or privileges granted or secured by the Constitution of Canada to the provinces, their legislatures or governments without first obtaining the agreement of the provinces?
3 Is the agreement of the provinces of Canada constitutionally required for amendment to the Constitution of Canada where such amendment affects federal-provincial relationships or alters the powers, rights or privileges granted or secured by the Constitution of Canada to the provinces, their legislatures or governments?

The answers to the Questions on Reference are as follows:
Freedman, CJM:
Question 1 – Not answered, because it is tentative and premature.

Question 2 – No.
Question 3 – No.
Hall, JA:
Question 1 – Not answered because it is not appropriate for judicial response, and, in any event, the question is speculative and premature.
Question 2 – Not answered because it is not appropriate for judicial response.
Question 3 – No, because there is no legal requirement of provincial agreement to amendment of the Constitution as asserted in the question.
Matas, JA:
Question 1 – Not answered, because it is speculative and premature.
Question 2 – No.
Question 3 – No.

FREEDMAN, CJM

Canada is a sovereign nation. It is so recognized throughout the world. But one vestige of colonialism still adheres to her national status, namely, that she is unable to amend her constitution. Such an amendment can only be made by the Parliament of the United Kingdom. The procedure for securing a desired amendment is for the Senate and House of Commons, in Parliament assembled, to pass a resolution for a Joint Address to Her Majesty the Queen requesting Her Majesty to cause to be laid before the Parliament of the United Kingdom a measure embodying the amendment. The measure in question will then in due course be enacted by the Parliament of the United Kingdom ...

Whether Canada's slightly diminished sovereignty is more a matter of appearance than of fact is something on which I need not linger. Even an appearance of incomplete sovereignty is something that calls for correction. This is especially so when it is realized that the process of effecting a change in the appearance is itself fraught with difficulty. So one should not underestimate the importance or the gravity of the constitutional problem here involved ...

Before proceeding with the consideration of the three questions I deem it useful to define the boundaries within which our inquiry should be conducted. Those boundaries are best defined negatively – that is to say, by indicating what does *not* fall within their scope. And clearly what does not fall within their scope is the political wisdom or unwisdom of what is contained in the Joint Address. The attempt by the Federal power to patriate the constitution unilaterally may be an act of high statesmanship or of political folly. That is not a determination that we are called upon to make ... We are concerned not with the wisdom or policy of the Proposed Resolution but only with its constitutional legality. We continue to function on this Reference as a court of law.

I turn now to Question 1 ...

A threshold problem must first be considered, namely, should this question be answered at all? Counsel for the Attorney General of Canada points to 'the tentative nature of the contents of the proposed Resolution' and submits that any answer we might give would therefore be 'speculative and premature.'

In my view there is merit in this submission. The proceedings before the [federal parliamentary] Joint Committee have already led to public declarations by the Attorney General of Canada that amendments to the subject matter of the proposed Resolution will be made. Indeed one of the undoubted purposes of the deliberations of the Joint Committee is to examine the proposals set forth in the *Constitution Act, 1980* and to recommend such changes therein as the Committee deems desirable. The very language of the motion appointing the Joint Committee makes this clear ... We therefore face a real likelihood that the amendments sought in the Proposed Resolution may be altered, deleted, or supplanted by other amendments before the Resolution is deemed ready for transmission to Her Majesty. In this situation there is a danger that if we answer Question 1, with the proposed amendments in their present form, we may later find that we have answered matters no longer before us and have not answered matters that emerged in their stead. The Court should not be exposed to the risk of such an adventure in futility ...

In saying this I am not being critical of either the Dominion or the Province. Manitoba brought this Reference before us on the only material that was then available to it. The Proposed Resolution tabled in Parliament was the basis of the Reference, and of course its subject matter had to be considered as it stood, even though it might later undergo alteration, perhaps even substantially so. As for the Dominion it had to make a start somewhere, and the *Constitution Act, 1980* represented that start. But to be wedded to every last provision of that document as rigid and unalterable would be to assume a posture unbecoming to a democratic state. So it accepts the idea of change.

Since the above was written the Minister of Justice of Canada, on January 12, 1981, placed before the Joint Committee a list of amendments to the proposals originally set forth. During the hearing before this Court I had referred to this very possibility and I invited counsel to indicate whether, in such case, we should deal with the original material or with the substituted material, always bearing in mind that in the latter case we would not have had the benefit of counsel's argument. [Counsel] for Manitoba, stated that we should deal with the original material, since it was that material alone which was referred to in the Reference.

I agree, and merely add that this strengthens the characterization of Question 1 as 'tentative and premature.' I therefore do not answer that question.

I move on to Question 2 ...

Is it a constitutional convention that the Federal power will not seek an amendment of the Constitution of Canada, of the nature described in Question 2, without first obtaining the agreement of the Provinces? In my view there is no such constitutional convention in Canada, at least not yet. History and practice do not establish its existence; rather they belie it. That we may be moving towards such a convention is certainly a tenable view. But we have not yet arrived there. As recently as December 21, 1979 the Supreme Court of Canada in the Senate Reference, *supra*, could write thus: 'The practice, since 1865, has been to seek amendment of the Act by a joint address of both Houses of Parliament. Consultation with one or more of the provinces has occurred in some instances.' This is not language appropriate to the existence of a convention full-blown, vigorous, and operative. A convention should be certain and consistent; what we have is uncertain and variable.

I therefore answer Question 2 in the negative.

I deal now with the last question. I need only summarize it: Is the agreement of the provinces constitutionally required for amendment, of the nature there stated, of the Constitution of Canada? Question 2 called upon us to determine whether there is a convention as claimed. Question 3 takes the matter one step farther. It rests on the submission that the convention has ripened or crystallized into a constitutional rule of law; or alternatively, that the convention has gained acceptance as an operative principle of our constitution, so that the Court should itself now crystallize it as a rule of law.

This argument need only be pursued if a convention has been found to exist. In that respect – and dealing with the questions as they have been submitted to us, and giving full effect to the main thrust of the argument submitted on behalf of the Provinces – I believe that the third question stands or falls on the answer to the second question. An affirmative answer to Question 2 paves the way for consideration of Question 3. But a negative answer to Question 2 – and I have given such an answer – requires the giving of a similar answer to Question 3. No convention, no rule of law. The matter is as simple as that.

My opinion could end here. But before leaving the matter in that way I wish to add some further observations.

Half a century ago a commentator wrote of 'the constitutional formula or legend which has come to be known as the compact theory of Confederation.' (Norman McL. Rogers 'The Compact Theory of Confederation,' ([1931] 9 Can. Bar Rev. 395). That theory has re-emerged on this Reference.

The essential meaning of the compact theory is that Confederation was brought about by a compact between its constituent parts. Any change in the nature of the union requires the consent of those parts. That is to say, it requires unanimity on the part of the Federal power and of the Provinces. Otherwise there would be a breach of the compact (or contract, or treaty) which was the basis of Confederation.

In my view the theory in question is supported neither by history nor by subsequent usage ...

Let us note that we are dealing here with something that is not the product of evolution. Moreover it is something that goes beyond the legislative sovereignty of the Provinces under Section 92 of the BNA Act. No one disputes the existence of Provincial legislative sovereignty of that character and within that domain. But the Provincial sovereignty here asserted appears to me to be something in the nature of an inherent right flowing from the fact of union. As such, it bears a direct relationship to the compact theory, on which I have already expressed my views.

In the result I certify to the Lieutenant Governor in Council my answers to the questions posed to us on this Reference, namely:
Question 1 – Not answered, because it is tentative and premature.
Question 2 – No.
Question 3 – No.

O'SULLIVAN, JA (dissenting)

... I accept the fact that there is a school of Canadian history which disputes the historical foundation of the compact theory, but there have been many able historians who have defended it. I do not know to what extent a court should enter into disputed historical points; my own historical studies have convinced me that there is solid historical foundation for it. I do not see how it is possible, in any event, to say there is *no* historic foundation for a concept which was explicitly expounded by all of the principal Fathers of Confederation ...

In any event, while Mr. MacGregor Dawson may be an authority in the historical field, he is not an authority on law. When he says that the compact theory has no

legal foundation, he ignores the course of Canadian jurisprudence. The compact theory has been recognized on many occasions by the highest courts with jurisdiction in
our country, and in my opinion must be accepted as a basic concept in determining
the constitutional law of the land ...

Each province has entered confederation on the understanding that our country is
a federal state, a federal union. Its fundamental terms cannot be changed without
unanimous agreement because a change in a fundamental term would change the
very nature of the federal union.

This does not mean that every amendment which affects dominion-provincial relationships requires unanimous consent, but only those amendments which affect fundamental terms of the union. What those terms are it is unnecessary to decide in this
case. The best way of determining what are the fundamental terms of the union is by
agreement of the constituents of the union; if, however, agreement cannot be
reached then the Supreme Court of Canada must be the final arbiter, as it was in the
Senate reference case.

I take it therefore to be a principle of the constitutional law of our country that the
federal power does not have the constitutional right to initiate or to obtain any constitutional amendment which would affect the fundamental terms of the union without
the consent of all of the provinces. Among these fundamental terms is the legislative
distribution of powers as between the federal and provincial spheres ...

2 Newfoundland

IN THE MATTER of Section 6 of The Judicature Act, RSN 1970, c. 187 as amended,
AND IN THE MATTER of a Reference by the Lieutenant-Governor in Council concerning the effect & validity of the amendments to the Constitution of Canada sought in
the 'Proposed Resolution for a Joint Address to Her Majesty the Queen respecting
the Constitution of Canada.'

COURT: Mifflin, CJN; Morgan, JA; Gushue, JA

March 31, 1981.

... Counsel for the Attorney-General of Canada, in defining the nature of the questions, submits that 'speculative and vaguely worded questions are not appropriate for
a reference procedure. Non-legal matters of politics or political science are not appropriate subjects for a traditional court action' ...

We agree with the Attorney-General of Canada that, as a broad generalization,
questions that are speculative and premature, and those that are purely political in
nature, are not appropriate for judicial response. The first question submitted may be
considered in part speculative and premature, and the second question undoubtedly
has some political connotation. They none the less pose questions that are of a constitutional nature and in our opinion require an answer ...

While the autonomy of the Provinces and the Federal Government within their
respective fields of authority was clearly defined by the British North America Act, it
could not be said until 1931, and the passing in that year of the Statute of Westminster, that Canada as a nation gained complete independence from Great Britain ...

The dissolution of the bonds with Great Britain was complete upon the passing of that Statute, and Canada, in the totality of its legislative powers, Federal and Provincial combined, attained sovereign independence, qualified only by Great Britain's role, retained at the request of the Canadian community, to enact amendments to Canada's constitution. However, there is no doubt that, to all intents and purposes, the Parliament of Great Britain renounced all external legislative sovereignty over the land and people of Canada ...

In our opinion, the intent, and the effective result, of that enactment was to place the Parliament of Great Britain in the role of 'a bare Legislative trustee,' as enunciated by Hon. Ivan C. Rand (then a retired Judge of the Supreme Court of Canada) ...

We adopt that statement fully with the important addition that the Parliament of Great Britain is a 'bare legislative trustee' for *both* the Federal Parliament and the Provincial Legislatures in relation to the matters within their respective legislative competence. Any amendment enacted by the Parliament of Great Britain affecting the legislative competence of either of the parties, without that party's consent, would not only be contrary to the intendment of the Statute of Westminster, but it could defeat the whole scheme of the Canadian Federal constitution ...

In our opinion, the constitutional status of the Provinces of Canada as autonomous communities was confirmed and perfected by (a) the Statute of Westminster giving effect to the constitutional principle declared by the Imperial Conference that both the United Kingdom and the Dominions are autonomous communities equal in status, in no way subordinate one to another in any aspect of their domestic or external affairs; (b) the recognition by that Conference of the division of power among the constituent parts that make up the Dominion of Canada by which each is autonomous, in no way subordinate one to another; and, (c) the surrender by the Imperial Parliament to the Provinces of its legislative sovereignty, over matters declared by the British North America Act to be within the exclusive legislative competence of the Provinces. The modification of that constitutional status was thereby withdrawn from future British parliamentary competence except with the consent of the Provinces.

While the Parliament of Great Britain, in the absence of notice to the contrary, is constitutionally entitled to accept a Resolution passed by both Houses of the Canadian Parliament as a proper request for a constitutional amendment from the whole Canadian community, it is nonetheless precluded, for the reasons stated above, from enacting an amendment restricting the powers, rights and privileges granted the Provinces by the British North America Act, and enlarged by the Statute of Westminster over the objections of the Provinces ...

[As to question 4, concerning the relation of the proposed resolution to the terms of union between Newfoundland and Canada, of 1949:] '... If Part V of the Proposed Resolution referred to in question 1 is enacted and proclaimed into force could

(a) the Terms of Union, including terms 2 and 17 thereof contained in the Schedule to the British North America Act 1949 (12–13 George VI, c. 22 [UK]), or

(b) section 3 of the British North America Act, 1871 (34–35 Victoria, c. 28 [UK])

be amended directly or indirectly pursuant to Part V without the consent of the Government, Legislature or a majority of the people of the Province of Newfoundland voting in a referendum held pursuant to Part V?' ...

As can be seen, the possibility for change exists, but an unqualified answer to the question posed could be misleading. We would therefore answer question 4 as follows:

1 By Sec. 3 of the British North America Act, 1871, *Term 2* of the Terms of Union cannot now be changed without the consent of the Newfoundland Legislature.

2 By Sec. 43 of the 'Constitution Act,' as it now reads, none of the Terms of Union can be changed without the consent of the Newfoundland Legislative Assembly.

3 Both of these sections can be changed by the amending formulae prescribed in Sec. 41 and the Terms of Union could then be changed without the consent of the Newfoundland Legislature.

4 If the amending formula under Sec. 42 is utilized, both of these sections can be changed by a referendum held pursuant to the provisions of Sec. 42. In this event, the Terms of Union could then be changed without the consent of the Newfoundland Legislature, but not without the consent of the majority of the Newfoundland people voting in a referendum.

3 Quebec

[Cour d'Appel, Province de Québec, District de Montréal]

DANS L'AFFAIRE d'un renvoi à la Cour d'appel relatif à un projet de résolution portant adresse commune à sa Majesté la Reine concernant la Constitution du Canada

COURT: Crête, CJQ; Owen, JA; Turgeon, JA; Bélanger, JA; Bisson, JA

April 15, 1981.

CRÊTE, CJQ (Translation)

... If the Canadian federation is created by a compact – and uniquely by a compact (I will return later to this notion) – the conclusion could impose itself that one of the parties to the compact could not unilaterally modify it or have it modified without the assent of the other parties to the agreement ...

In the last analysis, my conclusions can be summarised as follows:

1 Whether or not one is in agreement with the form or the content of the Resolution introduced before the two federal Houses, this Resolution is not open to review by the Courts, which, beyond that, do not have to pronounce upon the legislative measures that can or could be adopted by the British Parliament.

2 Whether or not one subscribes to the compact theory of federation, one has to agree that, at the legal level, the BNA Act is a law which can only be modified or abrogated by another law emanating from the same legislative authority which has adopted the original law, that is to say, the British Parliament ...

3 As to the formula utilised and consecrated by the practice since 1875, in order to invite the English Parliament to modify the Canadian Constitution, it is that of the Joint Address of the two Houses of the federal Parliament to Her Majesty The Queen.

As conclusion, I would add, always at the legal level, that the federal Government's constitutional approach – even if it be unilateral in character – is rooted in legality ...

OWEN, JA (CONCURRING)

...

The Compact Theory of Confederation
I agree with my colleague Mr. Justice Turgeon that this theory is not supported by history and has no juridical basis. I also agree with the Chief Justice of Manitoba in the Manitoba Reference ... who held that the theory is supported neither by history nor by subsequent usage or judicial practice.

In 1867 the three provinces, Canada, Nova Scotia, and New Brunswick which were united in a form of federation by the Imperial statute known as the BNAA, were not sovereign states which by agreement formed a federation.

In my opinion the Compact Theory of Confederation is unfounded ...

Federal Nature of Canadian Constitution
The Provinces argued that, as a consequence of the federal nature of the Canadian Constitution which divides legislative powers between the Federal Government and the Provinces, no amendment affecting these legislative powers can be made by the British Parliament without the consent of the eleven members of the Federation. The basis of this argument is that in an ideal federation the consent of all the parties is required to amend the terms of the federation. This argument is closely related to the compact theory. It does not apply in Canada because Canada is not the theoretical ideal confederation contemplated by text-book writers ...

The BNAA was passed by the British Parliament in 1867. Since that time it has been and it can be amended by the British Parliament without any legal limitation. The amendments made to the BNAA have consistently been initiated by means of a joint address of the Senate and the House of Commons of Canada in Parliament assembled to Her Majesty the Queen or His Majesty the King. There is no legal limitation, whether by statute, convention, or otherwise, to the type of amendment that can be requested by such joint address.

I would stress again that the above statements represent an opinion as to what the Senate and the House of Commons can do, from a *legal* point of view, in connection with the amendment of the BNAA.

The questions as to what the Government of Canada should do from a *political* point of view in connection with the amendment of the BNAA is entirely different.

It is a political not a legal problem.

TURGEON, JA (CONCURRING) (Translation)

... The Provinces assert that they are sovereign and that for this reason the British Parliament cannot, without their consent, damage their legislative competence at the request of the two Canadian federal Houses of Parliament. It is an argument which cannot be accepted ... If the Provinces were right in characterising themselves as sovereign states, how could one explain that it is the federal authority alone which can ask the British Parliament to legislate for Canada? ...

The Proposed Resolution of the Senate and of the House of Commons is not contrary to constitutional practice and to constitutional convention. On the contrary, it appears in conformity to constitutional practice and constitutional convention.

Certain Provinces assert that there is a constitutional convention to the effect that the consent of the Provinces is a prerequisite to any Address of the two Houses requesting the British Parliament to amend the Canadian constitution.

I am of the opinion that analysis of the procedure followed since 1867 in this regard, as much by the British Parliament as by the Canadian Parliament, shows clearly that there is no constitutional convention to that effect. On the contrary, if a constitutional convention exists, it confirms the Proposed Resolution ...

Certain Provinces have pleaded the 'compact' theory. The words 'compact, agreement or contract' have been utilized by certain courts the better to illustrate the circumstances which led the authors of the BNA Act to divide the competences as they did. But none of these judgments erected this theory into a rule of law. One must distinguish between 'compact' and 'political arrangements.' History does not support this 'compact' theory ...

At Confederation in 1867, the Provinces, such as they are now known, were colonies of the British Crown on which they were dependent: they were not sovereign. What they made between themselves was not a 'compact' but a 'political arrangement' which was then accepted by London which adopted the Canadian constitution ...

Thus one sees that the 'compact' theory is a purely political argument which has no legal base.

From the legal point of view, the only thing that concerns us, the BNA Act is a law which conforms, in its entirety, to the political arrangements determined by the representatives of the colonies concerned ...

We can thus affirm now that there is no rule of law flowing from a constitutional convention or otherwise that imposes the obligation for the Senate and the House of Commons to obtain the consent of the Provinces before asking the British Parliament to amend the Canadian constitution ...

As an additional point, even if there were a constitutional convention which would be violated, this violation could not be contested in law as to the procedure followed.

We have seen that the constitutional conventions are not rules of law and their violation does not entail judicial sanctions, but only political sanctions. The authorities in support of this proposition are numerous ...

BÉLANGER, JA (CONCURRING) (Translation)

... I cannot give my accord to the affirmation that one can find in certain opinions already expressed in the Reference re Legislative Authority of Parliament to alter or replace the Senate that it is incompatible with the federal system established by the Act of federation that the Canadian Parliament should be able to modify it in some part without the consent of the Provinces. On this account, one could also ask oneself if it is of the essence of this federal union that it remain stagnant and incapable of evolution in the face of the opposition of a single Province acting in its own special interests which are not necessarily compatible with those of the population in general which the central power represents ...

On several occasions, in the history of our Constitution, it has been a question of a compact to which certain English-language authors refer under the name of 'compact,' whether to confirm its presence or to deny it ... But I do not believe that one could find in the Act of federation the notion that it can not be susceptible to any amendment without the assent of each of the Provinces, for the simple reason that, at the time, the power of amendment of the Act of federation remained, according to all the evidence, solely in the British Parliament.

BISSON, JA (DISSENTING) (Translation)

... To recognise in the Canadian Parliament the juridical capacity to address itself to London (which, according to the federal thesis, could not refuse to agree to such a request) to seek – in spite of the objections of the Provinces – constitutional changes in domains which touch on subjects considered in the exclusive legislative competence of the Provinces or again which affect the statute of the Provinces in the federation, or likewise to permit Parliament to establish unilaterally an amendment formula to the constitutional law, would be equivalent to saying that Canada is, at the present time, a quasi-unitary State.

It would be equivalent to crushing the juridical concept of the exclusive legislative competence of the Provinces on the subjects which have always been recognised to them legislatively.

It would be equivalent to acting as if Canada was only a sort of legislative Union when the partners of the 1860s expressly rejected the legislative Union to opt for a federal union.

Supreme Court judgment
re resolution (extracts)

IN THE MATTER of an Act for expediting the decision of constitutional and other provincial questions, being RSM 1970, c. C-180
AND IN THE MATTER of a Reference pursuant thereto by the Lieutenant Governor in Council to the Court of Appeal for Manitoba for hearing and consideration, the questions concerning the amendment of the Constitution of Canada as set out in Order in Council No. 1020/80

The Attorney General of Manitoba (Appellant)
and
[The Attorneys General of Quebec, Nova Scotia, British Columbia, Prince Edward Island, Saskatchewan, Alberta, and Newfoundland, and Four Nations Confederacy Inc] (Intervenors)

v

The Attorney General of Canada (Respondent)
and
[The Attorneys General of Ontario and New Brunswick] (Intervenors)

The Chief Justice and Martland, Ritchie, Dickson, Beetz, Estey, McIntyre, Chouinard and Lamer JJ.

September 28, 1981.

[The 'group-of-seven' majority opinion]

THE CHIEF JUSTICE AND DICKSON, BEETZ, ESTEY, MCINTYRE, CHOUINARD AND LAMER JJ:

... The submission of the eight Provinces which invites this Court to consider the position of the British Parliament is based on the *Statute of Westminster, 1931* in its application to Canada. The submission is that the effect of the *Statute* is to qualify the authority of the British Parliament to act on the federal Resolution without previous provincial consent where provincial powers and interests are thereby affected, as they plainly are here. This issue will be examined later in these reasons.

Two observations are pertinent here. First, we have the anomaly that although Canada has international recognition as an independent, autonomous and self-governing state, as, for example, a founding member of the United Nations, and through membership in other international associations of sovereign states, yet it suffers from an internal deficiency in the absence of legal power to alter or amend the essential distributive arrangements under which legal authority is exercised in the country, whether at the federal or provincial level. When a country has been in existence as an operating federal state for more than a century, the task of introducing a legal mechanism that will thereafter remove the anomaly undoubtedly raises a profound problem. Secondly, the authority of the British Parliament or its practices and conventions are not matters upon which this Court would presume to pronounce.

The proposition was advanced on behalf of the Attorney General of Manitoba that a convention may crystallize into law and that the requirement of provincial consent to the kind of Resolution that we have here, although in origin political, has become a rule of law. (No firm position was taken on whether the consent must be that of the Governments or that of the Legislatures.)

In our view, this is not so. No instance of an explicit recognition of a convention as having matured into a rule of law was produced. The very nature of a convention, as political in inception and as depending on a consistent course of political recognition by those for whose benefit and to whose detriment (if any) the convention developed over a considerable period of time is inconsistent with its legal enforcement.

The attempted assimilation of the growth of a convention to the growth of the common law is misconceived. The latter is the product of judicial effort, based on justiciable issues which have attained legal formulation and are subject to modification and even reversal by the Courts which gave them birth when acting within their role in the State in obedience to statutes or constitutional directives. No such parental role is played by the Courts with respect to conventions.

It was urged before us that a host of cases have given legal force to conventions. This is an overdrawn proposition. One case in which direct recognition and enforcement of a convention was sought is *Madzimbamuto v. Lardner-Burke*, [1969] 1 AC 645. There the Privy Council rejected the assertion that a convention formally recognized by the United Kingdom as established, namely, that it would not legislate for Southern Rhodesia on matters within the competence of the latter's legislature without its government's consent, could not be overridden by British legislation made applicable to Southern Rhodesia after the unilateral declaration of independence by the latter's government. Speaking for the Privy Council, Lord Reid pointed out that although the convention was a very important one, 'it had no legal effect in limiting the legal power of Parliament' (at p. 723) ...

Quite a number of cases were cited on which counsel for Manitoba relied to support his contention of conventions crystallizing into law. The chief support put forward for the 'crystallization into law' proposition was the opinion of Duff CJC in *Reference re Weekly Rest in Industrial Undertakings Act*, [1936] SCR 461, better known as the *Labour Conventions* case when appealed to the Privy Council, [1937] AC 326, which took a different view on the constitutional merits than did the equally divided Supreme Court of Canada ...

What the learned Chief Justice was dealing with was an evolution which is characteristic of customary international law; the attainment by the Canadian federal executive of full and independent power to enter into international agreements. (Indeed, in speaking of 'convention' in the last quoted paragraph, he was referring to an international agreement ...

There is nothing in the other judgments delivered in the *Labour Conventions* case, either in the Supreme Court or in the Privy Council that takes the matter there beyond its international law setting or lends credence to the crystallization proposition urged by counsel for the Attorney General of Manitoba and, it should be said, supported by other Provinces and by observations in the reasons of the Newfoundland Court of Appeal. Other cases cited for the proposition turn out, on examination, to be instances where the Courts proceeded on firm statutory or other legal principles. This is as true of the observation of Viscount Sankey on the position of the Privy Council in *British Coal Corp. v. The King*, [1935] AC 500 at p. 510, as it is of the denial of injunctive relief in respect of disclosure of the Crossman diaries in *Attorney-General v. Jonathan Cape Ltd.*, [1976] 1 QB 752 ...

A close look at some other cases and issues raised on so-called crystallization reveals no support for the contention ...

Finally, there was an appeal to the Senate Reference decision of this Court. It is baffling how it can be said that this Court recognized convention as having *per se* grown into law. What was involved was a proposed federal enactment sought to be justified mainly under s. 91(1) of the *British North America Act*. This Court held that the proposal, at least in its main features, was beyond federal competence. Although the Court referred to certain historical background for perspective on the position of the Senate as it was dealt with under the *British North America Act*, its fundamental duty was to examine the validity of a proposed federal measure sought to be justified under a grant of federal power under that *Act*.

As to all the cases cited, it must be said that there is no independent force to be found in selective quotations from a portion of the reasons unless regard is had to issues raised and the context in which the quotations are found ...

The leap from convention to law is explained almost as if there was a common law of constitutional law, but originating in political practice. That is simply not so. What is desirable as a political limitation does not translate into a legal limitation, without expression in imperative constitutional text or statute. The position advocated is all the more unacceptable when substantial provincial compliance or consent is ... said to be sufficient ...

This is an impossible position for a Court to manage ...

Turning now to the authority or power of the two federal Houses to proceed by Resolution to forward the address and appended draft statutes to Her Majesty the Queen for enactment by the Parliament of the United Kingdom. There is no limit anywhere in law, either in Canada or in the United Kingdom (having regard to s. 18 of the *British North America Act*, as enacted by 1875 [UK], c. 38, which ties the privileges, immunities and powers of the federal Houses to those of the British House of Commons) to the power of the Houses to pass resolutions ...

For the moment, it is relevant to point out that even in those cases where an amendment to the *British North America Act* was founded on a Resolution of the federal Houses after having received provincial consent, there is no instance, save in the *British North America Act 1930* where such consent was recited in the Resolution. The matter remained, in short, a conventional one within Canada, without effect on the validity of the Resolution in respect of United Kingdom action. The point is underscored in relation to the very first amendment directly affecting provincial legislative power, that in 1940 which added 'Unemployment Insurance' to the catalogue of exclusive federal powers. Sir William Jowitt, then Solicitor-General, and later Lord Chancellor, was asked in the British House of Commons about provincial consent when the amendment was in course of passage. The question put to him and his answer are as follows (see 362 UK Parl. Deb. 5th Series, HC 1177–1181);

Mr. Mander: ... In this bill we are concerned only with the Parliament of Canada, but, as a matter of interest, I would be obliged if the Solicitor-General would say whether the Provincial Canadian Parliaments are in agreement with the proposals submitted by the Dominion Parliament ...

Sir William Jowitt: ... One might think that the Canadian Parliament was in some way subservient to ours, which is not the fact. The true position is that at the request of Canada this old machinery still survives until something better is thought of, but we square the legal with the constitutional position by passing these Acts only in the form that the Canadian Parliament require and at the request of the Canadian Parliament.

My justification to the House for this Bill – and it is important to observe this – is not on the merits of the proposal, which is a matter for the Canadian Parliament; if we were to embark upon that, we might trespass on what I conceive to be their constitutional position. The sole justification for this enactment is that we are doing in this way what the Parliament of Canada desires to do ...

In reply to the hon. Member for East Wolverhampton (Mr. Mander), I do not know what the view of the Provincial Parliaments is. I know, however, that when the matter was before the Privy Council some of the Provincial Parliaments supported the Dominion Parliament. It is a sufficient justification for the Bill that we are morally bound to act on the ground that we have here the request of the Dominion Parliament and that we must operate the old machinery which has been left over at their request in accordance with their wishes.

... This Court is being asked, in effect, to enshrine as a legal imperative a principle of unanimity for constitutional amendment to overcome the anomaly – more of an anomaly today than it was in 1867 – that the *British North America Act* contained no provision for effecting amendments by Canadian action alone. Although Saskatchewan has, alone of the eight Provinces opposing the federal package embodied in the Resolution, taken a less stringent position, eschewing unanimity but without quantifying the substantial support that it advocates, the Provinces, parties to the References and to the appeals here, are entitled to have this Court's primary consideration of their views.

The stark legal question is whether this Court can enact by what would be judicial legislation a formula of unanimity to initiate the amending process which would be binding not only in Canada but also on the Parliament of the United Kingdom with which amending authority would still remain. It would be anomalous indeed, overshadowing the anomaly of a Constitution which contains no provision for its amendment, for this Court to say retroactively that in law we have had an amending formula all along, even if we have not hitherto known it; or, to say, that we have had in law one amending formula, say from 1867 to 1931, and a second amending formula that has emerged after 1931. No one can gainsay the desirability of federal-provincial accord of acceptable compromise. That does not, however, go to legality. As Sir William Jowitt said, and quoted earlier, we must operate the old machinery perhaps one more time ...

The provincial contentions asserted a legal incapacity in the federal Houses to proceed with the Resolution which is the subject of the References and of the appeals here. Joined to this assertion was a claim that the United Kingdom Parliament had, in effect, relinquished its legal power to act on a Resolution such as the one before this Court, and that it could only act in relation to Canada if a request was made by 'the proper authorities' ...

It was contended, certainly with justification, that the 'proper Canadian authorities' were the Dominion and the Provinces and, presumably, it would be for them to decide whether it would be the respective Governments or Parliament and the Legislatures or both, and also what degree of agreement among the Provinces would be proper. It is, however, impossible to draw from this any legal rule of conduct because, ultimately, whatever political consensus might be achieved, there would still be the legal necessity of final United Kingdom legislative action ...

It is important in this connection to emphasize that the Government of Canada had, by 1923, obtained recognition internationally of its independent power to enter into external obligations when it negotiated the Halibut Treaty with the United States. Great Britain understood this by that time as did the United States. The subsequent Imperial Conferences added confirmation, sanctified by the *Statute of Westminster* which also put internal independence from Great Britain on a legal foundation. The remaining badge of subservience, the need to resort to the British Parliament to amend the *British North America Act*, although preserved by the *Statute of Westminster*, did not carry any diminution of Canada's legal right in international law, and as a matter of Canadian constitutional law, to assert its independence in external relations, be they with Great Britain or other countries. The matter is emphasized by the judgment of this Court in *Reference re Offshore Mineral Rights*, [1967] SCR 792, at p. 816. This is a relevant consideration in the appeals which are before this Court.

What is put forward by the Provinces which oppose the forwarding of the address without provincial consent is that external relations with Great Britain in this respect must take account of the nature and character of Canadian federalism. It is contended that a legal underpinning of their position is to be found in the Canadian federal system as reflected in historical antecedents, in the pronouncements of leading political figures and in the preamble to the *British North America Act*.

The arguments from history do not lead to any consistent view or any single view of the nature of the *British North America Act*; selective interpretations are open and have been made; see Report of the Royal Commission on Dominion-Provincial Relations (1940), Book 1, pp. 29 *ff*. History cannot alter the fact that in law there is a British statute to construe and apply in relation to a matter, fundamental as it is, that is not provided for by the statute. Practices which took account of evolving Canadian independence, did, of course, develop. They had both intra-Canadian and extra-Canadian aspects in relation to British legislative authority. The former have already been canvassed, both in the reasons on question 2 and question B and, to a degree, in these reasons. Theories, whether of a full compact theory (which, even factually, cannot be sustained, having regard to federal power to create new Provinces out of federal territories, which was exercised in the creation of Alberta and Saskatchewan) or of a modified compact theory, as urged by some of the Provinces, operate in the political realm, in political science studies. They do not engage the law, save as they might have some peripheral relevance to actual provisions of the *British North America Act* and its interpretation and application ...

In short, as in the attempt to argue crystallization of convention into law, there is nothing in the reference to theories of federalism reflected in some case law that goes beyond their use as an aid to a justiciable question raised apart from them.

So too, with pronouncements by political figures or persons in other branches of public life. There is little profit in parading them ...

The Attorney General of Canada was pushed to the extreme by being forced to answer affirmatively the theoretical question whether in law the federal Government could procure an amendment to the *British North America Act* that would turn Canada into a unitary state. That is not what the present Resolution envisages because the essential federal character of the country is preserved under the enactments proposed by the Resolution.

That, it is argued, is no reason for conceding unilateral federal authority to accomplish, through invocation of legislation by the United Kingdom Parliament, the purposes of the Resolution. There is here, however, an unprecedented situation in which the one constant since the enactment of the *British North America Act* in 1867 has been the legal authority of the United Kingdom Parliament to amend it. The law knows nothing of any requirement of provincial consent, either to a resolution of the federal Houses or as a condition of the exercise of United Kingdom legislative power ...

Nothing said in these reasons is to be construed as either favouring or disapproving the proposed amending formula or the *Charter of Rights and Freedoms* or any of the other provisions of which enactment is sought. The questions put to this Court do not ask for its approval or disapproval of the contents of the so-called 'package.'

What is central here is the untrammelled authority at law of the two federal Houses to proceed as they wish in the management of their own procedures and hence to adopt the Resolution which is intended for submission to Her Majesty for action thereon by the United Kingdom Parliament. The *British North America Act* does not, either in terms or by implication, control this authority or require that it be subordinated to provincial assent. Nor does the *Statute of Westminster* interpose any requirement of such assent. If anything, it leaves the position as it was before its enactment. Developments subsequent thereto do not affect the legal position ...

MARTLAND AND RITCHIE JJ [dissenting]:

... At the outset, we would point out that we are not concerned with the matter of legality or illegality in the sense of determining whether or not the passage of the resolution under consideration involves a breach of the law. The issue is as to the existence of a power to do that which is proposed to be done. The question is whether it is *intra vires* of the Senate and the House of Commons to cause the proposed amendments to the BNA Act to be made by the Imperial Parliament by means of the resolution now before the Court, in the absence of provincial agreement ...

In no instance has an amendment to the BNA act been enacted which directly affected federal-provincial relationships in the sense of changing provincial legislative powers, in the absence of federal consultation with and the consent of all the provinces. Notably, this procedure continued to be followed in the four instances which occurred after the enactment of the *Statute of Westminster* (herein the Statute of Westminster).

This history of amendments reveals the operation of constitutional constraints. While the choice of the resolution procedure is itself a matter of internal parliamentary responsibility, the making of the addresses to the Sovereign falls into two areas.

Resolutions concerning the federal juristic unit and federal powers were made without reference to any but the members of the federal Houses. Resolutions abridging provincial authority have never been passed without the concurrence of the Provinces. In other words, the normal constitutional principles recognizing the inviolability of separate and exclusive legislative powers were carried into and considered an integral part of the operation of the resolution procedure ...

In the result, if this process is examined from the point of view of substance rather than of form, what is being asserted is the existence of a power in the Senate and the House of Commons to cause any amendment to the BNA Act which they desire to be enacted, even though that amendment subtracts, without provincial consent, from the legislative powers of the Provinces granted to them by the BNA Act ...

The effect of the position taken by the Attorney General of Canada is that the two Houses of Parliament have unfettered control of a triggering mechanism by means of which they can cause the BNA Act to be amended in any way they desire. It was frankly conceded in argument that there were no limits of any kind upon the type of amendment that could be made in this fashion. In our opinion, this argument in essence maintains that the Provinces have since, at the latest 1931, owed their continued existence not to their constitutional powers expressed in the BNA Act, but to the Federal Parliament's sufferance. While the Federal Parliament was throughout this period incompetent to legislate in respect of matters assigned to the Provinces by s. 92, its two Houses could at any time have done so by means of a resolution to the Imperial Parliament, procuring an amendment to the BNA Act.

The Attorney General of Canada, in substance, is asserting the existence of a power in the two Houses of Parliament to obtain amendments to the BNA Act which could disturb and even destroy the federal system of constitutional government in Canada. We are not aware of any possible legal source for such a power. The House of Commons and the Senate are part of the Parliament of Canada. Section 17 of the BNA Act states that there 'shall be one Parliament for Canada, consisting of the Queen, an Upper House styled the Senate and the House of Commons.' Laws under s. 91 of the BNA Act are enacted by the Queen, with the advice and consent of the Senate and House of Commons. These two constituents of Parliament cannot by themselves enact legislation, nor could Parliament clothe them with powers beyond those possessed by Parliament itself ...

The federal position in these appeals can be summarized in these terms. While the Federal Parliament lacks legal authority to achieve the objectives set out in the Resolution by the enactment of its own legislation, that limitation upon its authority can be evaded by having the legislation enacted by the Imperial Parliament at the behest of a resolution of the two Houses of the Federal Parliament. This is an attempt by the Federal Parliament to accomplish indirectly that which it is legally precluded from doing directly by perverting the recognized resolution method of obtaining constitutional amendments by the Imperial Parliament for an improper purpose. In our opinion, since it is beyond the power of the Federal Parliament to enact such an amendment, it is equally beyond the power of its two Houses to effect such an amendment through the agency of the Imperial Parliament ...

Conclusions:
The BNA Act created a federal union. It was of the very essence of the federal nature of the Constitution that the Parliament of Canada and the Provincial Legislatures should have distinct and separate legislative powers ...

The fact that the status of Canada became recognized as a sovereign state did not alter its federal nature. It is a sovereign state, but its government is federal in character with a clear division of legislative powers. The Resolution at issue in these appeals could only be an effective expression of Canadian sovereignty if it had the support of both levels of government.

The two Houses of the Canadian Parliament claim the power unilaterally to effect an amendment to the BNA Act which they desire, including the curtailment of Provincial legislative powers. This strikes at the basis of the whole federal system. It asserts a right by one part of the Canadian governmental system to curtail, without agreement, the powers of the other part.

There is no statutory basis for the exercise of such a power. On the contrary, the powers of the Senate and the House of Commons, given to them by paragraph 4(a) of the *Senate and House of Commons Act*, excluded the power to do anything inconsistent with the BNA Act. The exercise of such a power has no support in constitutional convention. The constitutional convention is entirely to the contrary. We see no other basis for the recognition of the existence of such a power. This being so, it is the proper function of this Court, in its role of protecting and preserving the Canadian Constitution, to declare that no such power exists. We are, therefore, of the opinion that the Canadian Constitution does not empower the Senate and the House of Commons to cause the Canadian Constitution to be amended in respect of Provincial legislative powers without the consent of the Provinces.

Question B in the Quebec Reference raises the issue as to the power of the Senate and the House of Commons of Canada to cause the Canadian Constitution to be amended 'without the consent of the provinces and in spite of the objection of several of them.' The Attorney General of Saskatchewan when dealing with Question 3 in the Manitoba and Newfoundland References submitted that it was not necessary in these proceedings for the Court to pronounce on the necessity for the unanimous consent of all the Provinces to the constitutional amendments proposed in the Resolution. It was sufficient, in order to answer the Question, to note the opposition of eight of the provinces which contained a majority of the population of Canada ...

[The 'group-of-six' majority opinion]

MARTLAND, RITCHIE, DICKSON, BEETZ, CHOUINARD AND LAMER JJ:

... In these questions, the phrases 'Constitution of Canada' and 'Canadian Constitution' do not refer to matters of interest only to the federal government or federal juristic unit. They are clearly meant in a broader sense and embrace the global system of rules and principles which govern the exercise of constitutional authority in the whole and in every part of the Canadian State. They will be used in the same broad sense in these reasons ...

Counsel for several provinces strenuously argued that the convention exists and requires the agreement of all the provinces. However, we did not understand any of them to have taken the position that the second question in the Manitoba and Newfoundland References should be dealt with and answered as if the last part of the question read '... without obtaining the agreement of *all* the provinces?'

Be that as it may, the question should not in our view be so read ...

1- The nature of constitutional conventions

A substantial part of the rules of the Canadian Constitution are written. They are contained not in a single document called a Constitution but in a great variety of statutes some of which have been enacted by the Parliament of Westminster, such as the *British North America Act 1867*, ... (the *BNA Act*) or by the Parliament of Canada, such as *The Alberta Act*, ... *The Saskatchewan Act*, ... the *Senate and House of Commons Act*, ... or by the provincial legislatures, such as the provincial electoral acts. They are also to be found in orders in council like the Imperial Order in Council of May 16, 1871 admitting British Columbia into the Union, and the Imperial Order in Council of June 26, 1873, admitting Prince Edward Island into the Union.

Another part of the Constitution of Canada consists of the rules of the common law. These are rules which the courts have developed over the centuries in the discharge of their judicial duties. An important portion of these rules concerns the prerogative of the Crown ...

Those parts of the Constitution of Canada which are composed of statutory rules and common law rules are generically referred to as the law of the Constitution. In cases of doubt or dispute, it is the function of the courts to declare what the law is and since the law is sometimes breached, it is generally the function of the courts to ascertain whether it has in fact been breached in specific instances and, if so, to apply such sanctions as are contemplated by the law, whether they be punitive sanctions or civil sanctions such as a declaration of nullity ...

But many Canadians would perhaps be surprised to learn that important parts of the Constitution of Canada, with which they are the most familiar because they are directly involved when they exercise their right to vote at federal and provincial elections, are nowhere to be found in the law of the Constitution. For instance it is a fundamental requirement of the Constitution that if the Opposition obtains the majority at the polls, the Government must tender its resignation forthwith. But fundamental as it is, this requirement of the Constitution does not form part of the law of the Constitution ...

Yet none of these essential rules of the Constitution can be said to be a law of the Constitution. It was apparently Dicey who, in the first edition of his *Law of the Constitution*, in 1885, called them 'the conventions of the constitution,' ... an expression which quickly became current. What Dicey described under these terms are the principles and rules of responsible government, several of which are stated above and which regulate the relations between the Crown, the Prime Minister, the Cabinet and the two Houses of Parliament. These rules developed in Great Britain by way of custom and precedent during the nineteenth century and were exported to such British colonies as were granted self-government ...

The main purpose of constitutional conventions is to ensure that the legal framework of the Constitution will be operated in accordance with the prevailing constitutional values or principles of the period. For example, the constitutional value which is the pivot of the conventions stated above and relating to responsible government is the democratic principle: the powers of the state must be exercised in accordance with the wishes of the electorate; and the constitutional value or principle which anchors the conventions regulating the relationship between the members of the Commonwealth is the independence of the former British colonies.

Being based on custom and precedent, constitutional conventions are usually unwritten rules. Some of them however may be reduced to writing and expressed in the proceedings and documents of imperial conferences, or in the preamble of statutes such as the *Statute of Westminster, 1931,* or in the proceedings and documents of federal-provincial conferences. They are often referred to and recognized in statements made by members of governments.

The conventional rules of the Constitution present one striking peculiarity. In contradistinction to the laws of the Constitution, they are not enforced by the courts. One reason for this situation is that, unlike common law rules, conventions are not judge-made rules. They are not based on judicial precedents but on precedents established by the institutions of government themselves. Nor are they in the nature of statutory commands which it is the function and duty of the courts to obey and enforce. Furthermore, to enforce them would mean to administer some formal sanction when they are breached. But the legal system from which they are distinct does not contemplate formal sanctions for their breach.

Perhaps the main reason why conventional rules cannot be enforced by the courts is that they are generally in conflict with the legal rules which they postulate and the courts are bound to enforce the legal rules. The conflict is not of a type which would entail the commission of any illegality. It results from the fact that legal rules create wide powers, discretions and rights which conventions prescribe should be exercised only in a certain limited manner, if at all ...

This conflict between convention and law which prevents the courts from enforcing conventions also prevents conventions from crystallizing into laws, unless it be by statutory adoption.

It is because the sanctions of convention rest with institutions of government other than courts, such as the Governor General or the Lieutenant-Governor, or the Houses of Parliament, or with public opinion and ultimately, with the electorate that it is generally said that they are political.

It should be borne in mind however that, while they are not laws, some conventions may be more important than some laws. Their importance depends on that of the value or principle which they are meant to safeguard. Also they form an integral part of the Constitution and of the constitutional system. They come within the meaning of the word 'Constitution' in the preamble of the *British North America Act, 1867:* 'Whereas the Provinces of Canada, Nova Scotia and New Brunswick have expressed their Desire to be federally united ... with a Constitution similar in principle to that of the United Kingdom.'

That is why it is perfectly appropriate to say that to violate a convention is to do something which is unconstitutional although it entails no direct legal consequence. But the words 'constitutional' and 'unconstitutional' may also be used in a strict legal sense, for instance with respect to a statute which is found *ultra vires* or unconstitutional. The foregoing may perhaps be summarized in an equation: constitutional conventions plus constitutional law equal the total Constitution of the country.

II – Whether the questions should be answered
It was submitted by counsel for Canada and for Ontario that the second question in the Manitoba and Newfoundland References and the conventional part of question B in the Quebec Reference ought not be answered because they do not raise a justiciable issue and are accordingly not appropriate for a court. It was contended that the issue whether a particular convention exists or not is a purely political one. The existence of a definite convention is always unclear and a matter of debate. Further-

more conventions are flexible, somewhat imprecise and unsuitable for judicial determination ...

In our view, we should not, in a constitutional reference, decline to accomplish a type of exercise that courts have been doing of their own motion for years.

III – Whether the convention exists
It was submitted by Counsel for Canada, Ontario and New Brunswick that there is no constitutional convention that the House of Commons and Senate of Canada will not request Her Majesty the Queen to lay before the Parliament of Westminster a measure to amend the Constitution of Canada affecting federal-provincial relationships, etc., without first obtaining the agreement of the provinces ...

Requirements for establishing a convention
The requirements for establishing a convention bear some resemblance with those which apply to customary law. Precedents and usage are necessary but do not suffice. They must be normative ...

The precedents
An account of the statutes enacted by the Parliament of Westminster to modify the Constitution of Canada is found in a White Paper published in 1965 under the authority of the Honourable Guy Favreau, then Minister of Justice for Canada, under the title of 'The Amendment of the Constitution of Canada' (the *White Paper*) ... These precedents must be considered selectively. They must also be considered in positive as well as in negative terms.

Of these twenty-two amendments or groups of amendments, five directly affected federal-provincial relationships in the sense of changing provincial legislative powers: they are the amendment of 1930, the *Statute of Westminster, 1931*, and the amendments of 1940, 1951 and 1964 ...

These five amendments are the only ones which can be viewed as positive precedents whereby federal-provincial relationships were directly affected in the sense of changing legislative powers.

Every one of these five amendments was agreed upon by each province whose legislative authority was affected.

In negative terms, no amendment changing provincial legislative powers has been made since Confederation when agreement of a province whose legislative powers would have been changed was withheld.

There are no exceptions ...

The accumulation of these precedents, positive and negative, concurrent and without exception, does not of itself suffice in establishing the existence of the convention; but it unmistakedly points in its direction. Indeed, if the precedents stood alone, it might be argued that unanimity is required ...

In our respectful opinion, the majority of the Quebec Court of Appeal fell into error on this issue in failing to differentiate between various types of constitutional amendments. The Quebec Court of Appeal put all or practically all constitutional amendments since 1867 on the same footing and, as could then be expected, concluded not only that the convention requiring provincial consent did not exist but that there even appeared to be a convention to the contrary. (See the reasons of Crête, CJQ and Turgeon, JA at pages 92 and 124 of the case in the Quebec Reference. Owen JA agreed with Turgeon JA on this issue, and Bélanger JA with both Crête CJQ and Turgeon JA).

The Manitoba Court of Appeal was similarly misled, in our respectful opinion, but to a lesser extent, which perhaps explains that Freedman CJM wrote at p. 21 of the Manitoba Reference, speaking for himself, Matas and Huband, JJA on this point: 'That we may be moving towards such a convention is certainly a tenable view. But we have not yet arrived there.' ...

We have also indicated that while the precedents point at unanimity, it does not appear that all the actors in the precedents have accepted the unanimity rule as a binding one ...

Furthermore, the Government of Canada and the Governments of the provinces have attempted to reach a consensus on a constitutional amending formula in the course of ten federal-provincial conferences held in 1927, 1931, 1935, 1950, 1960, 1964, 1971, 1978, 1979 and 1980. A major issue at these conferences was the quantification of provincial consent. No consensus was reached on this issue. But the discussion of this very issue for more than fifty years postulates a clear recognition by all the governments concerned of the principle that a substantial degree of provincial consent is required.

It would not be appropriate for the Court to devise in the abstract a specific formula which would indicate in positive terms what measure of provincial agreement is required for the convention to be complied with. Conventions by their nature develop in the political field and it will be for the political actors, not this Court, to determine the degree of provincial consent required.

It is sufficient for the Court to decide that at least a substantial measure of provincial consent is required and to decide further whether the situation before the Court meets with this requirement. The situation is one where Ontario and New Brunswick agree with the proposed amendments whereas the eight other provinces oppose it. By no conceivable standard could this situation be thought to pass muster. It clearly does not disclose a sufficient measure of provincial agreement. Nothing more should be said about this.

A reason for the rule

The reason for the rule is the federal principle. Canada is a federal union. The preamble of the *BNA Act* states that 'the Provinces of Canada, Nova Scotia, and New Brunswick have expressed their Desire to be federally united ...' ...

The federal principle cannot be reconciled with a state of affairs where the modification of provincial legislative powers could be obtained by the unilateral action of the federal authorities. It would indeed offend the federal principle that 'a radical change to [the] constitution [be] taken at the request of a bare majority of the members of the Canadian House of Commons and Senate' ...

This is an essential requirement of the federal principle which was clearly recognized by the Dominion-Provincial Conference of 1931 ...

The purpose of this conventional rule is to protect the federal character of the Canadian Constitution and prevent the anomaly that the House of Commons and Senate could obtain by simple resolutions what they could not validly accomplish by statute.

It was contended by Counsel for Canada, Ontario and New Brunswick that the proposed amendments would not offend the federal principle and that, if they became law, Canada would remain a federation. The federal principle would even be re-inforced, it was said, since the provinces would as a matter of law be given an important role in the amending formula.

It is true that Canada would remain a federation if the proposed amendments became law. But it would be a different federation made different at the instance of a majority in the Houses of the federal Parliament acting alone. It is this process itself which offends the federal principle ...

Conclusion

We have reached the conclusion that the agreement of the provinces of Canada, no views being expressed as to its quantification, is constitutionally required for the passing of the 'Proposed Resolution for a joint Address to Her Majesty respecting the Constitution of Canada' and that the passing of this Resolution without such agreement would be unconstitutional in the conventional sense ...

THE CHIEF JUSTICE AND ESTEY AND MCINTYRE JJ [dissenting]:

... We cannot, however, agree with any suggestion that the non-observance of a convention can properly be termed unconstitutional in any strict or legal sense, or that its observance could be, in any sense, a constitutional requirement within the meaning of Question 3 of the Manitoba and Newfoundland References. In a federal state where the essential feature of the Constitution must be the distribution of powers between the two levels of government, each supreme in its own legislative sphere, constitutionality and legality must be synonymous, and conventional rules will be accorded less significance than they may have in a unitary state such as the United Kingdom. At the risk of undue repetition, the point must again be made that constitutionalism in a unitary state and practices in the national and regional political units of a federal state must be differentiated from constitutional law in a federal state. Such law cannot be ascribed to informal or customary origins, but must be found in a formal document which is the source of authority, legal authority, through which the central and regional units function and exercise their powers ...

As has been pointed out by the majority, a fundamental difference between the legal, that is the statutory and common law rules of the Constitution, and the conventional rules is that, while a breach of the legal rules, whether of statutory or common law nature, has a legal consequence in that it will be restrained by the courts, no such sanction exists for breach or non-observance of the conventional rules. The observance of constitutional conventions depends upon the acceptance of the obligation of conformance by the actors deemed to be bound thereby. When this consideration is insufficient to compel observance no court may enforce the convention by legal action. The sanction for non-observance of a convention is political in that disregard of a convention may lead to political defeat, to loss of office, or to other political consequences, but it will not engage the attention of the courts which are limited to matters of law alone. Courts, however, may recognize the existence of conventions and that is what is asked of us in answering the questions. The answer, whether affirmative or negative however, can have no legal effect, and acts performed or done in conformance with the law, even though in direct contradiction of well-established conventions, will not be enjoined or set aside by the courts. For one of many examples of the application of this principle see: *Stella Madzimbamuto v. Desmond William Lardner-Burke and Frederick Phillip George*, [1969] 1 AC 645. Simple convention cannot create such a power in either level of government. A Canadian convention could only be of negative effect, that is, to limit the exercise of such power. However, no limitative practice can have the effect of giving away such power where it exists in law ...

The general rule that the Governor General will act only according to the advice of the Prime Minister is purely conventional and is not to be found in any legal enactment. In the same category is the rule that after a general election the Governor General will call upon the leader of the party with the greatest number of seats to form a government. The rule of responsible government that a government losing the confidence of the House of Commons must itself resign, or obtain a dissolution, the general principles of majority rule and responsible government underlying the daily workings of the institutions of the executive and legislative branches of each level of government, and a variety of other such conventional arrangements, serve as further illustrations. These rules have an historical origin and bind, and have bound, the actors in constitutional matters in Canada for generations. No one can doubt their operative force or the reality of their existence as an effective part of the Canadian Constitution. They are, nonetheless, conventional and, therefore, distinct from purely legal rules. They are observed without demur because all parties concerned recognize their existence and accept the obligation of observance, considering themselves to be bound. Even though it may be, as the majority of the Court has said, a matter of some surprise to many Canadians, these conventions have no legal force. They are, in short, the product of political experience, the adoption of which allows the political process to function in a way acceptable to the community.

These then are recognized conventions, they are definite, understandable and understood. They have the unquestioned acceptance not only of the actors in political affairs but of the public at large. Can it be said that any convention having such clear definition and acceptance concerning provincial participation in the amendment of the Canadian Constitution has developed? It is in the light of this comparison that the existence of any supposed constitutional convention must be considered. It is abundantly clear, in our view, that the answer must be No. The degree of provincial participation in constitutional amendments has been a subject of lasting controversy in Canadian political life for generations. It cannot be asserted, in our opinion, that any view on this subject has become so clear and so broadly accepted as to constitute a constitutional convention. It should be observed that there is a fundamental difference between the convention in the Dicey concept and the convention for which some of the Provinces here contend. The Dicey convention relates to the functioning of individuals and institutions within a parliamentary democracy in unitary form. It does not qualify or limit the authority or sovereignty of Parliament or the Crown. The convention sought to be advanced here would truncate the functioning of the executive and legislative branches at the federal level. This would impose a limitation on the sovereign body itself within the Constitution. Surely such a convention would require for its recognition, even in the non-legal, political sphere, the clearest signal from the plenary unit intended to be bound, and not simply a plea from the majority of the beneficiaries of such a convention, the provincial plenary units.

An examination of the Canadian experience since Confederation will, bearing in mind the considerations above described, serve to support our conclusion on this question. It may be observed here that it was not suggested in argument before this Court that there was any procedure for amendment now available other than by the addresses of both Houses of Parliament to Her Majesty the Queen. It was argued, however, that this was a procedural step only and that before it could be undertaken by Parliament the consent of the Provinces would be required. It is with the frequency with which provincial consents were obtained or omitted, with the circumstances under which consent was or was not sought, with the nature of the amendments involved, and with provincial attitudes towards them that we must concern ourselves. As has been pointed out in other judgments on these References, here and in the other courts, there have been since Confederation some twenty-two amendments to the *BNA Act* ...

Prior to the amendment effected by the *BNA Act* of 1930 there were at least three amendments, those of 1886, 1907 and 1915, which substantially affected the Provinces and which were procured without the consent of all the Provinces ...

These precedents, it may be said, should by themselves have only a modest influence in the consideration of the question before the Court. It is clear, however, that no support whatever for the convention may be found on an examination of the amendments made up to 1930. None had full provincial approval.

The *BNA Act* of 1930 provided for the transfer of natural resources within the provincial territories to the Provinces of Manitoba, Saskatchewan and Alberta. It also provided for the re-conveyance of certain railway lands to British Columbia. In effecting this amendment the consent of the Provinces directly concerned, *i.e.* the four western Provinces only, was obtained, although the arrangement had received the general approval of the other provinces as expressed at a conference in 1927. This is a precedent of modest weight, but it is worthy of note that despite the fact that the interests of all non-involved provinces were affected by the alienation of the assets formerly under federal control, it was not considered necessary to procure any formal consent from them. It is of more than passing interest to note that in the amending procedure provided for in the *1930 British North America Act Amendment* there is no requirement for consent or participation by any of the other five provinces (as they then were) although their indirect interest in federal resources might be affected.

The amendments of 1943, 1946, 1949, 1949(2), 1950 and 1960 were not considered of great significance on this issue by the parties and little comment was made upon them but all, save that of 1960, were achieved without full provincial consent ...

After examining the amendments made since Confederation, and after observing that out of the twenty-two amendments listed above only in the case of four was unanimous provincial consent sought or obtained and, even after according special weight to those amendments relied on by the Provinces, we cannot agree that history justifies a conclusion that the convention contended for by the Provinces has emerged ...

Only in four cases has full provincial consent been obtained and in many cases the federal government has proceeded with amendments in the face of active provincial opposition. In our view, it is unrealistic in the extreme to say that the convention has emerged ...

A convention requires universal recognition by the actors in a scheme and this is certainly so where, as here, acceptance of a convention involves the surrender of a power by a sovereign body said to be a party to the convention. Furthermore, in recognizing uncertainty in specifying the degree of provincial participation, it denies the existence of any convention ...

If there is difficulty in defining the degree of provincial participation, which there surely is, it cannot be said that any convention on the subject has been settled and recognized as a constitutional condition for the making of an amendment. It is the very difficulty of fixing the degree of provincial participation which, while it remains unresolved, prevents the formation or recognition of any convention. It robs any supposed convention of that degree of definition which is necessary to allow for its operation, for its binding effect upon the persons deemed to be bound, and it renders difficult if not impossible any clear discernment of a breach of the convention ...

It was also argued that Canada was formed as a federal union and that the existence of a legal power of the central government to unilaterally change the Constitution was inimical to the concept of federalism. The convention then, it was argued, arose out of the necessity to restrain such unilateral conduct and preserve the federal nature of Canada ...

We are asked to say whether the need for the preservation of the principles of Canadian federalism dictates the necessity for a convention, requiring consent from the Provinces as a condition of the exercise by the federal government of its legal powers, to procure amendment to the Canadian Constitution. If the convention requires only partial consent, as is contended by Saskatchewan, it is difficult to see how the federal concept is thereby protected for, while those provinces favouring amendment would be pleased, those refusing consent could claim coercion. If unanimous consent is required (as contended by the other objecting provinces), while it may be said that in general terms the concept of federalism would be protected it would only be by overlooking the special nature of Canadian federalism that this protection would be achieved. The *BNA Act* has not created a perfect or ideal federal state. Its provisions have accorded a measure of paramountcy to the federal Parliament. Certainly this has been done in a more marked degree in Canada than in many other federal states. For example, one need only look to the power of reservation and disallowance of provincial enactments; the power to declare works in a province to be for the benefit of all Canada and to place them under federal regulatory control; the wide powers to legislate generally for the peace, order and good government of Canada as a whole; the power to enact the criminal law of the entire country; the power to create and admit provinces out of existing territories and, as well, the paramountcy accorded federal legislation. It is this special nature of Canadian federalism which deprives the federalism argument described above of its force. This is particularly true when it involves the final settlement of Canadian constitutional affairs with an external government, the federal authority being the sole conduit for communication between Canada and the Sovereign and Canada alone having the power to deal in external matters. We therefore reject the argument that the preservation of the principles of Canadian federalism requires the recognition of the convention asserted before us ...

We feel obliged to make a further comment related to the federalism argument. It was argued that the federal authorities were assuming a power to act without restraint in disregard of provincial wishes which could go so far as to convert Canada into a unitary state by means of a majority vote in the Houses of Parliament. A few words will suffice to lay that argument at rest. What is before the Court is the task of answering the questions posed in three references. As has been pointed out, the Court can do no more than that. The questions all deal with the constitutional validity of precise proposals for constitutional amendment and they form the complete subject-matter of the Court's inquiry and our comments must be made with reference to them. It is not for the Court to express views on the wisdom or lack of wisdom of these proposals. We are concerned solely with their constitutionality. In view of the fact that the unitary argument has been raised, however, it should be noted, in our view, that the federal constitutional proposals, which preserve a federal state without disturbing the distribution or balance of power, would create an amending formula which would enshrine provincial rights on the question of amendments on a secure, legal and constitutional footing, and would extinguish, as well, any presently existing power on the part of the federal Parliament to act unilaterally in constitutional matters. In so doing, it may be said that the Parliamentary resolution here under examination does not, save for the enactment of the *Charter of Rights*, which circumscribes the legislative powers of both the federal and provincial Legislatures, truly amend the Canadian Constitution. Its effect is to complete the formation of an incomplete constitution by supplying its present deficiency, *i.e.* an amending formula, which will enable the Constitution to be amended in Canada as befits a sovereign state. We are not here faced with an action which in any way has the effect of transforming this federal union into a unitary state. The *in terrorem* argument raising the spectre of a unitary state has no validity.

Notes

INTRODUCTION: FROM DUALISM TO REGIONALISM

1 *Quebec and the Constitution*, xii, 23, 32, 139
2 Ibid, 8
3 Ibid, 120
4 Special Joint Committee of the Senate and of the House of Commons on the Constitution of Canada, *Report to Parliament* (10 October 1978)
5 See Senate, Special Committee of the Senate on the Constitution, *First Report* (10 October 1978), in ibid, 129–31.
6 The Task Force on Canadian Unity, Report, Vol. 1, *A Future Together. Observations and Recommendations* (January 1979); Vol. 2, *Coming to Terms. The Words of the Debate* (February 1979); Vol. 3, *A Time to Speak. The Views of the Public* (March 1979)
7 *Une Nouvelle Fédération canadienne. La Commission constitutionnelle du Parti libéral du Québec* (1980)
8 Reference re Legislative Authority of Parliament to Alter or Replace the Senate, 102 DLR (3d) 1 (1979)

CHAPTER ONE: CONSTITUTIONAL INTERLUDE 1979–80

1 Jeffrey Simpson, *Globe and Mail*, Toronto, 5 February 1979
2 *Globe and Mail*, 7 February 1979
3 See Edward McWhinney, *Quebec and the Constitution 1960–1978* (Toronto 1979), 82–4.
4 *Le Devoir*, Montreal, 12 February 1980
5 *The Province*, Vancouver, 8 January 1980; and see also *Le Devoir*, Montreal, 24 September 1979.
6 Reference re Ownership of Off-Shore Mineral Rights, 65 DLR (2d) 353 (1968)
7 Cadre de référence pour le groupe de travail sur le renouvellement de la Fédération, *Le Devoir*, Montreal, 9 January 1980; and see also *Globe and Mail*, Toronto, 22 December 1979.
8 *Le Devoir*, 8 January 1980; *Globe and Mail*, 9 January 1980
9 On the rise and fall of the Clark government, generally, see Jeffrey Simpson, *Discipline of Power* (Toronto 1980).

CHAPTER TWO: CONSTITUTIONAL PARAMETERS

1 *Le Devoir*, Montreal, 4 July 1979
2 *Globe and Mail*, Toronto, 7 May 1981
3 *Globe and Mail*, 10 December 1979; *Vancouver Sun*, 11 December 1979
4 *Edwards* v *Attorney-General of Canada*, [1930] AC 124; *Attorney-General of Ontario* v *Attorney-General of Canada*, [1947] AC 127
5 *Le Devoir*, 14 December 1979
6 Ibid, 15 December 1979
7 Gérald Beaudoin, ibid, 20 December 1979
8 *Le Devoir*, 15 February 1980
9 Text not available when this book in press
10 *Globe and Mail*, 7 April 1981
11 *Anderson* v *Commonwealth*, 47 CLR 50 (1932)
12 *Thorson* v *Attorney-General of Canada*, 43 DLR (3d) 1 (1975); *Nova Scotia Board of Censors* v *McNeil*, 55 DLR (3d) 632 (1976)
13 Michel Roy, *Le Devoir*, 14 December 1979
14 *Le Devoir*, 17 December 1979
15 *The Province*, Vancouver, 14 December 1979; *Le Devoir*, 14 December 1979
16 *Le Devoir*, 24 March 1980

CHAPTER THREE: THE QUEBEC REFERENDUM

1 *Le Devoir*, Montreal, 24 December 1979
2 Ibid, 21 December 1979
3 Ibid, 4 January 1980, 23 February 1980
4 *Le Devoir*, 2 May 1980
5 76 DLR (3d) 455 (1977); 89 DLR (3d) 495 (1979)
6 *Le Devoir*, 21 August 1979
7 Donald V. Smiley, *Canada in Question. Federalism in the Eighties*, (3rd edn Toronto 1980), 305–6

CHAPTER FOUR: FEDERAL-PROVINCIAL DIPLOMACY, SUMMER 1980

1 Michel Roy, 'Un pari légitime mais incertain,' *Le Devoir*, Montreal, 24 May 1980; William Johnson, *Globe and Mail*, Toronto, 13 June 1980
2 Jean-Claude Picard, 'Lévesque s'engage à négocier de bonne foi,' *Le Devoir*, 24 May 1980
3 Jean-Claude Picard, 'Ni passif ni attentiste, Québec fondera sa position sur l'idée des deux peuples,' *Le Devoir*, 30 May 1980
4 Claude Turcotte, 'Trudeau désire obtenir des résultats dans 10 mois,' *Le Devoir*, 30 May 1980
5 John Fraser, *Globe and Mail*, 5 June 1980
6 The sidelined players denied a direct voice in the constitutional debate also included the Yukon and the Northwest Territories; editorial, 'The absent territories,' *Globe and Mail*, 6 June 1980. And see also Robert Décary, 'Qui parlera au nom de qui?,' *Le Devoir*, 26 June 1980.
7 Edward McWhinney, *Quebec and the Constitution 1960–1978* (Toronto 1979) 109

8 'Language Rights and the Constitution,' *Language and Society* (Ottawa, winter 1981), 23; and see also Gérald A. Beaudoin, 'Les droit linguistiques,' in ibid, (autumn 1980), 3.
9 *Le Devoir*, 11 June 1980
10 Ibid
11 Ibid
12 Ibid
13 Mary Trueman, *Globe and Mail*, 10 June 1980; Robert Sheppard, ibid, 11 June 1980
14 *Globe and Mail*, 12 June 1980
15 Jean-Claude Picard, *Le Devoir*, 17 June 1980
16 *Globe and Mail*, 8 July 1980
17 Margot Gibb-Clark, 'Rights charter greeted coolly at BNA talks,' *Globe and Mail*, 10 July 1980; Rodolphe Morissette, 'Le projet de la Charte des droits rejeté par la majorité des provinces,' *Le Devoir*, 10 July 1980
18 Jean-Claude Picard, 'Les mêmes divisions réapparaissent,' *Le Devoir*, 10 July 1980
19 Jean-Claude Picard, *Le Devoir*, 12 July 1980
20 *Le Devoir*, 11 August 1980; *Vancouver Sun*, 20 August 1980; Stan Oziewicz and Jeff Sallot, 'Ontario isolated, 9 provinces unite in export tax war,' *Globe and Mail*, 23 August 1980; Bernard Descôteaux, 'L'Ontario rompt l'accord des neuf autres provinces,' *Le Devoir*, 23 August 1980
21 'Who wrecked the negotiations? Bennett shares the blame with Peckford, some say,' *The Province*, Vancouver, 14 September 1980; 'Bennet, Peckford deny "disruption",' *Vancouver Sun*, 15 September 1980
22 Jeffrey Simpson, 'Vital elements to end the hang-up were missing,' *Globe and Mail*, 16 September 1980; Michel Roy, 'Le malheureux dénouement,' *Le Devoir*, 15 September 1980

CHAPTER FIVE: UNILATERAL FEDERAL ACTION

1 See, for example, the earlier hints at a federal referendum route to constitutional change: Michael Valpy, 'The last resort: a national plebiscite,' *Vancouver Sun*, 22 May 1980.
2 The Supreme Court's opinion makes a brief review, in passing, of the post-1867 approach to amendment of the BNA Act; but it is not a necessary element in the ruling, ie it could not be considered as part of the *ratio decidendi* (and therefore legally binding); see 102 DLR (3d) 1, at 7ff (1979).
3 See the historical review in the federal government white paper, Guy Favreau, *The Amendment of the Constitution of Canada* (Ottawa, February 1965).
4 The project for a federal bill of rights, directly entrenched in the BNA Act itself in contrast to the statutory bill of rights of 1960, had been associated with Trudeau from his earliest political life as justice minister in the Pearson government: see his white paper, *A Canadian Charter of Human Rights* (Ottawa, January 1968).
5 Edward McWhinney, *Quebec and the Constitution 1960–1978* (Toronto 1979), 56ff
6 The native peoples, though not mentioned in the preliminary drafts of the proposed resolution, turned up at the last moment in the first public draft (2 October 1980), by way of a special 'saving clause,' expressly preserving 'any rights or freedoms that pertain to the native peoples of Canada' (section 24). In the version of the joint resolution approved by the House of Commons and the Senate on 23–4 April 1981, this had been expanded to 'aboriginal, treaty or other rights or freedoms that pertain to the aboriginal peoples of

Canada,' citing the proclamation of 7 October 1763 and rights 'acquired ... by way of land claims settlement' (section 25).

CHAPTER SIX: THE PATRIATION PACKAGE

1 *Globe and Mail*, Toronto, 22 January 1981
2 John Gray, 'Tories' dragging of God into patriation row detestable: PM,' *Globe and Mail*, 25 April 1981
3 *Globe and Mail*, 23 January 1981
4 Ibid, 24 January 1981
5 Ibid, 27 January 1981
6 Ibid, 23 and 27 January 1981
7 Ibid, 23 January 1981
8 Ibid, 27 January 1981
9 *Vancouver Sun*, 22 January 1981
10 Geoffrey Stevens, 'A lamentable effort,' *Globe and Mail*, 22 January 1981
11 *The Province*, Vancouver, 24 December 1980
12 Editorial, 'A charter of loopholes,' *Globe and Mail*, 29 March 1981
13 Michael Valpy, 'A charter worthy of its name,' *Vancouver Sun*, 14 January 1981
14 *Globe and Mail*, 15 January 1981
15 See, for example, *Regents of the University of California* v *Bakke*, 438 US 265 (1978); *State of Kerala* v *N.M. Thomas*, AIR [1976] SC 490; and see generally Edward McWhinney, *Constitution-Making. Principles, Process, Practice* (Toronto 1981), 90ff.
16 *Canadian Industrial Gas and Oil Ltd.* v *Government of Saskatchewan et al.*, 80 DLR (3d) 449 (1978); and see generally Edward McWhinney, *Quebec and the Constitution 1960–1978* (Toronto 1979), 102ff.
17 See note 16.

CHAPTER SEVEN: CUTTING THE IMPERIAL GORDIAN KNOT

1 A.V. Dicey, *Introduction to the Study of the Law of the Constitution* (1st edn, 1885; 9th edn, by E.C.S. Wade, 1939), 171–2
2 United Kingdom, House of Commons, *First Report from the Foreign Affairs Committee, Session 1980–81, British North America Acts: The Rôle of Parliament*, Vols. 1 and 2 (21 January 1981)
3 Compare the vigorous editorial comments of *The Economist* (London), 11 April 1981, 52: 'Canadians, who for at least half a century have thought that their country was a wholly independent sovereign state, have been perturbed to discover that the British still have the last word about its constitution – and to see provincial lobbyists (even amazingly, some from Mr. René Lévesque's Quebec government) appealing to London in fine old nineteenth-century style ... Those British members of parliament who have lately been talking about "the imperial parliament's rôle as trustee" seem to have relapsed into thinking in 1867 terms. Canada passed out of British tutelage several generations ago.'
4 United Kingdom, House of Commons, *First Report*, Vol. 1, para 73, p xl; para 86, p xlvi; para 103, p li; and ibid
5 Sir Ivor Jennings, 'The Statute of Westminster and Appeals to the Privy Council,' 52 *Law Quarterly Review* 173, 187 (1936)
6 [1935] AC 494 (PC)

7 *Attorney-General for Ontario* v *Attorney-General for Canada*, [1947] AC 127 (PC).
8 United Kingdom, House of Commons, *First Report*, Vol. 1, paras 116–18, pp lvii–lviii
9 *In the matter of an Act for expediting the decision of Constitutional and other Provincial questions, being Chapter C 180, C.C.S.M.*, Court of Appeal, Manitoba, decision of 3 February 1981
10 *Globe and Mail*, Toronto, 4 February 1981
11 *The Times*, London, 10 December 1980
12 Ibid
13 United Kingdom, House of Commons, *First Report*, Vol. 2, 62–82, (Examination of Witnesses, 12 November 1980)
14 Government of Canada, Hon Jean Chrétien, Minister of Justice, *The Rôle of The United Kingdom in the Amendment of the Canadian Constitution. Background Paper* (March 1981), especially paras 51–4, pp 24–5 (Kershaw report: Inadequacy of Evidence)
15 Ibid
16 United Kingdom, House of Commons, *Second Report from the Foreign Affairs Committee, Session 1980–81. Supplementary Report on the British North America Acts: The Rôle of Parliament* (15 April 1981)
17 Ibid, v, note 2
18 Letter to *The Times*, 31 October 1980 (Jonathan Aitken, MP)
19 See the Public Advertisement to Members of the House of Commons and the House of Lords, London, published by the Inuit Committee on National Issues, in *The Times*, 3 December 1980
20 United Kingdom, House of Commons, *Second Report*, xxii
21 And see generally Prime Minister Trudeau's address to the Canadian House of Commons in the constitutional debate, 23 March 1981.

CHAPTER EIGHT: THE PREMIERS IN COURT

1 *In the matter of an act for expediting the decision of constitutional and other provincial questions, being chapter C 180, C.C.S.M.; and in the matter of a reference pursuant thereto by the Lieutenant-Governor in Council to the Court of Appeal for Manitoba*, Court of Appeal, Manitoba, decision of 3 February 1981
2 *In the matter of Section 6 of the Judicature Act, R.S.N. 1970, c. 187 as amended; and in the matter of a reference by the Lieutenant-Governor in Council concerning the effect and validity of the amendments to the Constitution of Canada sought in the 'Proposed Resolution for a Joint Address to Her Majesty the Queen respecting the Constitution of Canada'*, Court of Appeal, Newfoundland, decision of 31 March 1981
3 *Dans l'affaire d'un renvoi à la Cour d'appel relatif à un projet de résolution portant adresse commune à Sa Majesté la Reine concernant la Constitution du Canada*, Cour d'Appel, Province de Québec, decision of 15 April 1981
4 *Globe and Mail*, Toronto, 1 April 1981

CHAPTER NINE: THE SUPREME COURT RULING

1 *In the matter of an act for expediting the decision of constitutional and other provincial questions, being R.S.M. 1970, c. C-180*, Supreme Court of Canada, decision of 28 September 1981
2 A.L. Goodhart, *Essays in Jurisprudence and the Common Law* (New York 1931)

3 A.V. Dicey, *Introduction to the Study of the Law of the Constitution*, 1st ed (London 1885), 445ff. And see generally O. Hood Phillips, 'Constitutional Conventions. Dicey's Predecessors,' 29 *Modern Law Review* 137 (1966); Sir Ivor Jennings, *The Law and the Constitution*, 3rd edn (London 1943), 79ff.

4 *Liversidge* v *Anderson*, [1942] AC 206. And see the contemporary discussions of that decision, by Holdsworth, 58 *Law Quarterly Review* 1 (1942); A.L. Goodhart, ibid, 3; C.K. Allen, ibid, 232; Julius Stone, *The Province and Function and Law* (Toronto 1946), 193–4.

CHAPTER TEN: THE GUY FAWKES DAY COMPROMISE

1 *Globe and Mail*, Toronto, 29 September 1981
2 Léon Dion, *Le Québec et le Canada. Les voies de l'avenir* (Québec 1980)
3 Margot Gibb-Clark, 'Quebec left "weak, isolated" but Ryan doesn't cut PQ cord,' *Globe and Mail*, 11 November 1981
4 Robert Sheppard and Victor Malarek, *Globe and Mail*, 14 November 1981
5 Margot Gibb-Clark, '"Interesting" discussion delays Quebec House,' *Globe and Mail*, 5 November 1981; John Gray, 'Referendum gamble by PM powerful lever against Gang of Eight,' *Globe and Mail*, 5 November 1981
6 Margot Gibb-Clark, 'Duality of Canada a sham, bitter Lévesque declares,' *Globe and Mail*, 6 November 1981; Margot Gibb-Clark, 'Lévesque commits Quebec to ongoing patriation fight,' *Globe and Mail*, 10 November 1981
7 Michel Vastal, 'Trudeau arrache deux compromis aux provinces pour accomoder le Québec,' *Le Devoir*, Montreal, 19 November 1981
8 Premier Lévesque remained obdurate, however. See Jean-Claude Picard, 'Refusant de négocier avec Ottawa Québec ferme le dossier constitutionnel,' *Le Devoir*, 19 November 1981

CHAPTER ELEVEN: NEW PLAYERS, NEW PEOPLE'S POWER

1 Letter to the Editor, *Globe and Mail*, Toronto, 21 November 1981
2 Hugh Winsor, 'A pall on a style of politics,' ibid, 19 November 1981
3 *Globe and Mail*, 20 November 1981
4 Jeff Sallot, ibid, 19 November 1981
5 Marjorie Nichols, *The Vancouver Sun*, 21 November 1981; Allen Garr, *The Province*, Vancouver, 22 November 1981; *Globe and Mail*, 21 November 1981
6 *Globe and Mail*, 19 November 1981; *The Toronto Star*, 19 November 1981. And see editorial, 'Ten little premiers,' *The Vancouver Sun*, 21 November 1981.
7 *Globe and Mail*, 23 November 1981
8 *The Vancouver Sun*, 23 November 1981; *Globe and Mail*, 24 November 1981; ibid, 25 November 1981
9 Michael Valpy, 'Success or failure?,' *Globe and Mail*, 19 November 1981
10 Michael Valpy, 'They might lose,' ibid, 25 November 1981
11 *Western Sahara, Advisory Opinion*, ICJ Reports (1975) 12; discussed in Edward McWhinney, *The World Court and the Contemporary International Law-Making Process* (The Hague 1979), 65–97
12 *The Vancouver Sun*, 28 November 1981; *Globe and Mail*, 28 November 1981
13 'Bennett tells Trudeau to stop altering pact,' *The Vancouver Sun*, 28 November 1981; *Globe and Mail*, 28 November 1981

14 *Globe and Mail*, 28 November 1981; *The Vancouver Sun*, 28 November 1981
15 See, generally, Edward McWhinney, *Constitution-Making. Principles, Process, Practice* (Toronto 1981), 8–9, 90.
16 *Globe and Mail*, 28 November 1981; *The Vancouver Sun*, 28 November 1981
17 *The Vancouver Sun*, 5 November 1981; *Globe and Mail*, 6 November 1981
18 Jean-Claude Picard, 'Québec ferme le dossier constitutionnel,' *Le Devoir*, Montreal, 19 November 1981
19 *Globe and Mail*, 19 November 1981; *The Vancouver Sun*, 19 November 1981
20 *Globe and Mail*, 21 November 1981
21 Ibid, 3 December 1981
22 Ibid
23 Ibid, 2 December 1981
24 Ibid
25 *The Vancouver Sun*, 4 December 1981
26 John Gray, *Globe and Mail*, 4 December 1981; Linda Diebel, *The Vancouver Sun*, 4 December 1981; Jamie Lamb, *The Vancouver Sun*, 4 December 1981
27 *Globe and Mail*, 2 December 1981

CHAPTER TWELVE: THE CONSTITUTION AND THE FUTURE

1 See Edward McWhinney, *Constitution-Making. Principles, Process, Practice* (Toronto 1981).
2 See, generally, Federation of Canadian Municipalities, *Municipal Government in a New Canadian Federal System* (Ottawa 1980), 61ff.
3 Ibid, 121ff
4 As to Indian and native (aboriginal) issues generally, see P.A. Cumming and N.H. Mickenberg, editors, *Native Rights in Canada*, 2nd edn (Toronto 1972); Alexander Morris, *The Treaties of Canada with the Indians of Manitoba and the North-West Territories* (Toronto 1880); Richard Price, editor, *The Spirit of the Alberta Indian Treaties* (Toronto 1979); and L.C. Green, *Canada's Indians. Federal Policy, International and Constitutional Law* (Toronto 1969).
5 M. Duverger, *La Monarchie républicaine* (Paris 1974); A.M. Schlesinger, Jr, *The Imperial Presidency* (New York 1973).

CHAPTER THIRTEEN: CONSTITUTIONAL POSTSCRIPT

1 *British North America Acts: The Rôle of Parliament. Observations by the Secretary of State for Foreign and Commonwealth Affairs*, HMSO, Cmnd 8450 (London, December 1981), para 13, p 6
2 *Globe and Mail*, Toronto, 16 January 1982
3 Ibid, 23 December 1981
4 Ibid, 25 December 1981
5 Ibid, 16 January 1982
6 Ibid, 7 January 1982
7 Léon Dion, *Le Québec et le Canada. Les voies de l'avenir* (Quebec 1980), 221. And see also the present author's *Quebec and the Constitution 1960–1978* (Toronto 1979) 24ff; K. McRoberts and D. Posgate, *Quebec: Social Change and Political Crisis*, rev edn (Toronto 1980).
8 McWhinney, *Quebec and the Constitution*, 21ff

9 Letter from Prime Minister Trudeau (29 December 1981), quoted with the writer's permission. As to the 'notwithstanding' clause, see P. Weiler, *Dalhousie Law Review* (1980), 205; and, generally, see W. Tarnopolsky, *The Canadian Bill of Rights* (Toronto 1975).

10 *Globe and Mail*, 19 November 1981

11 *British North America Acts: The Rôle of Parliament*, para 14, p 7

12 *Globe and Mail*, 3 December 1981; ibid, 11 December 1981; ibid, 22 December 1981; ibid, 23 December 1981; ibid, 15 and 16 January 1982; *The Province* (Vancouver), 15 January 1982; *The Vancouver Sun*, 16 January 1982

13 *Globe and Mail*, 22 January 1982; *Toronto Star*, 22 January 1982

14 *The Vancouver Sun*, 22 January 1982; *Globe and Mail*, 23 January 1982

15 See note 14.

16 'Lévesque criticism harsh: Go back to sleep, Governor-General told,' *Globe and Mail*, 23 January 1982

17 *Toronto Star*, 22 January 1982; *The Vancouver Sun*, 22 January 1982

18 As note 17. And see Dr Forsey's letter to the editor, *Globe and Mail*, 2 February 1982.

19 *The Vancouver Sun*, 22 January 1982

20 See editorial, 'Silence is a virtue,' *Globe and Mail*, 23 January 1982.

21 *The Vancouver Sun*, 28 January 1982; *Globe and Mail* 29 January 1982

22 *Globe and Mail*, 29 January 1982

23 Ibid, 30 January 1982

24 *Globe and Mail*, 2 February 1982

25 Linda Goyette, *Edmonton Journal*, 3 February 1982

26 Ibid

27 Ibid

28 *The Times*, London, editorial, 'No reason to delay the Canada Bill now,' republished in *Globe and Mail*, 2 February 1982

29 Jefffrey Simpson, *Globe and Mail*, 9 March 1982

30 *Globe and Mail*, 27 March 1982

31 John Gray, ibid, 3 April 1982

Index